SEALY'S
CARIBBEAN
LEADERS

Theodore Sealy

LMH Publishing Limited

All LMH titles, imprints and distributed lines are available at special quantity discounts for bulk purchases for sales promotion, premiums, fund-raising, educational or institutional use.

AKNOWLEDGEMENTS

Preface:	Dr. Woodville Marshal
Cover:	CAP Designs
Cover redesign:	Lee-Quee Design
Illustrations:	Gerald Tyndale
Editing & Preparing Publication:	Elaine Melbourne Cindy Doyle MacRae – Kingston Publishers
Typesetting:	Twenty: O Four
Initiative:	Eagle Merchant Bank

Published by: LMH Publishing Limited
7 Norman Road,
LOJ Industrial Complex
Building 10
Kingston C.S.O., Jamaica
Tel: 876-938-0005; 938-0712
Fax: 876-759-8752
Email: lmhbookpublishing@cwjamaica.com
Website: www.lmhpublishingjamaica.com

Printed in the U.S.A.   ISBN 976-8184-62-0

www.ingramcontent.com/pod-product-compliance
Lightning Source LLC
Chambersburg PA
CBHW030922090426
42737CB00007B/292

Contents

Preface

by Professor Woodville Marshall

If slave emancipation can be regarded as a social revolution, the events of the decades, 1930-1960, about a century later, must surely rank as at least our second social revolution. This period of intense political ferment altered forever the features of the political landscape, producing party political and trade union organization, mass political participation and constitutional de-colonization. Above all else, it was a period of excitement, enthusiasm and activity on a number of levels: the character of the political succession allowed new social and economic possibilities to be brought within reach, social change was clearly accelerated, and various strains of nationalism flourished, then withered or mutated. For some, the greatest possibility and the deepest disappointment was the failure of Federation; but for most, the various developments represented, in Vic Reid's words, 'a new day'.

Unfortunately, no West Indian has yet attempted to tell the full story of those heady times - of the hopes and frustrations, the naive expectations and the emotional confusions; or of the attitudes and responses of all those students and teachers, professional people and civil servants, businessmen and politicians who, to a greater or lesser degree, were caught up in them. Gordon Lewis does catch some of the period's vigour and excitement in The Growth of the Modern West Indies; but so far the distinctively Caribbean voice and sensibility have been muted and fragmented, - in George Lamming's Season of Adventure, in Sparrow's early calypsoes, in C.L.R. James' editorials in PNM's Nation, in Arthur Lewis' pamphlets on the labour movement, industrialization and federation, in the memoirs of politicians and public servants. It remains for a social historian like E.K. Brathwaite or commentators on popular culture like Gordon Roehler and Rex Nettleford to synthesize the strands of an experience that spoke of optimism and self-consciousness, of a people and society on the move.

Theodore Sealy's biographical sketches of eleven Commonwealth Caribbean politicians is another valuable fragment, particularly for the young West Indian. The subjects of these pieces are Chief Ministers, Premiers and Prime Ministers of eight of these territories, from Belize in the west to Guyana in the south. All of these men dominated the political life of their units; some of them were also the giants of intra-regional politics and relations, most of them died, full of years and honours; and only three, Vere Bird, Cheddi Jagan and Eric Gairy still retain any political prominence. The sketches, based on reminiscences, on information in the files of the Gleaner and on interviews conducted mainly in 1963 and 1976, are, as one might expect, somewhat uneven in scope and quality. Predictably, given Sealy's range of contacts and domicile, there is far more information, insight and analysis in the pieces on Bustamante and Norman Manley; most of the rest are less coherent and informative, though the pieces on Grantley Adams, Eric Williams, Forbes Burnham and Jagan are superior journalism because of their intelligent comment on the leaders' relationships with each other and with political rivals.

Sealy is, of course, excellently qualified to sketch political lives. His professional activity as a journalist from 1928 spanned these tumultuous times and gave him a unique perspective from which to view the rapidly changing political and social landscape. Equally important, the professional eminence which made him almost as much an institution as the Gleaner which he edited for more than twenty-five years, conferred superior opportunities to cultivate close relationships with most of the high and mighty, opportunities which naturally were denied to most of his professional colleagues in the region. Moreover, his own involvement in the nationalist and regional movements as well as the mutual exploitation, which is part and parcel of the relationship between prominent journalist and politician, made him a man on the inside - with the type of access to leading politicians which could be described as intimacy, and which could lead to participation in decision-making. But this particular advantage, as can be seen in these sketches, is double-edged. Easy access to political leaders enables the journalist to refine his commentary on events while at the same time helping to shape them; but the price of access and intimacy is often restricted attribution and severely limited disclosure of vital corrobative materials. It is, therefore, unfortunate for scholars of the politics of those times that Sealy's scrupulous adherence to the implied bargain, imposes such a tight rein on his professional instincts as a journalist. We have only loud hints of what he must have known about what motivated particular decisions at critical points in Jamaican and regional politics. Perhaps, as his contribution to a fuller reading of his times, he might have considered amplifying some of these pieces, once death had weakened any obligation of confidentiality.

Nevertheless, the sketches do illuminate some of the dominant themes of this recent revolutionary era. First, they outline some of the characteristics of the *new* political leadership and document part of the reality of social change. Sealy is not content to merely recount the triumphs or to comment pungently on idiosyncra-cies. He attempts to place these men in their social and family contexts, to emphasize the ordinariness of their origins and upbringing, and to demonstrate that their success rested not on inherited social status or family wealth but on decent schooling and strict parental discipline, on their own driving ambition, sense of service and brain power. Therefore, his leaders are not larger than life; they are men who share many of the characteristics of their fellows - non-white if not black, often self-educated, mainly proletarian in class origins, if not always in their sympathies. They, therefore, represent possibilities that are open to the young, gifted and brown/ black.

Perhaps there is another message as well. It could be suggested that Sealy, as he reflected on his own achievements, realized that his life's trajectory was not much different from that of the political leaders whose careers were synonymous with success. Therefore, the sketches may suggest, while political changes had created opportunities for significant social mobility, those most likely to enjoy those benefits were the ambitious sons of the respectable, striving poor and lower middle classes. Therefore, almost like a latter-day Samuel Smiles, Sealy could be seen to be preaching the virtues of family cohesion, hard work, discipline and ambition.

Regional consciousness is the second major theme illustrated by these biographical sketches. The selection of subjects from the regional community, Sealy's obvious familiarity with them, and the ease with which he moves around each capital city in the region suggests more than a refined professionalism. The fact that during the short Federal years, Whitehall and Treasury Street of Port-of-Spain became as much his turf as Harbour Street in Kingston, makes the point. While he was chasing the lead story of the day, he was also following one of his dreams, as it moved out of committee rooms in London to Port of Spain in Trinidad. Therefore, his sketches of Manley, Bustamante, Williams and Adams are, in part, a personal statement of emotional commitment to that doomed experiment. For him, 'the whole sky came tumbling down' with the results of the Jamaican Referendum.

No doubt, here too, Sealy's personal history determined his orientation. He was a Jamaican by adoption but a Caribbean man by parentage and experience. Born in Belize of a Belizean mother and a Barbadian father, he grew up in Jamaica and travelled extensively as a child in Cuba and the Dominican Republic. Therefore, his sense of Caribbean regionalism may have been broader though not necessarily deeper than that of most of his contemporaries.

This brings into focus the final theme which the sketches help, perhaps unintentionally, to illustrate. That is, the extent to which ambivalence, if not contradiction and confusion, surrounded some of the critical issues of national and regional development during the era. Put simply, political leaders and their followers seemed to have committed themselves at one and the same time to unit-based de-colonization programmes *and* to a colonial form of regional integration without fully recognizing that the particular form of integration being contemplated during early stages of unit decolonization would inevitably conflict with the unit programme. Sealy's sketches, highlighting aspects of these simultaneous and divergent developments at unit and centre, allow us to establish the dramatic unity of scenes in that tragedy that was Federation.

In this regard, Sealy was perhaps as much a man of his times as the political leaders were. He was involved in the nationalist struggle in Jamaica, identifying to some extent with Bustamante, and he was a regional man, somewhat in the mould of Norman Manley. As a professional and a regionalist, he was always close to the Federal venture but, apparently, he never committed the full weight of his personal influence or that of his newspaper to the Federal cause. He too may have been ambivalent when it mattered most; and his sketches therefore may tell us as much about the author as about the leaders.

SIR GRANTLEY HERBERT ADAMS
C.M.G., Q.C.
BORN GOVERNMENT HILL, BARBADOS, 28 APRIL, 1898
DIED 28 NOVEMBER, 1971

CHIEF MINISTER OF BARBADOS (1948-1958)
PREMIER OF BARBADOS (1954-1958)
PRIME MINISTER OF THE WEST INDIES FEDERATION (1958-1962)

1

SIR GRANTLEY HERBERT ADAMS

"A PROPHET IS NOT WITHOUT HONOUR, save in his own country." That must have come bitterly true to Sir Grantley Adams in his last year or so while living down the failure of the Federation of the West Indies which had made him for four years the pre-eminent person of the Commonwealth Caribbean. He, in his own native land, was in some of the high places an object of derision. Fortunately, the Biblical saying was not true in its second respect, because Matthew said : "A prophet is not without honour, save in his own country, and in his own house." In that latter respect, Grantley Adams had honour and glory throughout all these dismal years of reverse and difficulty and disillusion. His was a home of pride in which his wife and son (himself a later Prime Minister of Barbados) sheltered him, protected him and later saw him gain new courage until the end came.

For some twenty years, Grantley Adams, barrister-at-law, trade union leader, politician, had held the mystique of Father of the Barbadian people and the Barbadian nation. But when the Federation came tumbling down about his ears, his rivals in Barbados rose in eminence and overshadowed him in so much that, at his funeral, the incumbent Prime Minister Barrow did not even attend. Thus, did the Barbadian government of the day treat the funeral of the patriarch of the nation.

Matters of deep personal hurt sometimes are nourished as fuel and engendered as impetus too. The funeral hurt may well have been part of the emotional powerhouse generated by Grantley's son, Tom, leading to his massive defeat of Prime Minister Errol Barrow in late 1976. It certainly must have been a matter of great pride to Grantley's wife, Grace (Lady Adams).

3

The Federation of the Commonwealth Caribbean was the spotlight in which Grantley Adams lived at the peak of his career. It also was, in a sense, his eclipse. Therefore, one might consider Grantley Adams, the Prime Minister of the Federation of the West Indies as the main personality before we even look at his upbringing and his other many-sided talents and careers.

When Grantley Adams came to the meeting of the Caribbean Labour Congress in Jamaica in 1947, he made a dramatic impact on a country which, up to that time, had been partially blinded by the excellence of the late Norman Washington Manley. Many of the young budding Socialists present at that conference were amazed at the poise, the magnetism and the persuasiveness of Grantley Adams. Indeed, to the surprise of many of Manley's supporters, the Conference made Adams the first President of this Caribbean organisation, which later led the islands into federation with Grantley Adams as Prime Minister. But it did not follow naturally; Adams was replaced as head of the Caribbean organisation by Manley along the way so that, by the time federation was to become a reality, the number one person again was Manley and not Adams.

A legal-political academic who remembers those meetings feels that Manley looked a pale second to Grantley Adams, who at that meeting seemed to have outshone all the other Caribbean delegates. Admittedly, Manley was not, even in Jamaica, a mass popular figure at that time. Manley appealed to academics and intellectuals whereas Bustamante was the mass leader.

Grantley Adams was a genuine intellectual but lazy in the sense that he would wait until the last moment to get things done. But he had a lot of energy and when he decided to act, he did things thoroughly. He was a first-class intellectual power, who could cope with the rest. He was not a subtle intellect, rather a sledge-hammer type, but an intellect that could understand intricate arguments and deal with them. Finally, in the long run, just when Federation was to come into being, Norman Manley declared that he would remain in Jamaica and not go to the federal legislature because of the dangers which might beset Jamaica if he left it for the Federal Government. And in that same announcement, Norman Manley chose Grantley Adams to be the one to lead the Federal Labour Party into the elections and conduct the Federation. The fact is that the reason then given by Norman Manley does not tally with what I know as a fact. For Edna Manley, Norman's wife, had declared quite firmly to me that unless Jamaica got the Federal capital, Norman could not go to Federation, where (as she put it), he would be living in a suitcase between two capitals a thousand miles apart.

Adams must have felt a sense of gratification that he was regarded as the suitable person to lead the Federal Labour Party with the promised Premiership and leadership of the West Indies Federation. He obviously felt that it was his duty to surrender his commitment to Barbados which was total and absolute, and go and lead the Federation of the West Indies.

4

A friend of his, commenting on this, says: "I think Grantley was probably right at that stage to go to Federation. He had done all he could for Barbados. One of the reasons why I was prepared to encourage him to go - a minor reason - was that I thought it was right that someone else should start doing things in Barbados, because Grantley's real contribution had been made. It was a real contribution but it had been a contribution of bulldozing. He had brought down the edifice that had been there. I didn't think he had the talent for the next job which would be architectural, to build the new edifice, the new society, the new economy. I did not see any obvious person there either, but as long as Grantley was there, they would never seek the other person. And so I felt in my own heart that his next move probably would be correct, a move to Federation, whether as the Leader or whether Mr. Manley was the Leader, but he could hardly not accept the choice if Manley wouldn't take it."

Grantley's great pre-Federal performance was the contribution he made in dethroning the plantocracy in Barbados. By the time the federal period came he was a nearly spent person. He was not a man who understood how to conserve his energies. He never slept enough; he never had regular hours. As a friend says, in those days, if you went to talk to Grantley, you could never get away, no matter what hour it was because he liked talking. He liked people and he just went on and on regardless of what he had to do next day. He would hastily postpone what the next thing was and went on from day to day in that way. He had little recuperative powers. He never practised the discipline which would enable him to recuperate. And so he wore himself out gradually. It was during the Federation of the West Indies that this obvious deterioration was taking place. Federation finished both Grantley Adams and Norman Manley. Manley has his own story but for Grantley Adams the context of his going to Federation meant that somebody else had chosen him to be the Federal leader. He did not like it. Obviously he would have preferred it otherwise, but he just could not let down the side. He believed in Norman Manley. He believed what Norman Manley had said as he believed anyone whom he had ever represented, because Grantley Adams only represented people in whom he believed. And so with his ambling gait, his heavy-headedness, his slow power, he took upon himself this great burden and, as seemed natural to me, failed.

At some of the earliest meetings of the Federal Parliament, Grantley was taunted that he was Manley's and Eric Williams' yo-yo. In those days, the wooden spool strung with cord which children spin, was popular: so the meaning was clear and this situation grew worse. Adams came under heavy fire from Opposition Members from the very start of the Federal Parliament with the accusation that Norman Manley, Premier of Jamaica and Eric Williams, Premier of Trinidad and Tobago, who had not sought election to the Federal Parliament, were in fact dictating terms to the Federal Prime Minister from the sidelines. Grantley Adams had hoped for a better atmosphere because on Friday, April 18, 1958 when he was formally elected as Prime Minister, he had thanked them all profusely saying, "Seldom have I heard such sincerity and general appreciation of the Leader of one side by the Leader of the other in Parliament." And he concluded: "I shall do my best from the start to work for the betterment of our people in the West Indies and I feel sure that both sides of the House will realise that the first few steps are essential if we want to gain the respect of other people."

But five weeks later Opposition spokesman Albert Gomes was accusing the Prime Minister of leading a Federation which was "a puppet and footstool for the little satraps who control some of the units, to dictate the terms and call the tune." And Opposition spokesman Ken Hill presaging a bitter attack on the Prime Minister, came into the Chamber with a yo-yo. His accusation, as was the general accusation, was that the Prime Minister was a yo-yo for Manley and Williams.

When Sir Grantley got up to reply amidst interruptions he lashed out: "Hon. Members may shout but before I finish a lot of them will be pretty dumb." And later he declared: "I have been accused in language that the legal gentlemen on the other side will agree is in some respects slanderous, absolutely slanderous; and however much I may be prepared to put up with ordinary rivalry - such is politics - I strongly object to the nasty way in which the Opposition has set out in this session of the Federal Parliament."

Sir Grantley went on to add: "You cannot begin to worry me. For more than a quarter of a century I have fought the political eagles of Barbados and now at this stage I will not allow the feeble flutterings of the fledgling wings of day-old chicks to worry me. And that is a fair comparison after listening to the debate and the ability of the Opposition. Day old chicks !"

There were lighter moments, of course, in Parliament when Grantley was able, in the right mood, to shed the heavy feeling of tragedy which seemed to haunt him.

In Port-of-Spain in those days, Federal Members of Parliament did not count too much with Trinidad authorities. So, as Prime Minister of the Federation, Sir Grantley Adams actually in defiance openly broke the laws of Trinidad in at least one instance. Trinidad law stated quite clearly that each motor vehicle must carry a number plate with the registration number printed on it, except in the case of the Governor General or the Governor whose vehicles had a crown on the registration plate. The regulations also stated that each new car should have a new registration number, except for the Premier or Prime Minister's which had always carried "PG 1".

Sir Grantley wanted to carry over his old number to a new car when he was given the new car to drive about in Port-of-Spain. The Licensing Authority refused to allow him a new number. So Sir Grantley drove about Trinidad and

Tobago with a blank number plate for many months until the issue was resolved in his favour. The Police did not touch him.

Sir Grantley, who once kept wicket for Barbados, was not to be interrupted whenever the subject of conversation was cricket. His Permanent Secretary, Mr. O.E. Henry, once spent a half-hour trying to get him to sign an important document at Federal House. Sir Grantley refused to listen to his Permanent Secretary while he talked on about the scores of whatever series was then in progress. On another occasion, the elevator door closed on Sir Grantley's hand while he was entering the lift. The tip of his index finger was sliced off. A secretary picked it up off the floor of the elevator, saying "But Sir Grantley, look your finger." The Prime Minister was quite unaware that anything had happened. However, he came out of the elevator with the tip of finger pressed against the stub, rushed to hospital and had it stitched on. At no time was there any show of pain. Sir Grantley was talking cricket.

During the life of the Federation I had many occasions to visit Sir Grantley Adams in Port-of-Spain. He had made the mistake of choosing someone as heavy-headed as himself to be his Public Relations Officer. Now, one thing that needed dynamism in a new federation was the public relations side, the creating of an emotional ferment in all the territories to let them feel a new sense of alliance and allegiance. But it was hopeless. I remember meeting with Grantley and his Public Relations Officer and saying to them that one of the few things they had was the postal service; one of the things they should do, simple things, was instantly to fly the Federal Flag at all post offices in the Federation, issue new stamps, start doing the things which give the people a feeling that something had happened; but there was no response and little was done.

Mr. Shridath Ramphal of the Commonwealth Secretariat said in London that while the Commonwealth leaders had accepted the Commonwealth, the Commonwealth people themselves did not necessarily feel the same way. That was the position in 1958 where the leaders of the Caribbean had become Federalists but the people knew not Federation. Sir Grantley must have had a lonely agonising time in those years when he was seeing the Federation, of which he was the first and only Prime Minister, come slowly to grief. In Parliament he was often doggedly brilliant. He fought every battle to the standstill. He was a massive opponent to face but he had started on a losing side.

Lord Hailes, the Governor General, was an ill-chosen partner for a Prime Minister of Sir Grantley's disposition. Hailes was fancy and glamorous and not likely to arouse the new patriotisms which his position would require of him in these far-flung islands. Indeed, the Gleaner once described Grantley and Hailes as "the evil twins of Federation." But despite his inward sadness, outwardly Grantley Adams remained seemingly indomitable. He carried on bravely at all times. But things came to a nasty pass with Jamaica's Norman

7

Manley about duties deferred on an industrial plant (which was really a Federal prerogative). Grantley Adams threatened that the Federation would use retroactive measures to counter units which gave away revenue as an industrial incentive, which should really be a Federal decision. The very Norman Manley who made it unavoidable and obligatory that Adams should go to lead the Federation now became the main stumbling block. And it seems that around that time Manley himself had decided that the Federation might be wrong for Jamaica. So the man who sent Adams there was now pulling the rug from under the whole Federation.

However, Adams remained outwardly self-confident, fighting every inch of the way to the very end, the fateful day when Robert Bradshaw, Finance Minister in the Federal Government, moved the terse adjournment of the Federal Parliament of the British Caribbean for the last time. It was the 11th of April, 1962. He moved "the adjournment of this Honourable House" sine die for the last time and added: "We have been privileged to lay the foundation of West Indian unity. Let us, in the words of the American poet, Lowell, hope that "After us some purer scheme will be shaped out by wiser men than we."

Indeed, when Adams had become aware that the British Government itself was in connivance with the destruction of Federation, he said in the Parliament on the 13th of February, 1962: "Nobody in this House is going to speak more critically on what I consider an immoral and monstrous act by the British Government to the West Indies." At that moment he had in mind the fact that the British Government had made the suggestion that Adams give way to Manley (though this has not been recorded) at the Constitutional Conference over which Iain McLeod presided as Secretary of State for the Colonies in London. Adams was invited down to Chequers that Sunday with Ian McLeod and offered a peerage if he would relinquish the post of Prime Minister in favour of Manley. It is said that McLeod told him: "I have a Peerage in my pocket and a pension." Sir Grantley has never admitted this publicly, and even to close political colleagues, the most he said was, "Remember I had the offer of a pension and a Peerage." The fact is McLeod had already given Norman Manley the attributes of nationhood; Jamaica knew that it could become independent.

Of this offered peerage, Adams' widow told me "There was a vague offer - I don't think Grantley even considered it; in fact I think he was rather amused at the offer."

Clearly from all those things, Britain wished to save the Federation even if Grantley Adams had to be sacrificed. And so, if Sir Grantley had agreed, he would have died a Peer and Manley, conceivably, would have been the Prime Minister of the West Indies Federation. But since Sir Grantley had not accepted it, it meant that Manley had the freedom to take Jamaica out of the Federation. This he did by calling upon the Jamaican people to support Federation and to vote for it in the Referendum. He knew that if the people voted no, Jamaica

8

would have the right to leave Federation. If they voted yes - which most people considered unlikely - then the Federation could continue.

Lady Adams tells a sad story of the night in Port-of-Spain, the Federal capital, when they were all waiting on the results of the Jamaican referendum. She says : "At the time of that Referendum Sir John Mordecai was acting as Governor General in Trinidad and a dinner party had been fixed for that very night, thoughtlessly perhaps. Anyway, the dinner party went on and it was during the dinner that the results were pouring in from Jamaica. Mordecai, I think, fully expected Manley to make it; I expected him to make it; Grantley wasn't sure what he expected. The Deputy Prime Minister Carl LaCorbinierre said that there were so many obstacles that Manley couldn't make it."

"Anyway, as the results came in and I sat next to Mordecai. I could see the depression lowering that man's spirits. His wife who sat opposite to me had her eyes fixed on the door through which the messages were coming in. It was a most traumatic experience and I am afraid that some people were disgusted with Manley because it never should have happened. And even although I know that if Manley won the Referendum, Grantley would be replaced by Manley, I still felt very sorry that something we all dreamt about had gone. And I felt sorrier because that was a downward path for the whole West Indies. And we have gone further and further down and further and further apart."

Eric Williams, Lady Adams says, made quite certain that the Federation could not continue. She added in our conversation "I wonder how Manley felt that night. For we in the Southern Caribbean were sure that Manley would make it and I have a number of letters from Manley to Grantley saying he wasn't sure this was the right time. It was rather surprising and I am very critical of the British Government of the time. They promised Manley Independence so it did not matter whether he won the Referendum or not, Jamaica would be independent."

When it was clear that Federation would collapse, Mr. Bradshaw, the Federal Minister of Finance, had the Legal Draughtsman, a Canadian legal draughtsman, Harvey daCosta, Attorney General and Sonny Ramphal draft a Pension Law for the Prime Minister without the Prime Minister knowing. It went to Cabinet and it went through the House without opposition because, Bradshaw told me, "we had taken the precaution at the Constitutional Conference which was held in '61, to add a paragraph that the Federal Government would have power to legislate for pension for the Prime Minister. It is recorded elsewhere "Paul Southwell had raised that point at the conference and got these pension powers established. On Sir Grantley's death, arrangements were made for a pension to his widow but the Widow's Pension is comparable to the widow's mite."

9

The pension that the widow receives is so small - especially now that the pound continues to fall - that when I visited Lady Adams at age 72, she was marking exercise books at her home on a Sunday because she still had to earn a living by her lifelong profession - teaching.

Grantley Adams was at the peak of his career when he was in the Federation but his eminence arose from his earlier work as a barrister in Barbados which gave him access to the means of aiding in the struggle for the workers. It was that which laid the foundations of his subsequent political career. So it should be interesting to take a look at Grantley Adams, Barbados scholar, Oxford graduate, barrister-at-law (Grays Inn).

One of his first cases was *R. versus Payne* which was significant in political terms. Sir Hugh Springer, junior to him by many years, said about this case that :

"When Payne started the riots - inadvertently I think - I don't think he meant to start the riots but the tinder was there and it was lit and Grantley Adams found himself defending Payne as an ordinary practitioner. He was paid a fee. From there on it was clear that once Grantley takes on something he put everything in it. He was never known to admit that any client he has defended was guilty. Even 50 years after he would argue with you that the client was innocent. Nobody else might believe that, but if he took on a case, it was in toto. So he took on Payne. That was a very important psychological fact, Grantley being the kind of man he was. He was now Payne's advocate. He found himself leading deputations to the Governor about the case. I think that this more than anything else decided him in his total career. He was always admired as an advocate and so he was eagerly sought after and that forced him into politics, although at that time Grantley was a liberal and not a radical. That was how he was drawn into the radical movement with the Progressive League and all that. He became the most important person. He wasn't at that time President of the League because he had just come in but he became the most important person in the group....events had really overtaken him.

"As an advocate, in matters of law only, Grantley had another side to him. He would just sometimes dabble in the situation and ideas would come into his head as he was standing addressing the Court. One Counsel recalls a case in which the facts were not understood. It was largely a question of law and high technical procedural law and it was suggested that the Counsel agree between themselves on the facts and then narrow that down so that they could argue on what was really in dispute and save the Court's time. Grantley agreed but never got down to doing it. When Grantley did get up it was appalling for about 20 minutes - Grantley was really talking nonsense and the Court was getting very impatient. And Grantley was getting angry because he knew he was talking nonsense and he knew that the Court knew that. So, Grantley kept on for a while, treading the water, so to speak, because he had not done his preparation. But standing on his feet suddenly he discovered the right move to be made, made it, and the Court was with him "Yes, Mr. Adams; yes, Mr. Adams" and Grantley won. He hadn't prepared the case; he worked it out on his feet because he wasn't going to give in; he was going to go on and on until he got something to work on. And the idea came to him right there on his feet. That's the sort of chap he was."

A distinguished member of the Bar of Grantley's time declares: "Grantley and I were poles apart so there is a possibility - and I put it no higher than that - that I might misjudge him. But let me assume an objective outlook, as an advocate, as a lawyer, there are two approaches; one, was Grantley a good lawyer like say a man like Hannays, or a man like Manley? If you have a difficult matter, do you go to him feeling that if there was at all a Law, he could find it for you and expound it? Secondly, was he forensically an able advocate. The two things are entirely different. I say this: Adams was undoubtedly a pertinacious advocate, very pertinacious. He was a good cross-examiner - I have known better - but you could not fault him at the cross-examination. And when it came to the sequence of his arguments, he had an undoubted skill in hiding the weak parts of his case; he had the knack of shaping his language and his tone to the level of the Court - by Court I mean either a Court of Judges or a Court with a jury. It would be unfair to say less than that of him. Whether he was as sound a lawyer, I have known other lawyers, men of the type of Henry Walter Reece who was one of the greatest in the West Indies and Henderson Clarke, brilliant lawyer and advocate, and Hannays. But someone said that a lawyer need not know necessarily all the law himself but know where to find it. But once the law has been found he has to take the necessary trouble to make the requisite research. Grantley Adams undoubtedly had that.

"Most people nowadays think of Adams as a politician and not as a lawyer. That is understandable because lawyers in Barbados and in the West Indies have had very little power in shaping the nature of existence, in shaping legislation, in shaping public opinion. But there is one aspect of Adams' career which I have not heard commented upon which is that I think he was instinctively more a lawyer than a politician - which does not mean he was not an able politician. That would be gratuitously depriving him of something which was entirely his, which was undoubtedly his; but the fact is that his arguments, his approach, his tactics, reminded one who is familiar with work in the Courts with the approach and the tactics which he would employ as a pleader in Court.

11

"The fact is you never felt that he was, let us say, advancing a cause on grounds of high principle - that is not to criticise him for lack of principle. But he did not appear so much to be an exponent of principle as an advocate or shall we say, a seeker for particular advantage. For instance, he would take risks in politics which were analogous to risks one might take in cross-examination but which, in a politician, especially a leader, as undoubtedly he became, might not justify his own interest, nor the group or Party which he represented. You got the impression he was adventurous and had the sort of audacity you look for in an advocate."

Were there any low points at the Bar in Grantley Adams' work? My informant said he had heard from practitioners who were senior both to Grantley and to himself. Grantley returned to Barbados before my informant did, and Grantley was cross-examining in a case before Judge Herbert Greaves, a man who had had considerable experience and practice. It was a case relating to forgery and handwriting and so on, and Adams was emphasising the great impossibility of a witness distinguishing between one pen and the other.

"Sir Herbert Greaves called for the two pens and placed them on his desk. Then later he told the Clerk to pass them to Mr. Adams' Bench, which was done. When the pens were placed there, Mr. Adams promptly took up the pen which was his and put it in his pocket. Then he realised what had happened. He had shown that one of the pens could be distinguished from the other. In other words, a man will know his own pen."

As to high points, my informant declares: "I know he was a good advocate. There was a case in which Adams appeared in relation to a collision. In those days the law in relation to collisions on land was a bit murky and there had been a book on the Law on collisions on land which had come out and Adams had got hold of it and had researched and lit upon the precise point on which the case would turn.

"He was a good cross-examiner and he was adept at bringing out the point; and he appreciated not only the point but the way in which to elaborate it and apply it to the facts in the case. Naturally, he won the case and it illustrates the high mark of advocacy which was his when in form."

Another Barbadian, who up to the time of his death was very close to Barbadian affairs, the Parliament and the Courts, declares that "Grantley was a first-class advocate. In his time there may have been his equal as lawyers but as an advocate he was exceptional. Henderson Clarke was the outstanding barrister of those days but Henderson Clarke hardly took cases of the masses against the ruling classes. Adams always took those cases. In 1937 when Henderson Clarke refused to appear for the people charged in the rioting, Adams appeared and did what he could. Grantley Adams actually also took a case and won it against Henderson Clarke for assault of a journalist.

"In summary, his legal work brought him into the limelight as a figure challenging the past to build a new future and he totally succeeded at the Bar. But the summit of that success was his absorption into political life in Barbados in which the talents of a great lawyer were combined with the talents of a politician, in first of all making Barbados a new country and then going to the Federation of the West Indies. Though the latter has perished, it may yet make a contribution to the future of the Commonwealth Caribbean."

Now, what of Grantley Herbert Adams as a person, as man and boy? Born to a family of definite quality but of modest means, he had a firm and enlightened upbringing. His father was headmaster of St. Giles Elementary School, which all the seven children (three were girls) attended under their father's own eagle eye. Their life as a family had no lavish frills but they suffered no need or lack of opportunity to be educated. For although their father as a teacher earned in those days no magnificent stipend, they made do and all the children received a secondary education.

Grantley's mother was a near-white woman of great charm (she had white half-sisters). Her marriage to Grantley's father, who was dark-skinned, caused quite a flutter at the time; just as happened when Grantley himself years later caused a social flurry when he married a white wife.

His mixed lineage gave Grantley Adams what might be called a Mediterranean look - dark but not black, with prominently large head, pronounced ears, silky hair, he had an impressive visage, but kindly look. Tall and well-built, he had a good personality and although large feet and loose-set knee joints gave him an ambling gait, it became so much a part of his manner and poise that his physical image was always one of strength and determination.

Friends of those days recall the cricket lover that Grantley was all his life. He was never happy in the field, except as wicket-keeper, which made the most of his reach, but did not tax his feet with too much running, except when he went to bat, at which he was also recognised as competent.

At school and at Harrison College where he gained the Barbados Scholarship in 1918, Grantley was a popular lad and good sport, but compatriots recall an individual stubbornness about him which grew more pronounced as he matured.

At Oxford he was a success, though not brilliant. Being of roving inquisitiveness, he did not follow strict patterns of study but enriched himself by the companionship and leadership which a great University provided. So, called to the Bar at Gray's Inn, home he came, soon to meet Grace Thorne and they were married.

Says Grace (now Lady Adams) when I later talked with her: "I met

13

Grantley soon after he came out from England as a young barrister and I had just left school. We met at a birthday party and I immediately asked somebody, "Who is he?" And I think he did the same thing about me. And that was the beginning."

"And what attracted you to him?" I asked. "He was tall and slim - I couldn't say good looking, but arresting looking, and over the years I had a special affection for the shape and gentle touch of the back of his head."

When they were married in 1929, four years after Grantley's return to Barbados, he had already made a reputation for himself both in the Courts and as a hard-hitting controversialist. But things were not to be all smooth. The white people of Barbados liked his progress and his personality but they objected to his marriage to Grace Thorne, daughter of a director of Austin and Company, head of which was Sir Harold Austin. Indeed it had been through cricket that Austin had formed a liking for Grantley and invited him to his home where he often saw Grace.

Mrs. Thorne and several of the white families objected to the romance. Mrs. Thorne came from the Clarke family, the head of which at that time was Sir Frederick Clarke, Speaker of the House of Assembly. A contemporary told me. "Although it was never said publicly, the white people objected to him marrying into the family of a white director of a big firm."

Says Lady Adams to me on that subject: "We were married in 1929 - and I am afraid my family disapproved of the marriage considerably. I left home and we just married as we intended. And we had no family troubles with his family. But for many years we had no connection with my family. Eventually we got back together."

During the early years of marriage Grace gave up her job as a teacher. As she says, "In those days when a girl got married she gave up her job and became a housewife. So I did that too. Our first (and only) child, Tom, was born in 1930. It was such a difficult birth that I was told by my doctors that another child would certainly be the end of me - and certainly I like life too much to want to end it."

The child grew and prospered and developed into a person of prominence and importance, becoming Prime Minister of Barbados in September, 1976.

Life for the Adams' was happy at home, but for Grantley, he was most of the time in the midst of contentions of the nation, in which he more than held his own, becoming a Member of the Assembly in 1934 and member of the Executive Committee and eventually Chief Minister in 1948. But there were some very dark days, times of mortal peril.

14

The most hazardous of these times was in 1937 when he had to rush to London to see the Secretary of State for the Colonies - moreso to be out of his Barbados enemies reach physically. Hugh Springer, who was then still in London and was Treasurer of the League of Coloured Peoples, helped make appointments and fix speaking engagements for him. As Springer said, it was not a case of Grantley fleeing Barbados, but there had been shooting at him and that sort of thing. (The following year Springer went back to Barbados and teamed up with Grantley, who had then taken the leadership of the Barbados Progressive League, which became the Barbados Labour Party - a partnership which ended when Springer left Barbados to become the first Registrar of the University College of the West Indies in Jamaica).

Joe Broome, now deceased, veteran Barbados journalist, tells in more detail of the dangers which Grantley had faced. In 1937, he recalls, a car with policemen in it passed Grantley's residence "Tyrol Cot" and fired shots through the window. Later Grantley told Joe about it. "You know," he said, "I didn't know what the hell to do. All Grace and I had to do was to go down on the floor so that we could be protected by the two feet of wall below the window sill."

On another occasion an attempt was made to set fire to his house. Says Joe: "I met Grantley at the Police Station carrying the acid, glass and apparatus the arsonists used. He had taken these things to prove to the Inspector General of Police that he was in danger. It was only then that the police put patrols round his house. In those days when Grantley was in real danger, friends used to travel with him to the outlying districts so that at least there could be witnesses if anything happened."

Those days also took their toll on housekeeping. Grantley had previously had a lucrative practice. Then all of a sudden he no longer got those briefs because of political hostility between the old establishment and the new movement. His income suffered considerably. So Grace Adams had to go back to work as a school teacher. "But I liked teaching," she recalls so there was no hardship. But the salaries of those days were very, very small, so that my contribution to the household keep was very, very little."

Eventually the tide turned, and peace returned, and a measure of prosperity. Grantley was totally absorbed in public life. Recalling Grantley's image in those days, Cameron Tudor says: "My abiding impression of Grantley was that he was first and foremost intensely Barbadian. I think all of his instincts, his prejudices - if you like to put it that way - were Barbadian. Certainly his outlook on life was that of a Barbadian, nurtured in the soil and caring most about the Barbadian scene and the Barbadian people in a sort of personal way. I do not think that he was in any sense an internationalist. He had of course world-wide sympathies, but I think he saw everything in the context of the Barbados he knew, the atmosphere in whch he was born and grew up. That

15

I think might be described as his purview. This is not to say he was a "Little Englander." He had interests of course outside Barbados, but he saw everything in the context of being Barbadian."

Cammie Tudor emphasised also that on the personal level Grantley was a charming man - that is, if you got him outside of politics - in any conversation, particularly on cricket and sports generally, or on his reminiscences. He could be very urbane, and occasionally extremely witty - especially in after-dinner speeches.

Tudor thinks, however, that in politics, Grantley took a rather conservative view. "He was, I think, in politics more concerned with what I might call the form of society rather than its substance. You could arouse all his passion and interest in any discussion on constitutional matters, the niceties of it, the do's and the dont's, the distribution of power, and the manipulation of power. But as to what a constitution meant in terms of social development, I think that he had a weakness there."

As to Grantley's image with the people, Cammie says: "To the man in the street in Bridgetown or Christ Church or wherever, he did exercise a fantastic influence over ordinary folk. This came from many sources. First of all, he was a black man, springing up to speak out of the disturbances of the thirties and forties. Then he was a lawyer, a very good one. And on the professional side, he had the reputation of being a sort of bulldog fighter, holding on and not letting go. And I think that it was this aspect of his character as a lawyer which was more or less transmuted into his stance as a politician; and that gave him charisma."

To this assessment should be added, however, that in the memory of others, Grantley could be quite vicious as a Parliamentary opponent. Robert Bradshaw of St. Kitts, Minister of Finance in the Federal Government, recalls, "There was one occasion when the Prime Minister insulted me on the floor of the House. We were going through a detailed Bill which had taken quite a bit of time. The Prime Minister seemed to have been hurrying to leave to attend some function or to go somewhere. He addressed the Speaker and said we could leave the Bill as it was and "let the Clerk adjust the commas."

Says Bradshaw, "The thing seemed to me so ridiculous, as Clerks don't make Law, so I got up and pointed this out. The Prime Minister brushed me aside saying 'If the Minister of Finance wants to argue with me, let him meet me outside.'"

And in the Barbados Legislature, when a member of the Executive Committee, Grantley was leading the introduction of tax increases to finance the new social order, Sir George Walton was persistently criticising the new measures. His bete noir, says a journalist who was present, was the succession duty.

16

Sir George expressed the view that the imposition could only have been devised by an ogre who sought to rob the dead in their graves, to plunder men who in their lifetime had contributed to the wealth of Barbados; to plunder their widows and children.

Grantley Adams, it is recalled, tore into him with great virulence and described him as the kind of person, descended from the lower class of the old-time Bajans who wanted to keep down the black people.

Walton reacted with panic. He gathered up his papers at his seat in the House and walked out. Passing the press table, he said sotto voce : "This man wants me to get a bullet in my neck. If he goes on like that, the people out there will shoot me or kill me somehow." (This was thought to be a reference to the death of a former Speaker of the House, Sir George Pile, who was shot one evening after he left the House of Assembly to go to his home in St. George).

Amidst all the strident events in the political arena, Grace (Lady Adams) says life at home was serene. She says that around the house Grantley was lazy, except that he loved tinkering with electrical gadgets. He was more at home outside in the garden. He loved the garden and grew roses; he would spend hours in the garden when he could spare the time.

I suggested that Grantley was not a domesticated person as such, although he was happy at home.

Said Grace, "I wouldn't say he was not domesticated. He had very good taste in regard to furniture and pictures and arranging the house. He had very good taste indeed."

I recalled that there had been a suggestion that their home Tyrol Cot, because of its aesthetic excellence of home and garden, should be made a national residence for leaders of Government - like Chartwell House in England. Lady Adams said nothing had ever come of the idea. "I think the present Government is very reluctant to have anything named after Grantley." Their son, Tom, renamed the International Airport in memory of Sir Grantley.

The late Sir Hugh Wooding had told me a rather fey story about Sir Grantley Adams at home one night when a thief was heard in the shrubs round the house. He said Grantley took his gun and went out and held the man, brought him into the house, sat him down on a bench and said, "Wait until I call the police." Grantley went to the telephone and when he came back he seemed amazed that the man had fled.

Said Lady Adams, "That's a Wooding story. The fact is Grantley told me he took the fellow by his hand and took him to a bench to sit down. He said

17

the man's hand was almost as small as a child's - a little man, rather oldish. Grantley just frightened him; he didn't want anything to happen to the little man. Grantley may have had a revolver, but it wasn't loaded. He had never fired a shot in his life. But he and Hugh were such good friends and they used to pull each other's legs."

The story also has a moral. Which other Caribbean Prime Minister (except perhaps Bustamante in his prime) would have gone outside his house at night to apprehend an intruder? The story is typical of a certain 'Barbadianess' of those days expecially. Home was a castle. Barbados was mostly a peace-loving society, and a man would protect his own, without necessarily telephoning for the police, except to take over the felon! And Grantley's home was always his castle, his retreat, his place of intensive care, for relief from the buffetings of the angry and trying world of political leadership, of poisonings from rival venom.

This was his Eden, to which he returned (as Paradise regained) when the Federal world came tumbling round him. Listless for a long time, it was like a miraculous hibernation out of which Grantley returned.

Lady Adams recalls that just after the Federal collapse she found a book marker in a volume of poems which Grantley (most unlike him she said) had been reading. The marker was at the resurgent poem "Invictus" by Henley:

> "Out of the night that covers me
> Black as the pit from pole to pole
> I thank whatever gods may be
> For my unconquerable soul
> in the fell clutch of circumstance
> I have not winced nor cried aloud
> Under the bludgeonings of chance
> My head is bloody, but unbowed."

His personal confidence returned but torpor remained, then two grievous illnesses, both of which threatened to be fatal, struck. But he suddenly made what Lady Adams says was indeed a marvellous revival.

The ferment of politics in Barbados had come back to a simmer and a boil with the fixing of the date for the 1966 elections.

Says Lady Adams "It has always been a mystery to me. The minute that Grantley heard that the election date was fixed he was absolutely galvanised into action.

"I would not allow him to go to meetings alone - not that I could have prevented him - but I always drove him. And some nights he spoke on four different platforms.

18

"He even managed to climb up on these lorries where they make their speeches, despite his knees which gave trouble."

Thus did the veteran once again become a member of his beloved House of Assembly in 1966 at the age of 68, and back again to the fighting stance of Leader of the Opposition. But neither his age nor his unequalled sacrifices gave him protection from Prime Minister Barrow's accusation that Adams had come back to try and destroy Barbados. Grantley's counter-attack led to his suspension from the House; and undismayed he resumed, though obviously he had had enough. So in October 1970, the old warhorse called it a day; he died just over a year later.

In 1937 when he had just returned from his successful protest mission to London, Grantley's grassroot supporters had collected their pennies and bought for him a second-hand Hillman car so he could better serve the cause of the masses. The presentation was made at Queens Park, Bridgetown. In his speech of acceptance Adams permitted himself the boast and confession that Sir Conrad Reeves, one of the first black men to be knighted in the Commonwealth, was his exemplar and that he had promised himself not only to equal the record of Sir Conrad Reeves, but to surpass him. This Grantley Herbert Adams certainly did, as history perhaps will say, he surpassed all the rest of his contemporaries of his beloved Barbados.

THE RIGHT HONOURABLE
ERROL WALTON BARROW Q.C.
BORN ST. LUCY, BARBADOS 21 JANUARY, 1920
DIED 1 JUNE 1987.

PREMIER OF BARBADOS   (1961-1966)
PRIME MINISTER OF BARBADOS, (1966-1976 and 1985-1987)

2

ERROL WALTON BARROW

It IS SAID THAT THERE ARE TWO STRAINS that have come down in Barbados politics. There is the Adams strain of which the great prototype was the late Sir Grantley Adams, after an interregnum succeeded as head of the Barbadian government by his son, Tom. The other strain one might say is the Barrow strain, exemplified by Errol Barrow, twice recently Prime Minister of Barbados having served as head of that island's government for some 15 years in the first instance and then again from 1985 until his death in 1987.

Barrow himself belongs to the lineage of Dr. Charles Duncan O'Neal who was not only an outstanding medical practitioner but who had great political insight, great even in the context of the thirties, a forward-looking Socialist, the first person ever in the island of Barbados to lift the banner of Democractic Socialism. It was Dr. O'Neal who founded the old Democratic League which was an attempt to galvanize the masses, the black working people into some conception of what their life could be if society were changed in their direction. Errol Barrow inherited that same sense of mission, which was his guiding light in politics.

Of course, Sir Grantley Adams merged into the Socialist stream after a while but at the start and in many respects, Grantley was more conservative than the O'Neal strain of Socialist and so, it is these two great strains of political instinct, insight and service that have brought Barbados to its modern state. In a sense one can use for comparison the differences between these two great Barbadians. Grantley Adams was anti-Garvey and Barrow was pro-Garvey. So in this sense the black streak, stream and vein of politics was Barrow. Grantley Adams was a moderate, a liberal, but he could not (even years after Garvey was dead) say anything good about that black Jamaican who spread the world philosophy of a new deal for the black man from Africa. Barrow could hardly be anti-Garvey; indeed his father was a black priest in the Anglican Church, who became the Head of the Garveyite African Church. But that's another story.

Errol Barrow told me that his earliest recollections are not of Barbados at all; for his father was posted to the U.S. Virgin Islands. At that time in Barbados when Errol was born, his father was the only black priest in the Anglican Church. And his father before him was one of the Church wardens in one of the inland parishes and had retired from being Quarter Master of the West Indian Regiment. Errol's grandfather had seen service in the Boer War and in the Ashanti War and in the West Indies as an active soldier and then he was a church warden. "My father being the eldest boy," says Mr. Barrow, "and my grandfather being a strong churchman, he was sent to Codrington College when he was quite young, about 17 years old. He was ready to be ordained to the Anglican Priesthood before he was 21. Then the Rev. Barrow was sent to one of the most northernmost parishes, St. Lucy, as a Curate of the Parish Church. Turbulent, he was always challenging the establishment in the Church. "So they sent him to the Virgin Islands" says Errol.

Rev. Barrow, with Errol's mother, nee O'Neal (that's the link with the O'Neal strain) went with the rest of the family to the U.S. Virgin Islands. Errol was then three months old; he has no childhood recollection of Barbados.

The Virgin Islands had just been bought a couple of years before from the Danish Government by the U.S. Government and the Virgin Islands were then administered by the Admiral of the U.S. Fleet. It was not a very democratic society; it was run as a sort of naval station.

Looking back on those days, Errol says"

"My father got very involved with the Trade Union Movement with a lawyer, Hamilton Jackson, who lived in the same building belonging to my mother. He was a militant trade unionist and he was one of the first men I grew to admire. I suppose he must have influenced me from I was two or three years . I stayed in the Virgin Islands for seven years and then because of his involvement in the Trade Union movement with Hamilton Jackson (who subsequently became a Judge) my father was invited on board an American warship and taken away surreptitiously. That was the last we saw of him for years. Eventually he found his way to the United States to put his case, but he stayed on there and having been taken away under those circumstances, he joined the Garvey Movement and the African Methodist Episcopal Church in the United States."

A sister was born to the family in the Virgin Islands and in 1927, when

24

he was aged 7, his mother and all five children (one brother and three sisters) went back to Barbados. Back in Barbados, his uncle Dr. Duncan O'Neal, his mother's brother, had founded the Working Men's Association in Barbados. So the family were in a political atmosphere all the time. Young Errol was sent to Combermere School and then to Harrison College. Says Errol:

"During this time my uncle was very active in politics. My mother went to the United States somewhere along the line and joined my father, when I must have been 11 years old. But just then the depression was on and she stayed there and I stayed in the house with my uncle.

"Of course, I was too young to run for election, but there was a Socialist organisation called the Democratic League and there were only three black men in the House of Assembly out of 24. Grantley Adams was not in the movement at that time; as a matter of fact, he was the lead writer and editor of a very conservative newspaper called the Agricultural Reporter. Then after that he wrote for the Barbados Advocate, which was very conservative as well.

"Grantley Adams, did not agree with the policies of the Democratic League; because he did not believe in strikes and that kind of thing. We called a strike on the waterfront and Grantley Adams attacked the concept of dock workers holding up the whole of the rest of the community. Thus I was growing up in a home with my uncle completely absorbed in these matters and I went around with him to his political meetings (certainly during the respectable hours) and I was very involved in his elections and that kind of thing in my early teens."

Then Errol Barrow's uncle, Dr. Duncan O'Neal, died around 1936 and Errol's cousin, Hugh Springer, came back from England and Errol got involved with elections from 1938. In 1940 Errol Barrow was involved with elections again and was campaigning with his cousin Hugh Springer for a seat in St. George's which Hugh won. Hugh Springer was the second General Secretary of the Barbados Progressive Movement. Eddy Thomas was the first. Originally the Progressive League had a union side and a political side; then the union side became dormant but started again after 1939 when the Trades Disputes Act was enacted enabling proper unionism to function.

During all these kinds of activities in the Union Movement and in politics Errol was still a minor. Then the war came along in 1939 just about the time Errol left school, and in December of that year he won a scholarship for Classics to Codrington College.

Errol says he did not want to do Classics so he joined the Royal Air Force. There were not many West Indians in the Air Force at first - two of the first Jamaicans he remembers were Richard Tucker, a young lawyer who died, and Huntley daCosta, also a lawyer.

So, transplanted to London, Errol Barrow grew up in the Royal Air Force, a West Indian uprooted from home. He met lots of other people at Ivory House, which was a sort of hostel for West Indian students, among them John Carter from Guyana. It was a very small West Indian community. Then Errol went away to Canada to complete his training and came back to London in 1944 when he became involved in flying until the end of the war. Just before the end of the war, however, Flight Lt. Errol Barrow left operations - "I had had more than my share" he says - and went to the Communications Centre in Belgium looking after transport of mail and V.I.P's and all that, Cabinet Ministers, Generals and that kind of war person.

Then the war came to an end. Lt. Barrow then joined the staff of the Commander-in-Chief, Field Marshal Montgomery and when Montgomery was called back to the United Kingdom as Chief of Staff, Lord Sholto Douglas became Military Governor and Commander-in-Chief in Europe. Barrow remained with Sholto Douglas until 1947 when he was posted back to the Air Ministry in London to assist with arrangements for the education and training of ex-servicemen.

"I was in charge of the programme of getting people out of the services", Errol says, "and into the universities. I worked between the Colonial Office and the Air Ministry."

Subsequently, Errol Barrow asked to be released from the R.A.F. and from the Colonial Office where he was doing this work and went to London School of Economics where he met as his classmates, Michael Manley, later Prime Minister of Jamaica; the two Mills boys, Gladstone and Donald, the one Professor of Government of the University of the West Indies, the other, Jamaica's former Ambassador to the United Nations, among other things. There was quite a contingent of West Indians at London University. For some time before there had been no West Indians coming into the British Universities, although some came in 1946, for instance, Forbes Burnham, later Prime Minister of Guyana.

"Around that time," says Barrow, "we started the West Indies Students' Union and we roped in students from the other universities in England, Ireland and Scotland, and we had quite a strong Socialist organisation. We were not just school boys; we were people with a certain amount of maturity. There we met people like Leacroft Robinson and David Coore (both of Jamaica) at the Students' Union. It was a vital organisation and played a tremendous part in West Indian and Caribbean leadership in later years."

And so, having got his B.Sc in Economics at the London School of Economics and having been called to the Bar at Lincoln's Inn, Errol Barrow returned to Barbados in 1950. He was a mature scholar, citizen, positive thinker at 30 years of age. Thus and then he became committed to political life while, of course, carrying on his practice as a barrister-at-law.

26

"Well in 1950 I came back home and in 1951, largely through the persuasion of Dr. Cummings - I was reluctant, but they were short of candidates - I stood for election and won my seat. I had wanted to do research and planning instead. Cameron Tudor who had just come down from Oxford, joined with me, and the two of us together wrote the 1951 Manifesto and a chap called "T.T". Lewis, a white Barbadian but a very strong character and very much a Socialist, was with us. Grantley Adams assigned to us the job of writing the Manifesto and for the first time the Barbados Labour Party got a clear majority in the House. Before that the Barbados Labour Party had had 12 members, but one had to be Speaker, which meant that they had a minority on the Floor. In this 1951 election we got 16 seats then. Frank Walcott was with the Labour Party, but by that time Hugh Springer had gone to the University of the West Indies since 1948 and Frank Walcott had taken over as General Secretary.

"We were happy, that we got the majority but after that it was like a colonial administration. Because on the Executive Council of the Barbados Government, the Financial Secretary was an Englishmen and the Attorney General was another Englishman and four members of the House of Assembly - and that included Grantley Adams. It amounted to representative government; although we had Universal Adult Suffrage we did not have full responsibility in government. That was not a situation that we liked; so a lot of friction began to develop. In 1952 Cameron Tudor was the first person to quit; he did not win a seat in 1951 but he had run in 1953 as an Independent. In 1955 we formed the Democratic Labour Party. It had its ups and downs but eventually came into office and held office for 15 years."

This in short compass is the summary of the political emergence of Errol Barrow to be Prime Minister of Barbados.

What of the barrister-at-law? Mr. Barrow had a very fine career at the Bar in Barbados. Contemporaries say he had a very brilliant and successful career in the Courts. He understood what had to go into a case for it to be properly presented. Most people enjoyed his style of address; not just a matter of oratory, but for the clear and direct ideas which he brought to his listeners' minds. Well versed in most branches of the law, his reputation, however, grew mostly as a criminal defender. He probably began to gain this reputation from the famous Pirate Murder Case.

A senior contemporary referring to Mr. Barrow's talents at the Bar says:

"We sometimes were at loggerheads in matters of interpretation of the law, but Barrow has the knack of seeing all round - not just his own case - but all round the legal points involved, which is unusual in advocates."

27

"Most advocates see their own point and see it with crystal clarity in a way almost blinding, which prevents them from seeing anything else. But Barrow not only could see his own case but could anticipate the points which his adversary would be making, the law on the point, and what interpretation the law was capable of bearing in the direction of the circumstances."

Of his style and manner this jurist said:

"Barrow can be reasonably restrained, usually, but on occasion he can be hostile and offensive and a flash of fury.

Frank Walcott, a cardinal personality in Barbadian politics said:

"I think he is a man of powerful resources; he is a very resourceful man. I would say that in my view as an all rounder he is one of the most resourceful men I have come across in the Caribbean. He is the sort of man that reminds me very much in resources - mental resources - of Norman Manley, but without Manley's charm. He does not have Manley's charm. But he can reach people. What he lacks, I think, is that he came at a time when things were running so good for him that he did not know what it was to run a government against difficulties and did not think that he was forced to build up a corps of let us say, advisers, people who would have been with him for a long time. He started with a lot of fledglings, so to speak, so he has run into difficulties. Speaking as a man now, I wonder how much he listens to anybody and whether there is anybody who could advise him. I think one of Errol's difficulties is he might have reached the stage of being on top for so long that, well, who is to advise him? And you can get very lonely. That's the impression I get; that he does not seek advice and I think - all of us have our weaknesses - I think he has an idiosyncrasy of operating on the basis of surprise. He likes these surprise packages and sometimes that does not work so well."

Barrow's life-long friend and colleague, Cameron Tudor, has a different description. He agrees that Barrow was noted for very strong methods. Said Mr. Tudor:

"The peculiar thing about Mr. Barrow's personality is that he is a single personality. There are some people who are public persons and then private persons and then in between. He is neither. It is a single well-oriented personality and his outlook and his ways of dealing with people are the same whether it is in connection with public life or his private life. He is forthright, straightforward, intensely compassionate though he will go to any lengths to disguise his compassion and gentleness. But he is a straightforward person all through.

"There is another aspect of his character which, of course, people don't realise - and that is the irony of it - that he is more a private person than he is a public person. If you want to get close to his true personality you have to see him away from public life. What makes him appear to be strong and not only appear to be strong but gives him the strength of purpose and character in public life is that firstly he is an intensely serious and efficient person. If he has work to do, it must be done and it must be work of a certain quality. The second thing is that he has a sense of mission."

"I do not know if you are aware of the life and work of his famous uncle Dr. Charles Duncan O'Neal. That sense of mission comes from the O'Neal lineage.

"As a speaker on the hustings Barrow's style is again very direct. He is a trained polemicist."

"I think Errol acknowledges that he owes almost all of what he is to the O'Neals. His mother was Ruth O'Neal, the sister of the great leader. The whole O'Neal family were gifted. All of them without exception made a contribution to the public life of Barbados. But more than that, they were a sort of leading light in their community; in education, in the arts and matters of the mind as well as in practical affairs. His mother, Ruth, was one of the best educated women of her generation, and an outstanding musician. She was a firm church-woman, Sunday school teacher, and had a very beneficent influence on young women of the generation that came after her. And I think all of her children - of course everyone knows Errol's sister Nita who earned great distinction for her country by her career as a nurse and in the international field generally - were brilliant. This is the sort of family background which Errol Barrow was heir to. I think his mother played an exceptional part in the moulding of his character and in shaping the outlines of his career. Unfortunately for him she died while he was still a young boy and I think it must have been one of his chief regrets that she did not live long enough to see how well she had brought him up. And of course his mother's mother, Kathleen O'Neil, she was a matriarch and it was largely due to her influence along with her daughter's that shaped Errol's destiny."

In the 15 years of Barrow's first administration in Barbados what was achieved? It seems that social democracy in bringing the people to be bene-ficiaries of the new kind of state, freed as it is from the plantocracy, was the guiding spirit of his administration. The educational process was democratized and free education introduced at all levels. The remaining pockets of segregation in education had been defeated. School meals on a nutritional basis, improved health services of many kinds were the welfare side of it but on the economic side there was industrial development and considerable expansion of the tourist industry.

29

When I saw Mr. Barrow in Barbados mid-1976, these were not the issues which loomed as the elections came nearer. An obvious dispute between Prime Minister Barrow and the Ministers of the Gospel had been raging. Thick-set, cool - almost cold - Mr. Barrow told me that all parties and organisations had had opportunity to examine his proposals for constitutional amendments but for some strange reason the Dean of the Anglican Church sent him a stern reply which was published in the Barbados Advocate before the Prime Minister even got it.

"I thought that ill-mannered and made no reply" says the Prime Minister, "because the churches had apparently been organised by the Opposition and by the conservative elements. The question of the appointment of the Chief Justice (which was largely the contention) had always been done by the Governor General on the advice of the Prime Minister and he had made the proposal now that the Puisne Judges should also be appointed by the Governor General on the advice of the Prime Minister. This would mean that when a Chief Justice came to be named from among them it could not arise that they were Puisne Judges approved by the Judicial Services Committee only, (independent of the Prime Minister) who might not be acceptable later on for appointment as Chief Justice. The government's proposal that Puisne Judges, like the Chief Justice, be appointed on the advice of the Prime Minister, created hostile criticism. The critics claimed that it was a tendency to interfere with justice, beginning with dictatorship and the like. The Dean had published virulent statements on that."

Mr. Barrow said that previously, arising from the referral of the Constitution proposals to organisations and to the Ministers of Religion, twenty-seven proposals for amendment had been received by the Government but the Opposition only concerned themselves with five of them. In London where the British Government tended to side with the Opposition on the proposals, Mr. Barrow said he had decided not to allow them to delay independence by sticking out. So he had compromised on some matters knowing that when the nation was independent these could be sorted out. The opportunity came when his Party had the necessary two-thirds majority to implement the changes.

Asked about his not attending the funeral of Sir Grantley Adams, Mr. Barrow said to me:

"In the Caribbean we are rather ghoulishly concerned about funerals, but that was not my only reason. In fact years ago there was a great member of the Socialist elements of the Barbados Labour Party, Christopher Braithwaite, who died; and when it was sought to have the House of Assembly adjourn early so that Members could attend the funeral, Premier Grantley Adams refused to agree to the adjournment. By contrast, when Stalin died Adams took the occasion to a make a big speech 'about this great man', but he did not consider that upon the death of his own Barbadian it was worthy of Parliament adjourning early to enable Members to attend the funeral"

Obviously little love was lost between Errol Barrow and Grantley Adams. As Sir John Mordecai has written, "Barrow habitually never missed a chance of not meeting Sir Grantley."

Those were the urbane, if not conciliatory, views on these contentious matters held by Prime Minister Barrow just a few months before the 1976 election. But as it turned out, the contention and the rift in the nation was deeper than seemed to have been envisaged, and Barrow was heavily defeated.

Local analysts after the election contended that the Barrow Government lost the support of the conservative middle-class. The issue over whch that confidence was lost was the dispute - the bitter dispute - with the clergy and others.

Prime Minister Barrow was crucial in the attempts which were made, when Federation failed, to try and rescue the remainder by creating a Federation without Jamaica. Says Mr. Barrow:

"After the referendum by which Jamaica left the Federation, I went down to Tobago to see Dr. Williams and to give him the assurance of anything I could do to help him to keep the Federation together. I had known Eric Williams for a long time and Frank Walcott and I had done a lot to encourage him when he left the Caribbean Commission, to get some political organisation going to fill the vacuum that then existed in Trinidad. Frank Walcott had taken Eric to Geneva to the International Labour Organisation on one occasion as his adviser. And, of course, Dr. Williams was also very close with Arthur Lewis who had been at university with him. Then we had met in Jamaica with Norman Manley in 1956. But when I met Dr. Williams in Tobago he discussed everything else but Federation. I could hardly get to say anything. He did most of the talking but said nothing about what was going to be done. When we tried to draw him out, he said his Cabinet had not yet had an opportunity to discuss it. So it was a very disappointing meeting."

"Shortly after that, Mr. Maudling the Secretary of State came down to discuss what could be done to keep the rest of the Federation together, what was left of it. Of course, Barbados said it would go along - I was a very ardent Federalist at the time - not now. Then Maudling went to Eric Williams and did not receive a very good response. Arthur Lewis was then advising us in Barbados and there was a conference in London about setting up a Regional Council of Ministers. Eric did not like the idea of going back to the Colonial Office. Then the question of finance was an important one because most of the small territories were grant-aided and so Eric wanted to know what kind of financial support the Central Government was going to have, otherwise the burden would have to fall on Trinidad. This dragged on and on and on and it was very unsatisfactory."

"Instead of meeting together by ourselves as we now do in CARICOM, we had the Governor of Barbados as chairman. I wouldn't say he was a weak chairman certainly he was very strong in so far as the British Government's interests were involved - he was very strong on that. But we never got any guidance as to how far we could go on certain points. Just at that time Grenada had elections and they had been made a promise by Trinidad and Tobago that they could expect some help from them. That did not come off. And then St. Lucia had elections. John Compton had never been in favour; he preferred a unitary state. Well, in 1965 we published a White Paper on Barbados and its place in a federal structure. As soon as we did that the Opposition, which had never taken any interest in the discussion on Barbados and the Leeward Islands getting together, started an island-wide campaign against it. They said it was going to be too costly and we were going to set up a republic and we were going to abolish elections, the same kind of thing they are doing right now, saying that when you have established a strong majority, you have started a one-Party state."

"This is damned nonsense, of course. Grantley Adams was mixed up in all this. Then, we had an election in 1966, he ran and won a seat and was the Leader of the Opposition. They insisted on sending a strong delegation to London although they never even attended the Barbados House of Assembly to discuss the draft Independence Constitution. They and the conservatives who still had a couple of members in the House of Assembly had a joint delegation. They opposed everything in the Independence Constitution. There were a lot of things which we compromised on which we knew were not consistent with more advanced Constitutions given to countries recently becoming independent. But because we wanted to get the thing out, we said we could argue about that point later. It appears that the Secretary of State, on the advice of the Governnor of Barbados, was looking for an excuse to say we could not reach an agreement on Independence and thus to postpone it. But we were determined to have Independence in 1966 because we had been elected on an Independence Manifesto. So we compromised on one or two matters and we went off to a West Indian conference in August 1966 and we had Independence in November when we won the elections."

Garvey and Garveyism are a very deep-rooted part of black Barbadian thinking. As we have seen, Prime Minister Barrow's father was a Bishop in the Garveyite Church. Mr. Barrow told me that when he was a young boy, Marcus Garvey came on a speaking tour of Barbados and though small and young he could stay at his parents' home and listen to Garvey's meeting across the way. He remembers with interest how Marcus Garvey came in a procession on foot from the waterfront to the meeting place and Garvey was wearing a felt hat in the hot sun and a coat with a fur collar, all in this great tropical heat and he marched with his companions up to the place for the meeting.

Says Mr. Barrow: "I will never forget that meeting because that was when I heard Garvey say: 'The trouble with the black man is that he goes to bed too early and he wakes up too late.' From that time until now I took the decision that would not happen to me and five hours sleep a night has been adequate for me, because Garvey impressed me with that philosophy."

At any rate the Back-to-Africa movement had been strong in Barbados before Garvey's time. Indeed, Barbados claims that the first Back-to-Africa movement from the coloured peoples of the new world started not in Jamaica with Garvey, but in Barbados.

They say it started in Barbados in 1840. The President of Liberia who had been to the United States, President Roberts, stopped in Barbados and had long consultations with a man called Anthony Barclay, who by the way is the father of George Barclay, who later on became President of Liberia. Anthony Barclay was an exceptional man who had his complete family history and who knew the tribe of Africa from which he came. And it was said he could not only go and find the exact area but the exact tribe from which he sprung. Well, actual migration took place, but not until about twenty years later when they started an organisation called the African Progress Union when a number of Barbadians, including Barclay and his sons, migrated to Liberia.

Barrow seems from childhood to have had a skill at crucial action. For instance, in the Sixth Form at Harrison College they had a Master called Evans who was somewhat eccentric but a brilliant, classical scholar. One of the boys of the scholarship class had caught his notice and he used to give this boy extra attention in tuition to get him ready for the Barbados scholarship. But this young man had offended him in some way and one day in class Evans said to this young man: "I can't understand what's wrong with you people. You come to my house, I spend all my time with you, I teach you by taking up time I could use more profitably, and this is the ingratitude you show me."

One of the boys of the class still surviving told me: "This upset all of us but we none of us knew how to react to it, but Errol Barrow who was in class with us said: 'I will deal with him'. Then he advised: 'All the books he has ever lent all of us, you bring them back and put them back on my desk after the lunch period.' "We did as he told us. When the lunch break was over and we resumed classes, Errol Barrow took all the books up and just struck them down on the teacher's desk."

"It was a dramatic gesture of defiance", says the narrator of this anecdote of schooldays, and adds "I think those of us in the class then saw the first beginnings of leadership in him."

THE RIGHT HONOURABLE
VERE CORNWALL BIRD

BORN ANTIGUA, 1903

CHIEF MINISTER OF ANTIGUA (1960-1967)
PREMIER OF ANTIGUA, (1967-1971, 1976-1981)
PRIME MINISTER OF ANTIGUA, (1981-

3

VERE CORNWALL BIRD

VERE CORNWALL BIRD, whose name has been almost synonymous with Antigua for a very long time, is an unusual West Indian character, in that he does not have a show-off style, neither is he the academic type; he is a straight worker-leader individual. Very tall, his height is accentuated by the ever-present felt hat with black band which perhaps is his only affectation. He can be seen at a glance in any crowd, because he stands tall above most people. Not given to melodramatics, he is homespun, but like so many homespun leaders he is tough, resilient and almost indestructible.

His sombre complexion has been marked in later years by discolorations on parts of the face which tend to give his look even greater strength, and he might be said to have some of the look of a benign dalmatian - strong, gentle and impressive.

Sensitive about his age, it is difficult to get him to state when he was born. I ventured asking him his age and got no answer, whereupon I said to him, "I was born in 1909. Were you born before or after 1909?" He chuckled. He said: "You set me the conundrum. I don't think it was before and I don't think it was after." It seems, however, that he was born in 1903 and stalwart as he is, you would hardly believe it. Opponents rather maliciously, it would seem, once published a photograph of Premier Bird, when, according to the Opposition newspaper, he was 66, showing him in the company, seemingly affectionate, of a most attractive young girl. This was published obviously to scandalize the Premier but, indeed, it improved his stocks with the populace because it gave him an aura of warmth and human affection. His people, of course, have known him all these years. But the thought that the Opposition must have had

37

in publishing that photograph seeing that they are mostly young men, was a strange kind of political gimmick and did not pay off.

Mr. Bird, who was then in Opposition, came through to win the General Election and was returned to office as Premier of Antigua, Barbuda and Redonda, the three islands which form the state of Antigua. As the books say, 'Antigua' is a place of peace and freedom and friendship. Visitors find it so, but the Opposition Press belies that. It is hard to find duplicates in the Commonwealth Caribbean for the bitter journalism of Antigua. But in the midst of all that, like a tall ship, steady at sea, Vere Conrad Cornwall Bird remains dispassionate, ruthless no doubt, but always charming.

Like so many other Commonwealth Caribbean political leaders, Vere Bird grew up in relative poverty. He grew up in the New Street area of St. Johns. Nowadays, it has been cleaned up, but in those days it was squalid. Those poor circumstances in New Street impressed him with the necessity for improvement, not only there but in all Antiguan communities. As he put it: "So that those coming up afterwards would not have the same bitter experience."

There were five sons in the Bird family and, as he says, very reservedly: "Let us say we had very low fare. That is what we people had in those days. So low it was in those days that I do not even think of it now."

Vere Bird went to school at St. Anne's Boys' School, an elementary school, and there he got a basic education. After that, at 18 years of age, he became a Salvationist, serving in the Salvation Army for some time. In Trinidad, where he went for training in the Salvation Army, he became renowned as a preacher. Indeed, his political stance is very much that of a preacher. He has for so long been accustomed to speak to large crowds without a microphone, that his voice booms over the largest crowd as clear as a drum.

I said to him: "So your eloquence was notable from your teenage days?" He modestly replied: "I tried in those days, I tried as I saw the need."

One would wonder how, from little Antigua, he did not feel attracted to staying on in Trinidad where he was gaining his reputation as a Salvation Army preacher. I asked him: "Didn't you fall in love with Trinidad?" He said: "No, I didn't. At a very early time I made up my mind that I would only serve in the Salvation Army for a number of years after which I would return to Antigua and enter ordinary life again."

And so, after serving in the Salvation Army in Trinidad and in Grenada, he came back to Antigua when he was about 22 years old. But, he says he has remained religious. When he goes to worship publicly, he goes to the Salvation Army Hall. Says Premier Bird: "I think of the time I spent in the Army in my youth and I am still satisfied with the training I got then. I am quite satisfied with my experience as an officer, a Captain in the Salvation Army, the highest post to which I could aspire then. And I was very much impressed by the spirit of service in the Salvation Army."

So, after the discipline of a religious movement such as the Salvation Army in 1939, Vere Cornwall Bird entered the hall of the Antigua Trade and Labour Union in which he was to find his feet as a people's leader and as a national leader. At first he was a member of the Executive Committee and after two years he became President and served in that capacity for 25 years.

In between his return from Trinidad and Grenada he had served in commercial firms doing clerical work which gave him some experience in the routine of an office, and so, with that experience behind him and the discipline of the Army, he went into the Union and from there on to political pre-eminence.

He says, however, that he did not have politics in mind when he went into the Union. The political leaders in Antigua at that time were Harold T. Wilson, Major Hole and Reginald Sinclair Stephens. Bird's mind was set on the Union and the improvement of the lot of workers of Antigua. This leadership of the workers, of course, led to conflicts with the plantocracy and as he recalls it, very often the Union and the workers would win but the planters, being of the Legislative and Executive Councils, were able to go into these Councils and take back or reduce what had been gained for the people.

Then it was that the Union and himself realised and saw the need of getting into where the policies were formulated. So that is how they decided that they would have to get into the Legislative Council. They made the effort and they broke through. The 1940 general elections to the Legislative Council of Antigua was the turning point. Strangely, it led to crisis inside the Union because the first vice-president of the Union at that time, Joseph Oliver Davis, wished the Union to consider persons not necessarily of their membership but persons who had wider experience. Members disputed this and went against Davis, dropping him, and going on to select the Union candidates that they thought capable of serving. And so Vere Cornwall Bird, D. Leonard Benjamin, Edmund Hawkins Lake, Hugh O. Pratt and Ernest E. Williams were chosen to stand for election; all five of them were elected. They had contested all the seats available and were victorious in all of them. Joseph Davis contested as an independent candidate and was badly defeated, whereafter he gave up active politics. Vere Bird was chosen to sit on the Executive Council, but he was the only Union member chosen to sit there, so that he had little support in the Executive for his views.

Premier Bird recalls that from their seats in the Legislative Council and using his presence in the Executive Council where he served for some time, the Unions agitated for greater representation and succeeded in getting the number in the Legislative Council increased. Then they agitated to improve the conditions, because to stand for election, or to vote, one had to have so much property value or so much money. Next they succeeded in getting a majority in the Legislative Council of elected persons. Having achieved that, they worked on, first the membership system, then they came up with the various steps for the committee system, and then on to the ministerial system.

So Vere Cornwall Bird worked along that line, step by step. The great bug-bear of the workers in Antigua at that time was A. Moody-Stuart who was the leader of the plantocracy. There was to be many a conflict between Vere Bird and Moody-Stuart.

Mr. Bird recalls:

"Moody-Stuart in 1951 thought that the Union had petered out after all those years, so when 1951 came for negotiations, he said no, he wasn't dealing with any trade unions. He boasted: 'I always said this thing would not last; and now we think the time has come to break it, to break it once and for all."

Moody-Stuart said all he needed was police protection and he was going to starve the people into submission: he said that in the presence of the Governor of Antigua, Sir Kenneth Blackburne, and Premier Bird recalls the Governor saying to Moody-Stuart "Take care you don't butt your head against a wall." Moody-Stuart repeated that all he needed was police protection. So they all left the meeting and the Governor told Moody-Stuart that he could have his police protection and he, Moody-Stuart told the Governor: "I will break them in three months."

And so the plantocracy and Moody-Stuart had their police protection and they would not deal with the trade union representatives. The people remained out of work because Moody-Stuart wanted the workers to return to work unconditionally. They declined and the strike went through one month, then another month, then the third month. At the end of the third month when Moody-Stuart realised that the people were not bowing under as he thought they would, he came to the trade union leaders and suggested that they go out among the people and hold some mass meetings.

Premier Bird relates:

"So we went first to the tamarind tree by Bethesda Village. A great amount of people gathered. Moody-Stuart wanted to speak first and he did so and told the people that the sugar industry was losing a lot of money and the people were losing a lot of wages and he thought this suffering should not continue, and he thought they should go back to work."

40

It is exceptional in Caribbean circumstances that such a mass meeting would have been addressed jointly by the leader of the sugar industry and by the leaders of the sugar workers. But that is part of the genius of Bird's and Antigua's history in such matters.

"At the meeting, however, the people said:

Oh no! You were going to starve us into submission. Never again will you be able to say that to us. The workers, who had not been working for three months had made up their minds that they were not going to work for the other nine months of the year.

Premier Bird says that with that determination they left the meeting at Bethesda for another mass meeting at Betty's Hope in another part of the island where another great assembly of people were. Moody-Stuart again spoke first and tried to say the same thing to the people. But the people were of the same resolute mind.

It was a very determined stand the people took. They did not work again for the whole of 1951. Says Mr. Bird:

"They went into pastures and they would cut bush and boil the bush to make a soup; they went to the seaside, to the beach and they would pick up some cockles and that is how they lived for the whole year 1951. First three months and then nine months more. It lasted the whole year of 1951."

That broke Moody-Stuart and the planters. When the next year came, the day after New Year's day in 1952, Moody-Stuart rang Vere Bird and said he wanted an early negotiation. This was agreed to and they met on the 5th of January. And, as they met, Moody-Stuart asked the Union officials: "What do the people want that could satisfy them and let them go out to work?" The Union leaders said: "We wanted an agreement and the people wanted a 25% increase on their wages." Moody-Stuart said: "Let them have it." And so the negotiations were finished there and then, and the people went back to work.

Mr. Bird said: "I think Moody-Stuart and all of us were very satisfied with the amount of work that was done now, clearing out the canes that had remained standing since the year before and putting back the industry into full production."

I asked Premier Bird: "Tell me something, sir, how did you and your workers maintain a spirit so equable and quiet that after three months you and Moody-Stuart could go and address them at the same time and there was peace and order?"

41

Mr. Bird replied:

"Well, probably from the way we ran our organisation here; there was not a lot of violence. There was some, and some people went to prison, but very often it was not violence, but going around and advising people not to work. Then they were just charged with incitement. Those were the days too, when you couldn't get lawyers to represent the workers and our officers. I myself had to go before the Court with Judge and jury and without a lawyer to defend myself. They had charged me with contempt of court, with inciting the people - because it was in times like those that I would have to go out and hold public meetings and advise the workers as to how they should act. The authorities were not satisfied with this so they carried me before the court. I couldn't get a lawyer to represent me and so I defended myself and in the end I was acquitted."

One would have thought that after all these critical things and the year's strike and its eventual settlement and the good work done by the workers in bringing back the sugar industry that Moody-Stuart would have changed his attitude. Premier Bird says:

"I don't think he ever changed. He was conscious of the master and servant relationship; that could not come out of him."

Asked how Governor Blackburne took it all, Premier Bird says:

"I think Governor Blackburne did a good job here. When he was coming here a lot of people told us he was a Conservative and they didn't feel he would get on with us. But when he came, Governor Blackburne said all he wanted was to place whatever there was on the table and let us go over it and whoever is right he would support them."

"And I must say," Premier Bird declares, "that on most occasions when our matters went before the Council, or whatever it was went on the table, we were most often right and so we succeeded quite often."

About Governor Baldwin's days which were quite interesting, Premier Bird says that Baldwin came and gave encouragement to the people. He was a Socialist and he gave us heart. "And very often we were able to go and discuss matters with him . Of course, admittedly, there were those who frowned on the Governor encouraging men like myself to come to Government House but I don't think the Governor supported their view and he would continue to invite the labour leaders and the followers very often, and so some from the other groups disliked him very much for that," Premier Bird recalls.

"We had some heated matters here which led to his recall to England. I had to go there and make representations to the British Government telling them that we felt it was an unfair thing being done to Baldwin and so they sent him back to Antigua."

At this I said to Mr. Bird: "Imagine you with all the struggle behind you, going to London to appear on behalf of a British Governor on trial."

Said Premier Bird: "Yes and I told them why I was doing it; that I wasn't satisfied that Baldwin was doing anything especially to help labour's cause against the rights of the other classes and against the planters and for them to withdraw him at this stage without proper explanation was to create a lot of doubt."

Asked whether there were days of extreme violence over all these years of union growth while this change in the life of Antigua was taking place, Mr. Bird said no. He remembers an occasion when the Welsh Fusiliers were brought to Antigua and he says: "When we heard they had come in, we the leaders went round to the people and we advised the people not to go near them. We felt it was uncalled for to have them there. There had been no riot; there had been no uprising. So we told the people: 'Stay away from them and those who brought them here will have to answer why they brought them here.'"

At that time Mr. Bird says there was an inquiry going on. He remembers men like Richard Hart of Jamaica who was there to give a hand and appear before the Board of Inquiry. "Sir Clement Malone was the chairman of the Board of Inquiry. And after we heard that they had brought in these soldiers, our executive at the Union decided that we would not appear before the Commission with the soldiers present. We felt we were being intimidated and so when the time came Mr. Richard Hart went and he notified the Commissioners that the leaders of labour had decided that due to the presence of the military, the bringing in of the Fusiliers, we would not be attending as long as the soldiers were present."

"I remember the Governor calling us up and trying to mouth-fight us and we told him we were very sorry but that we had made that decision and we were determined no inquiry for us as long as the soldiers were in Antigua. The Governor was Sir Brian Freyston and after a time as a result of the Unions' determination the soldiers were withdrawn. It was then that the Union leaders returned to the Board of Inquiry and concluded the proceedings."

Looking back over the years Mr. Bird thinks that Antigua has proceeded very well. On the industrial side they have been able to increase wages quite a lot. "I remember when it was what 10d. a day for men and 8d. for women and in the small gangs boys and girls were paid 5d. a day. Tradesmiths were paid 2/6d. a day. We succeeded in raising those rates to a very great extent and we have had a fair amount of prosperity in Antigua. In the political

43

arm we have been able to introduce a lot of industries. We have had full employment, the rates of wages were good and there was lots of money in circulation. I think Antigua was a happy place in which to live."

Discussing the question of his having held both the office of President of the Union and then Chief Minister and then continuing in both posts, Mr. Bird said there were people who preached that he should not be both President of the Union and be the head of the Government. "But it never troubled me because whenever there was any question to be decided I am sure I decided it in a manner that gave justice, and being President of the Trade Union did not help or hinder one way or the other. Justice was done at all times and that was why I was able to continue for so many years as both President of the Union and Chief Minister and later Premier of the island."

"That went on for some time, but I gave it up after there was this agitation that I should not hold both positions."

The late Robert Bradshaw, Premier of St. Kitts-Nevis was not so sure that Mr. Bird wasn't wrong in giving up his Union leadership and retaining only his post as head of government because he felt that was why ultimately Mr. Bird was defeated by Mr. Selwyn Walter. Mr. Bradshaw recalled advice which was given by Jamaica's Alexander Bustamante to him and to Mr. Bird in the bar of the Country Club in Montego Bay in 1952. They were there attending that year's meeting of the Caribbean Commission. Bird asked Busta how it was that he, Busta, was able to retain the dual positions of President of the Bustamante Union and Chief Minister of Jamaica at one and the same time. Bustamante said: "They tried to discuss it and to talk to me about it, but I refuse to discuss it, I refuse to discuss it. You think I am a goddam fool? The people who elect me as President of the Union are the very people who elect me to be Chief Minister of Jamaica. I refuse to discuss it."

Bradshaw said:

"I kept that advice. Grantley Adams did not take the advice and as a result his party lost because he tried to separate the Trade Unions from politics which does not work out here because political representation has grown out of the labour movement. Maybe it is unfortunate but there it is, a fact of life. If I were to say to my people in St. Kitts today that I am going to withdraw from the Presidency of the Union to which they elected me and retain the Premiership of the State, the people's reaction would be violent and predictable. 'Oh, you get too big for us now, eh?' It is as simple as that."

Mr. Bradshaw added that "when Selwyn Walter started his opposition to Mr. Bird, he used the same thing, criticising Mr. Bird for being President of the Union and Premier of the country at one and the same time. But what did Mr. Bird do? He gave up the presidency of the Union. The result was predictable; he went out of power. And no sooner did Selwyn Walter get in, he himself promptly also formed a Union. That is something to remember."

Federation found Mr. Bird sticking to his beloved Antigua. "I remained at home in Antigua. I was one of those who remained in the individual territory. Novelle Richards and Grantley Carrot went to the Federal Parliament. They were among our leaders and they went for us to the Federal Parliament. I felt," Mr. Bird says, "my job was here in leading Antigua and that job was not completed; there was work to be done, like bringing in the oil refinery; like bringing in the cement works, bringing in a lot of factories here. There were those who felt that the smaller territories should not concentrate upon these things but I remained at home and succeeded to a very great extent in having the island industrialised."

Asked what he thought caused Federation to fail, or who caused Federation to fail, Premier Bird says: "It was a matter of wanting to walk too fast. When they agreed to federate I was one of those who supported the view that we should take the subjects that were possible and in the course of time the Federation would strengthen. There were those who felt they wanted a strong central government. But after all these numbers of years these islands having been under the Colonial Office, I don't think they were ready to have the Colonial Office transferred from London to a federal capital. They would have done better to leave a fair amount of autonomy with the territories and let the people see the benefits of federation and then from year to year strength would have been added and the federation would have been still here today. I feel it was that feeling of wanting to take too much from the territories that caused some amount of fear among the people of some islands and made them support the dissolution of the federation."

On the question, however, of whether Mr. Bird's defeat in 1971 did not arise from his decision to give up the leadership of the Trades Union, Mr. Bird says: "Well, as far as I am concerned, for the many years that I served as President of the Union and as leader of the political side, I would say the results are there. Let those who want to judge, judge."

Asked how he spent his time while the other Party was in power, Premier Bird said:

"I am always very happy and comfortable reading magazines. In the early days I used to read books a lot, but nowadays I read mostly magazines and newspapers. And provided I could get them I kept myself informed about the world, especially about Africa.

"I also looked on at what the new government was doing here; the members of the new government were all of them formerly our secretaries and organisers and so on who had won the election. I gave them an opportunity to see what they could do and I was not troubled in any way."

45

Asked whether having been accustomed to a full day's work of government and Union did he not take up any other hobby during that interregnum, he said no. "I don't need hobbies; once I have books and magazines and all that, I study what's going on in the various spheres of politics in the world."

I then said to him: "So in those days you were worrying about the world and Africa and what was going on?"

"Very much so," he replied. "When it comes to the African question I regard myself and all coloured people as part of the common problem facing black people all over the world; whether it is the 25 million in the United States or the 20 million in South America (although they talk there about equality, I don't accept that). Once they are coloured the problem is the same all over. In the Caribbean or even at home in Africa I always take a very keen interest in what goes on among our people all over the world."

This reminded me that speaking about Premier Bird, the late Mr. Bradshaw of St. Kitts had told me that Mr. Bird had a lot of conviction in whatever he did. He was a determined Antiguan. "With him Antigua comes first but what is more he is very racial. He loves his race very, very much."

Said Mr. Bradshaw: "When he went to Africa in 1954, he was in Kenya and was invited to speak. He was then attending the Commonwealth Parliamentary Association meeting in Kenya. The British authorities in Kenya had taken him to a Mau Mau camp and what he said to the camp upset them so much they complained to the Colonial Office. John Stow was then in some official capacity. Then later on Mr. Bird went to what is now Southern Rhodesia and demanded and got service in a white restaurant, on the basis that he was an African who had returned home and that if he did not get service in his own homeland he was going to mash up the restaurant.

"Now looking at mild Mr. Bird, you would never think that, but it is true and also when he went to a post office to buy stamps he was not standing in line with Africans, for he insisted that there should be no separate lines." That is a definition of Mr. Bird by his late long time friend and Leeward Island compatriot Robert Bradshaw.

Asked about his general political philosophy, Mr. Bird insists that he has always been on the side of Socialism. He admits that the future of Antigua needs to be looked after.

"The economy is in a bad way, so that is the priority. The national debt is very high. All our factories and industries have been closed. The unemployment is 47% and with that being the position, our hands are full to find something to put the people back to work to get the economy moving again."

46

He considers that when that has been attended to, will be time to deal with the question of independence. "We are going all out. We are making every effort to put the factories back into operation. I think we have a good programme and I am quite satisfied that it is going to be successful. The tourist industry - all industries - went down here very much, so that is one of the things we have to do right away."

Asked whether he thought that the Selwyn Walter government had caused the decline, Premier Bird said: "I thing the story is well known; they helped alot to cause what has happened." Mr. Bird thinks the federal idea will come back. He said:

"As I see it we are going ahead with CARICOM and we are seeing about common shipping and marketing and airlines; all these things. They are all good and are going in the right direction showing the great need of these territories to work together. We will watch and see what will be the outcome."

At Lancaster House, London, in 1961, at the break up of the Federation of the West Indies, Mr. Bird was regarded as one of the most thoughtful speakers. After Iain McLeod's 'bracing' opening, Sir John Mordecai recalled Mr. Bird of Antigua leading a point of special timeliness. "He thought that the trouble was that some leaders, having seen the form of Federation differently from others, and having convinced their followers that theirs were the only lines, we were finding difficulty in agreeing to anything that was not 100% in line with what they had advocated earlier. Mr. Bird felt that such leaders were under-rating two factors.

"Shorn of all that they were told, the people of the West Indies want Federation.....and are expecting their leaders to reach agreement.... Secondly, none were sufficiently realising that the public leaders who followed in the future would, in any event, be bound to put Federation into a form somewhat different from what was now being insisted upon.'"

Finally, he told me in 1976: "All I will add is we are all going to continue the fight as long as we are able to, and we will see, we the people in the Caribbean."

ROBERT LLEWELLYN BRADSHAW

BORN ST. PAUL'S, ST. KITTS, 16TH SEPTEMBER, 1916
DIED 24TH MAY, 1978

CHIEF MINISTER-OF ST. KITTS-NEVIS-ANGUILLA (1962-1978)

4

ROBERT LLEWELLYN BRADSHAW

ROBERT LLEWELLYN BRADSHAW, was head politician of the State of St. Kitts-Nevis-Anguilla for 20 years, firstly as an elected member and when the Ministerial system was introduced as Minister of Trade and Production. In 1958 he was elected as the State's representative in the West Indian Federation and subsequently the Premier of the State of St. Kitts-Nevis-Anguilla.

Impressions of Robert Bradshaw vary not only in his own home state but throughout the Commonwealth Caribbean. Some emphasised his aggressive nature, others his diplomacy; some made much of his foibles of dress, but all respected and almost held him in awe as a man of work, study and application to the job in hand. He had a fighter's face with a clipped officer's moustache which sometimes gave him a grim, forbidding look. When he chose , he would break quickly into the smile of diplomacy which could just as quickly fade away.

Bradshaw figured prominently during the Anguilla episode by which Anguilla seceded (and succeeded in doing so) from the dominion of the government of St. Kitts-Nevis-Anguilla. That is a very interesting episode out of which Robert Bradshaw emerged as a sort of swash-buckling-politician turned-security-force-leader, because, as he put it, the Constitution of St. Kitts-Nevis-Anguilla was still intact, though the British Government in London had interposed another government of Anguilla, without dissolving, in his judgment, the government of St. Kitts-Nevis-Anguilla.

51

But back to Robert Llewellyn Bradshaw. He was born at St. Paul's, St. Kitts on September 16, 1916. His family was poor even taking account of the existing living standards of those days. Let us hear him, in the 1970's , relate something about his early childhood:

> "St. Paul's at that time was one of the poorest parts of St. Kitts. My mother was unmarried; my father a blacksmith. I was brought up mostly by my late grandmother who did the best she could for me. She ensured that I had training in behaviour, etiquette and things of that description and she saw to it that I went to school. She herself took me to school the first day.

Of his early childhood there were some other recollections. His mother's only child, he had a fair diet and life. Childhood meals were the usual vegetables; a fair amount of meat, because in the countryside there were pigs and goats which were slaughtered and corned (salted), and they had fruit; ordinary fare, but good. There was no great luxury and trimmings but the food was fresh and plentiful. At school he played bat and ball, pitched marbles, spun top or gig, the usual thing, as he says, "getting the worst of it sometimes, winning sometimes." He was expert at nothing particularly but he liked cricket. There were no real cricket fields so it was really "bat and ball", using young breadfruit, pear seeds, mangoes, anything. A typical Caribbean worker's child.

> "Ours is a poor family - still poor - because if you go to the village today, you will still find some of my relations working in the canefields. So to the extent that blood is blood, I have not quite left the fields, I am still attached to the earth.

> "Our lives were the same as other people in the village: no rich people there; the biggest people were the shopkeepers and above them the estate owners and overseers. The village was totally set on estate lands, the result being that people were not quite free. Because, if they offended the owners of the estates on which they lived, the usual punishment was swift and severe, namely, they had to remove their houses to another location which was not easily found."

Robert Bradshaw says that this was something which attracted his attention from the very early days as being manifestly unjust, cruel and inhuman. He said he simply could not do anything about it then because he was a child. It was during his school days that he became aware of something called a Union because his grandmother, who worked on one of the two estates - the one called Belmont - and with whom he went mornings to weed cane before going to school, gave him every Monday morning, either a penny or a threepenny bit as her Union dues. This was paid to the local Union representative who lived just at the entrance to the school; a man called Gabriel Douglas.

"I didn't know what the Union was all about, but my grandmother insisted that she had to pay. But that habit of contributing to the Union entered into my childhood mind and lived with me as I grew up."

About his school days, Robert said: "The Head Teacher was female. She certainly did the best she could for all of us - not for me in particular - but she was our second parent. My mother, who went out to work as a domestic servant, contrived to send me to study music. The organ it was, with the head teacher. I got through primary school and within a few weeks was apprenticed to the foreman of the machine shop at the sugar factory. I became a machine apprentice in 1932 when I was 16."

Of his days as an apprentice, very eventful days, and contributing considerably to his outlook on life and on the world, Premier Bradshaw said:

"Well, I worked at the factory and stayed with my mother, who by that time had become caretaker of the Guest House at the sugar factory where the directors who came out from England stayed on their annual visits. That was the St. Kitts-Basseterre Sugar Company which owned the sugar factory and which in great part was my adversary in life, as I grew up in Unionism.

"I was able, between 1932 and 1938, when my mother migrated to Curacao, to see the other side of life in the island. The Guest House was located where the staff lived. I could see how those people lived, who were all white as against how my own black people lived and I felt again that something was wrong."

What brought things to a head in his mind, he said, was a simple event which took place one evening when one of the directors was in the house on his annual visit. A man called Moodie-Stuart (his father and himself were managing directors of the company and were involved in the conception and execution of the factory programme) was in the house. Young Bradshaw then had the habit of collecting stamps. He, therefore, went to the waste-paper basket, as he often did, to see what envelopes had been thrown away from which he could take the stamps.

Robert Bradshaw, recalling this incident, said: "I found a document torn in two. I like reading, so I took the torn document to my quarters which were right in the house, put them together and read them, read the whole thing. The document was the annual account for the sugar factory, showing profit and loss, things I didn't understand at that time, but I had a general idea of what it meant for it showed the profits the factory was making , which when I compared with the wages we were paid, confirmed in my mind that the people - my people - were being exploited and I felt that when I grew up I would have to involve myself in whatever was going to redress that sort of wrong."

It was not long after young Bradshaw had been apprenticed to the sugar factory machine shop that a welder, Adam Claxton, told him about the St. Kitts Workers' League, headed at that time by an estate owner called Manchester, a very liberal minded man. There were other people like Edgar Challenger and Alford Seaton.

"Claxton, my boss in the machine shop, said it was all right and that I should join the St. Kitts Workers' League."

So Robert spoke with his mother and she agreed that he should join. And thus Robert Bradshaw joined the Workers' League on the recommendation of his machine shop boss. His membership was seconded by Mr. Harry O'Day, who was also in charge of the machine shop. And then a frightful event occurred which could have easily destroyed the career of young Robert Bradshaw.

He was sitting on a bench in the machine shop when one of the other boys pushed him violently and he fell against a glass window, causing his right hand to go through the glass. All the tendons in his forearm were cut. That put Robert Bradshaw in hospital for a long time. It was a terrible experience, he said. It cut short his career as a machinist because he could no longer handle the tools and manipulate the machines and, as he said: "What is more, my musical career also came to an end abruptly and terribly."

I spoke to his 90 year-old mother, Mary Jane Francis about this. She said "When the lad pushed him from the bench crashing him into the window, the glass slashed his right arm, severing the tendons. Doctors stitched the arm with 15 stitches, but he was not able to use it at all, until a doctor who was rescued from a shipwreck saw him in hospital and operated further, which enabled him to use it somewhat."

She said tearfully: "When Bob, going 18, came to realise that his right arm was never going to get better really, he said to me: 'Mama, I can't use my arm so I have got to use my head.'"

So his mother paid eight pounds for a correspondence course for him from England and two of the Grammar School boys who worked in the sugar factory lab helped him in his lessons. He studied all the time, she said. He had a resoluteness about him. He never turned back. He had been a bright boy in school. When on one occasion his mother expressed anxieties for the boy, the teacher said to her, "Dear Miss Francis, oh my! you have a bright boy and you don't seem to know it." Indeed, Bob, before he was 16, was teaching in the very school he attended, although his ambition was to become a Mechanic.

Premier Bradshaw told me that after he had got out of the hospital, the boss of the shop very kindly put him to work in the office, the toolroom of the machine shop. There he learned to write with his left hand which he had begun to do even before the right hand was injured, because he felt that if a person could write with their right hand they should also be able to write with their left hand.

There came a drastic turning point during Robert Bradshaw's early twenties. He had remained in the toolroom at the machine shop until the Union was formed in 1940 (after the British had caused Trade Union Laws to be passed which enabled the proper functioning of Trade Unions). At that time in 1940, the Union had asked at the workshop for an increase in pay because the cost of living had risen terribly high as a result of the war. They were told no, and so they went on strike, admittedly an unauthorised strike. Indeed, Mr. Bradshaw said he was not even sure that the Union was then registered. The strike lasted seven weeks at which time he was told, along with some others, that he had no job.

He had been earning the lordly sum of 2/3d. a day which was roughly the same as many other people in the sugar factory. There were some people, especially in the fields, who were working for a shilling a day. That was the level of wages until 1940.

After being fired from the machine shop Robert was taken on at the Union as a clerk. His work then became union work. He worked with the Union until 1944 when he became its President. By that time, Mr. Challenger, the great pioneer, had resigned and had been succeeded by a man called Sebastian, a member of the Legislative Council, who died. Thus Robert Llewellyn Bradshaw became President of the Union in 1944, a position held for many years.

By the time he had become President of the Union he had developed a total commitment to work and responsibility. Always a student, he studied a lot, read a lot (as evidenced in his speeches which were very often enriched by sentiments, phrases and idioms from the larger world).

In 1946 the Workers' League was founded, becoming the political arm of the Labour Movement and he stood for election to the Legislative Council. He was unopposed and remained a legislator until his death. So Robert Llewellyn Bradshaw had an unbroken record in both Union and Legislature for 38 and 32 years respectively. In those days in St. Kitts-Nevis-Anguilla, there was a British Administrator as the President of the Legislature. There was also, over and above that, another structure called the Leeward Islands Legislative Council. That was a combined colony composed of Dominica, Antigua, Montserrat, St. Kitts-Nevis-Anguilla and the British Virgin Inslands, each group being called a Presidency. Each of the Presidency Legislatures elected representaives to the general Leeward Islands Legislature, whose laws applied to all the Presidencies.

Robert Bradshaw became the first Deputy President of the General Legislative Council just before it was dissolved in 1956 in order to make way for the Presidencies to join the West Indies Federation. All of them joined except the British Virgin Islands.

Asked whether party politics played any part in life in St. Kitts-Nevis-Anguilla in those days, Premier Bradshaw said no.

"They did not know party politics as it was later known. It was individual service to the people based largely on trade unions, the sacrifices made for the workers and the like. The beginnings of party politics did occur round about 1935 when the elective principle in the legislature was re-introduced. There was a time when the Legislatures in the Presidencies were totally nominated but, in 1944, when adult suffrage came to the Commonwealth Caribbean region, a new attitude in politics became apparent."

Bradshaw recalls that in 1944 when Jamaica gained adult suffrage, he and a friend, Mr. France, went to the high ground of the cemetery in Basseterre which is top of the town, to listen on the radio to the first swearing-in of the House of Representatives in Jamaica, where Alexander Bustamante became the first Chief Minister of Jamaica.

Robert Bradshaw's major triumphs were, being elected to the Union Presidency and continuous re-election to the Legislature. He did not regard them, he says, as personal triumphs in a general sense. He regarded them really as inevitable - particularly the legislative one - because it was just a question of the people having chosen him to lead them on the labour front and then saying, you must do the legislature also. He was happy that the people felt that he could serve them and that he had their trust.

Asked whether that produced any reactions of persecution among the entrenched elements of the sugar industry, characteristically Premier Bradshaw said: "Yes and no. It made me their enemy but it was an enemy they could not avoid. So they had to make the best of the fact of me being there. There was never really any terrible clash with these people and the fact that I had had some sort of legislative authority blunted the edge of whatever might have happened."

I asked the Premier to reflect on the West Indies Federation, his participation in it, his days in Port-of-Spain and the collapse of Federation.

"We were first made aware of Federation in my time by the speeches of people like Marryshow, and also what our own leaders told us from time to time, particularly at workers' meetings. Marryshow came to St. Kitts with Elmore Edwards, a Vincentian. Later Edwards served in St. Kitts as Attorney General. At that time one looked at the Federal idea as something very good to be achieved because it would bring all our people together. And so even before the Montego Bay conference of 1947, Manley had come to Antigua where he met us and we spoke about Federation. We spoke about various other things all having to do with bringing our people together."

Then there was a Montego Bay conference at which Mr. Bradshaw was not a delegate. He was in Jamaica having gone there for the Caribbean Labour Congress. St. Kitts' representative at the Montego Bay conference was a man named Morris Davis, a member of the Legislative Council of the Leeward Islands who was senior to Robert Bradshaw, and later Chief Justice of the Associated States Supreme Court.

Robert Bradshaw recalls:

"A committee was set up to work out the broad outlines of the Federal Constitution. Bustamante did not think enough of it to appoint a member of their House but sent the Clerk, Clinton Hart, and that committee was conducted under the chairmanship of Sir Hubert Rance, the last British Governor of Burma, who then went to head the Colonial Development and Welfare body in Barbados and eventually became Governor of Trinidad and Tobago.

"The job of this committee took them two years but in those two years one heard a lot about Federation. In the Leeward Islands we had a sort of mini-Federation so that the idea was not totally alien. I took part in the Federal talks as from 1956 and we came to Jamaica in 1957 to choose the Federal capital. At that time the work of making the Federal Constitution and making the pre-Federal arrangements fell to a committee comprised of representatives of all the territories which were to take part, chaired by the gentleman who was then the Controller of Development and Welfare, Sir Steven Luke. John Mordecai, of Jamaica who worked with Development and Welfare on the Regional Economic side was Secretary. So we did all that was necessary to be done. Nevertheless, Trinidad was chosen as the capital against the advice of the Capital Fact Finding Committee which said we should avoid Trinidad because of various things such as graft and corruption. Nevertheless, Trinidad was chosen and the time came when one had to decide whether one would leave one's own bailiwick and venture into Federal politics.

I chose the latter, believing that I had a duty to make available to the nation which we set out to form whatever little experience I had gathered in public life from 1946 until then. So I gave up my position in St. Kitts and was succeeded by Mr. Paul Southwell.

I went to Trinidad. Life for the first year or so wasn't too bad but within that year Dr. Eric Williams had put his teeth into the Chaguaramas issue - the bases issue with which I was associated as a member of the sub-committee which had to do with the formation of Federation. The committee had been sent to England to start negotiations with the British about the termination of the U.S. Bases Agreement. There were bases in Trinidad, Barbados, St. Lucia, Antigua, Jamaica, Turks and Caicos Islands.

Mr. MacMillan was then Prime Minister and it was there that Dr. Williams began to tear at the guts of the business and never turned back. But the Federal Government paid the price because as soon as Dr. Williams realised fully what it meant to have a superior government - to put it like that - on his own Trinidad soil, he began to give us trouble."

As an example Mr. Bradshaw said:

"Just about three months after the Federal Government had taken over, a man we all know arrived on a visit to Trinidad. He was married to a Trinidadian, Professor W. Gordon Lewis of the University of Puerto Rico a lecturer in Political Science. A Welshman, he arrived in Trinidad by air and was interviewed by the Press and was asked what he thought the relationship between the Federal Government and the Unit Governments would be. He said words to the effect that like man and wife there is bound to be friction between the Federal Government and the Unit Governments. These could be resolved but there would be friction. Even in the United States, he said, which has the longest running example of a Federal structure, a State will feel that its rights are being infringed on by Federal authority.

"Dr. Williams and Dr. Lewis" said Mr. Bradshaw,

"were friends so far as I knew, and it was just as if what Dr. Lewis said was a signal. Because the very Saturday of that week Dr. Williams gave a Press Conference where Lewis' utterances were thrown at him. And from that time he started to hound and harass the Federal Government until the Federation collapsed. And despite the fact that the majority of people here and abroad blamed the Jamaican referendum for the collapse of the Federation, I have said and will ever maintain that Dr. Williams did more to break up the Federation than did anybody else.

Men from Jamaica like Frank Ricketts of St. Ann's Bay who was one of the Federal Ministers and Senator Byfield, later President of the Senate in Jamaica and elected M.P. , having been in the Federal Cabinet and lived in Trinidad during the life of the Federation- 1958 to 1961 - can attest to what I have said.

For instance, we could not visit a Trinidad Government project unless we first notified our Trinidadian counterpart that we were going there. So that if there was a project along any one of the high-

58

ways at which you might and stop and visit in passing, it was reported that Federal people had been there and it was regarded as an infringement. It was strange because Trinidad and ourselves were of the same Federal Party. Anyhow, despite this harassment, we did the best we could.

Sir Grantley Adams made the terrible *faux pas* which was taken out of context and magnified - this thing about retroactive taxation. It came because of a decision which had been announced in Jamaica to give a 25-year tax holiday to someone who intended to establish an oil refinery in Jamaica. When asked about this at a Press Conference, the Prime Minister, Sir Grantley Adams, said this should not happen because in time such companies should be subject to Federal taxation. It could have been dealt with otherwise, by retroactive legislation; but Sir Grantley Adams said: 'I as a lawyer do not like retroactive taxation.' But then he went on to say that nevertheless all of us should get together and work out a set of incentives in which all of us could participate so that a foreign investor would not be able to play off one against the other.

Now that has come to fruition, because in the CARICOM, rules have been worked out for the incentives. After all these years - and that was all Grantley Adams had in mind at the time.

And so I repeat that despite the Jamaican referendum, Trinidad had done more, in fact, had done most to wreck the Federation. We had hoped to go on from Federation to Nationhood and at one stage we met Dr. Williams (Manley and Bird were present) in Grantley Adams' office in Trinidad, and Williams said we should bring the Federation to Nationhood before the divisive forces gained the upper hand. So that, even though we might not have an independence and set up our Constitution Commission, set up a constitution for independence. And he was annoyed because we did not do it that way. That can be said to Dr. Williams' credit but by and large he did so many things to upset us in the Federal Government."

Asked how did he take the collapse at the end personally,   Premier Bradshaw said:

"Let me see if I can express it in just a few words. When I was leaving, on my last day in the office which was late in May, one of the messengers said to me: 'Mr. Bradshaw, this is like a funeral.' I felt we were ruining the one great opportunity we had of making ourselves a recognizable grouping on a national scale in the world. I say this because it would have given us a much greater say in world affairs and much more respect; and by now we would have known each other better. People say the populations were too far apart so they did not know each other; but the populations had given their leaders a mandate to form the Federation and bring it to Nationhood. The fact that we did not do so meant that we failed the people; whoever it was and however it was, we failed the people."

I suggested to Mr. Bradshaw that in fact Jamaica did not give a mandate to its leaders to go into Federation because, in Jamaica, the Federal Party lost the Federal Elections. In other words, Manley's party, the pro-Federation Party, was defeated in the very Federal election itself.

Said Premier Bradshaw:

"Yes, but the Party that defeated it assumed the role of Opposition in the House. And the Leader of the Party himself, Sir Alexander Bustamante, came down to Trinidad for the inauguration so that in fact the pro-Federation Party and the anti-Federation Party both participated so that it can be said that Jamaica did give a mandate. And you could say the same thing about Trinidad because of the ten seats for Trinidad, the Opposition got six and the PNM, which was a pro-Federal Party, was beaten. That's strange but both these principal countries, their electorates opposed and voted against the Federal Parties."

On the Referendum in Jamaica, called by Norman Washington Manley, Mr. Bradshaw recalled that the late Hugh Wooding and himself had gone up to Irish Town to see Bustamante after a University Council meeting. They were both very friendly with him and Sir Alexander told Hugh with respect to the referendum: "I knew my cousin Norman was a fool, but I didn't know he was such a goddam fool, but Jamaica was already in the Federation, already in the Federation."

With regard to CARICOM, Premier Bradshaw was asked: "Is that a Federation in embryo? What are its hopes and fears?" He answered:

"I don't know." Then he added pensively, "It is an effort but it has been a most expensive effort to keep us linked in some sort of way. I say it is expensive because had the Federation subsisted, survived, the work that is being done by the CARICOM Secretariat would have been done by the Federal Ministry of Trade. We would have had long ere this a common external tariff *(sic.)*. The studies to do all these things to bring us together had already been done, you know. I can think of two great volumes on the question of common external tariff and integrated trade. All that was there and it was done even before the Federation came into being.

"So today when we have these big gatherings, CARICOM

meetings of Finance Ministers, meetings of Labour Ministers, meetings of Education Ministers *et cetera, et cetera,* we are spending more money. Count the number of meetings and count the number of people who are attending and their advisers and measure it against what they have to pay just for hotel alone. The thing is absolutely fantastic.

So we break up the Federation and are now spending a whole pile of money just to keep some sort of link. However, CARICOM has the advantage of bringing in Guyana which was not in the Federation, bringing in Belize which was not in the Federation and of including the Bahamas which were not in Federation. So if on no other ground it has done a good thing in bringing together all of us formerly British, in one organisation."

Premier Bradshaw added, however, that CARICOM is an organisation which so far has been beneficial to the more developed units. He would put the main beneficiaries as Trinidad and Tobago, Jamaica, Barbados and, rice apart, Guyana.

Premier Bradshaw was asked about St. Kitts' independence (which was then imminent) and the bugbear of secession by the islands, the tide of secession which his Opposition was causing to flow. What in those circumstances were his hopes, plans and purposes? The Premier replied:

"Yes, we are hoping that the people who are talking secession this time in Nevis will come around to the fact that secession is not on. We have Anguilla round our necks and the British have used superior force to make nonsense of the Constitution. They have made a constitution within a constitution which to me is nonsense and totally intolerable. I have said that I regard Anguilla in the same way that Communist China regards Formosa and it is only a matter of time when Formosa will once again be brought back to where she belongs. Britain has said that Formosa is part of China because she voted to expel Formosa from the U.N., saying that Formosa has always been a part of China. Having done that I cannot see how she can now say that Anguilla is not part of the state of St. Kitts-Nevis and Anguilla."

On the question of independence, Premier Bradshaw said that he expected independence for St. Kitts-Nevis-Anguilla to be formally proclaimed before the end of 1976.

One of the most colourful and controversial of Caribbean political characters, Robert Bradshaw was a man of flair, portentous speech, and yet a man of cultivated dalliance. As often as the opportunity occurred, he fitted himself out in Court dress, or other very formal attire. Indeed he related that at the opening of the Federal Parliamant in Port of Spain, Bustamante twitted him about his gaiters and general formality of dress, saying to him "Man, you look like a masquerade," at which Robert Bradshaw laughed with happy amusement. As Deputy President, whenever he took the sessions of his Legislature, he wore a large theatrical full bottom wig and a fancy, designed tunic. He loved to dress up for a part. None of this was reason for considering him anything but a most serious and thorough student of all affairs. He did his homework and every official or other person who worked with him came to realise that whether it was a Draft Bill or a Government Paper of Finance or Estimates, Robert Bradshaw was a serious critic and appraiser of what was going on.

For Mr. Bradshaw's first Budget speech in the Federal Parliament in 1959, he turned up in pin-stripe trousers, black coat, wing collar and tie and bag with the Budget speech. He had no more than about $9M to spend. Most of the expenditure was already committed to the Federal Civil Service, the Federal Parliament, travel and regional services. He had no power to tax. But he gave the speech the same attention and treatment as if he were presenting a billion dollar budget. Then with a theatrical gesture, after about 15 minutes, he paused, rummaged under the Despatch Table, and as the House watched in total silence, he brought out a coffee cup, a flask and a small decanter. He poured from the flask and a small decanter. He poured from the flask into the coffee cup, then from the decanter, shook the cup gently, sipped, then drank as a roar of laughter burst from Members. Robert Bradshaw did not even smile. He resumed his speech and paused every so often and repeated the process of the coffee cup.

Afterwards, newsmen asked him what he had been drinking. He proceeded to describe his coffee cup made of the most delicate china, the flask and the decanter and said it was Blue Mountain Coffee. Asked what else was put in the cup, said Mr. Bradshaw: "I can't tell you that." The reporters persisted: "Was it rum, whisky, gin? What was it,?" they asked. Said Robert Bradshaw, "Just say the cup was suitably laced." It made the newspapers as a happy side story on this Federal budget.

When a mutual friend went to Anguilla in 1967 on a team of officials to investigate and to report on the Anguilla episode, my friend was a bit apprehensive as to how Mr. Bradshaw would accept his interference. He says :

> "The morning after we arrived I looked out from the hotel window which faced the Government offices across the street and saw a vintage Rolls Royce cruising slowly down the street. The Rolls stopped so I waited to see who was the owner. A khaki-uniformed figure emerged with carbine slung over the shoulder. It was none other than the Hon. Robert Bradshaw who had assumed the rank of Lt. Col. of the army of about 70 men."

Says my friend: "Later in the day he received us quite courteously in his office, his carbine leaning an arms' length away and his Colonel's cap resting nearby. He promised any help that we might need and did everything to see that we were not hampered in any way. However, throughout our visit he never appeared in civilian clothes."

It is not surprising that these idiosyncracies of Robert Bradshaw gave fuel to his critics' continued attacks upon him. Nevertheless, he prospered like a green bay tree.

His detractors considered him a master at getting people to react the way he wanted so that he could use them to further his ends, that he liked to play on the sympathy of the people. For example, he would go on the radio to make a broadcast during which he would thank some old lady for giving him a remedy for a cold and hoped that his listeners would bear with him. He liked to listen to people , but few people were ever able to have their way with him. Even his detractors admitted that he showed interest in everything that went on. If a road was being built, he would direct the work. If a netball stand was being erected, he would be present. And, later, the radio report would say that the Premier directed the building of the netball stand. Detractors would, however, express the opinion that this was all done for a political reason. In a cynical sense, that amounted to saying that Robert Bradshaw had the skills of a grass-root politician.

Friends and critics alike agree that Robert Bradshaw was a very outspoken man, who tended to become furious and over-emphatic in his statements when faced with any obstructions to his plans. Because of this attitude, antagonists often branded him as despotic. But his reply was that obstruction to plans for the progress of his people had to be firmly dealt with.

A totally serious and dedicated public leader, Robert Bradshaw did not marry until he was 48. He told me that, when he was younger, one could not be very serious about romantic activities, one was too poor, and one had to think of the responsibilities of having children and having a wife. But, eventually, he married a Kittitian-Lebanese, Millicent Sakely and they had a happy marriage which produced one daughter.

LINDEN FORBES SAMPSON BURNHAM

O.E., S.C.
BORN KITTY, GUYANA, 20 FEBRUARY, 1926
DIED 6 AUGUST, 1985

PREMIER OF GUYANA (1964-1966)
PRIME MINISTER OF GUYANA (1966 -1980)
EXECUTIVE PRESIDENT OF GUYANA (1980-1985)

5

LINDEN FORBES SAMPSON BURNHAM

LINDEN FORBES SAMPSON BURNHAM declared himself to be the head of the most Socialist government in the Commonwealth Caribbean - Guyana. To give the nation its proper title, it is the Co-operative Republic of Guyana a title it took on February 23, 1970, the 207th anniversary of the Berbice slave rebellion, when also Cuffy, slave, statesman and warrior, was named National Hero.

Guyana, the only nation on the South American continent whose official language is English, is a land of prairie and mountains, vast rivers some 83,000 square miles. As a matter of contrast, Hog Island in the Essequibo River was larger than Barbados, until Barbados did a reclamation scheme which enlarged it by a square mile. Yet this vast territory is populated by only some 800,000 people. The Socialist Co-operative Republic of Guyana, despite the rugged and inhospitable nature of much of its hinterland, has considerable room for economic development.

Mr. Forbes Burnham told me:

"It is inevitable that the present social structure will vanish; for the two alternative governments are left-wing. The more important problem would be the achievement of racial harmony. The tensions between the race groups, I predict, will heal and eventually vanish, when further political education spreads and people vote for programmes rather than ethnic origins of the respective parties."

67

When I saw Mr. Burnham in the 1970's he emphasised this point and said:

"I take strong objection to the suggestion that my government is racist, too African. You cannot win an election in Guyana on the black vote. We just aren't enough black people. More than 42% of the population of Guyana are Hindus or Muslims and many of the Christians are also from India originally."

Mr. Burnham put his confidence in ultimate fusion nationally between all of Guyana's major racial aspects, the Indian, the African and the some 50,000 Amerindians - one of the largest aggregations of Amerindians in South America.

His National Youth Service, more popularly known as the Pioneers, required all young Guyanese to give service in a semi-military training organisation, based primarily on giving service to the hinterland.

At the semi-military parade I attended, thronged by 40,000 to 50,000 Guyanese and fair representation of diplomats and visitors from other countries, it was stimulating to watch the vigorous and ardous physical training which both boys and girls in the Pioneer Corps have to undergo. It is co-educational and multi-racial: that is the intention and it seemed well on the way. As the Prime Minister saluted and took the salute at the March Past, and as the uniformed columns moved off to the sound of the band, the music was standard world army music so well known from the original British and American military. But as they were marching off, the Band shifted its beat and instead of Kneller Hall formal military band rhythm, there came the shuffling sound, the easy accented beat of the Calypso merged into the military music. The marching columns suddenly changed their march from a stride to a Carnival road march shuffle, to the delight of the vast crowd which showed unbounded enthusiasm for the recognition of their Caribbean innovation added to the military glamour of the occasion.

Said Mr. Burnham at the last independence celebrations:

"We did not achieve political freedom for the mere emotional satisfaction and the outward trappings. We did not achieve political freedom to continue in the even tenor of the old colonialist system of exploitation and discrimination in old or new forms. We sought first the political kingdom to add at the appropriate time the social and economic kingdoms. Under the philosophy of ownership and control of Guyanese resources for and by Guyanese, there followed the nationalisation of Demba, Guyana Timbers, Reynolds, Jessel's, Sprostons and others. And then Booker's.

68

These acts of sovereignty are not empty emotional vauntings. If mere emotion lay behind them, in most cases we would have paid no compensation when we reflected on the exploitation of our forefathers and ourselves. But in each case, we have, as a result of negotiated agreement, paid compensation in accordance with fixed and well-known criteria. Justice has been even-handed and ascertainable, and reasonableness the hallmark of our approach. There could not be two governments in one state - the Booker's economic power and the people's government."

About the early period Prime Minister Burnham said:

"I came back home in 1949 and soon after joined the Guiana Labour Union, the start of my own political and trade union interest. There was Hubert Nathaniel Critchlow, the famous Critchlow, whom I had known from my childhood, the President, on and off. While I practised at the Bar, I worked with the Trade Union Movement and I was their lawyer as well. I never charged them really, but I remember once there was a long enquiry and the boys felt that 'well you know, they ought to give the Comrade something for acting as lawyer. I have never seen so many cents, pennies and in those days I still think we had the four-penny bit and the six-penny bit. I have never seen a collection of so many small coins in my life. At the end of every week I had to give it to my clerk to let him count out what it was. I think the enquiry lasted about eight weeks and in all I think that I must have got in about $200 in coins. But it was fun.

In 1949 I also met Jagan whom I had not previously met because he had come back shortly before I left. I think it is the week after I came back Jagan and I met at my father's house. There were some others brought in like Ashton Chase, Ramkarran, Martin Carter, and so that's how the People's Progressive Party was born. Some of these fellows had been working with Jagan before, but Jagan had heard about me, I think, through Richard Hart of Jamaica, in England. I had heard of him and we got together. Incidentally on my way back home, I went to Jamaica where I was the guest of the PNP. And so, looking at the PNP's constitution and seeing how they organised their politics and so on, I came down to Trinidad, spent a week and then came home. Then came the Union and out of that grew everything else. To be very frank, I did it because I was interested in Unionism and Mr. Critchlow was my father's friend. I had met Critchlow again when we went to the World Federation of Trade Unions conference in '45 when I was a student. He passed through London and I remember him saying to me: 'Look, we need young men like you.' So when I came back we met again and I have been with the Union since and, except for one two-year period, I have always been President of the Guyana Labour Union. But since I have been in office as Prime Minister, I have been President-on-

69

leave. I attend special meetings and also the biennial conference, but apart from that I do not actively take part in their business."

At this point, I said to the Prime Minister: "You are like Bustamante." He replied rather sharply: "Well, I think I am a little more active than Busta." (Referring of course to Busta having been for so long an invalid). Then Mr. Burnham went on to explain:

> "It is not because I feel there should be this division between politics and unionism, but because you really cannot as Prime Minister have the time to run the Union. I have only remained president because the members insist. They insist. They say: 'Look, we are going to elect a good first vice-president but will you please stay on?' So it has become a sort of tradition and I think too they feel that because there is a Prime Minister who had got a trade union background and still maintains at least a theoretical contact with a particular union, they would get more sympathetic consideration. Another thing is that, even if I were not president, I would have maintained my membership because the Guyana Labour Union which controls the waterfront, was my first political base. It was from there that my political base spread and it would be in the nature of ingratitude to have cut my relations with the Union."

Prime Minister Burnham then went back to his return when Jagan was secretary of the party. Indeed, Jagan was Parliamentary Leader because, explained Mr. Burnham,

> "at one time it was Jagan and a fellow named Theophilus Lee ; he left the PPP so Cheddi was the only member of the party who was a member of the then Legislative Council. So, he was political Leader, I was Chairman. His wife, Janet, was Secretary. I think the rest is history. Came the 1953 elections, the suspension, the split in the Party in '55 and the subsequent elections up to 1973."

At this point I asked Prime Minister Burnham why the British sent troops to Guiana in 1953? Said Mr. Burnham:

> "Well, first of all, you must remember, it was the Cold War. They thought that Guiana was following an unusually radical line as against the line that had been taken by Grantley Adams in Barbados, Gomes and his group in Trinidad and Bustamante in Jamaica. I am not criticizing them. I am just telling you how I analysed it. Then we used to be reading and selling Socialist and Communist literature. So the British, I believe, under pressure from the Americans, felt that this Guiana was going to be a Communist enclave which would endanger democracy in this part of the world; and they suspended the Constitution. They trumped up all sorts of things in order to do that."

70

I asked whether Premier Jagan hadn't at that time made it appear that he was about to make a bid to seize government. Said Burnham:

"No. He was the most senior elected Minister. All of us were champing at the bit because although we were six ministers, the Finance man, the Attorney General and the Chief Secretary held the real power. We were all champing at the bit and in that respect I don't think there was any difference between Cheddi and myself as to wanting elected ministers to have the full powers. That was our philosophy and policy, but there was no build up or intention to act physically.

Between you and me, as a politician and a revolutionary, the circumstances then were not right for us to attempt a unilateral declaration of independence. I don't know what Cheddi had in mind but he certainly never told me he would. I definitely did not have that in mind because the circumstances weren't right. If the circumstances had been right I am not going to fool you that I would not have opted for UDI."

Concerning the history of the two parties and the two leaders, Mr. Burnham said:

"Jagan was Premier in 1963 under the Constitution that came into operation in 1961 by which time we were in different parties. I think Cheddi made a mistake in the 1963 Constitutional Conference when he allowed Duncan Sands to say to us: 'Well, look, since you three leaders cannot agree (the three leaders being Jagan, Burnham and D'Aguiar) would you sign a letter to me giving me the right to decide'. At that stage our quarrel was mainly about the electoral system. At that time Jagan had about 42% of the vote and 60-something percent of the House. I had 41% of the vote and 15% of the House and I was saying to Jagan that we should have an electoral system which reflects popular support.

"I remember when we were writing the 1961 Constitution in London, he refused to appoint a Leader of the Opposition. He said there was no need for that, - he who now talks about opposition. And at that time, that fellow Iain MacLeod bent over to him - because by that time I think the British had decided that they could play ball with Cheddi. Anyhow, there was the issue of the next stage of the constitution, that is a constitution under which independence would come. He would not agree to proportional representation but he signed this letter. He signed it, D'Aguiar signed it, and then after about three or four hours Duncan Sands said, 'Well, Mr. Burnham, if you don't sign it, the conference is at an end and independence would be posponed indefinitely'. So then I signed.

71

"I subsequently learned that one of the reasons for Jagan's signing was that he could not exercise power in a hostile Georgetown which I controlled - though he did go on the BBC-TV and say that he signed because he had great faith in the British sense of fairplay and justice - which I thought was rather naive for a politician of his ideology, his ilk and experience.

"I mean for instance, he would declare an emergency and I would break the emergency and say 'lock me up if you want.' And he dared not.

"So then we had the election in '64 which was supervised by a fellow named Hucks which some of Cheddi's supporters found an excellent word for rhyming with a four-letter word, and said he was doing that to the people. Cheddi got the highest plurality. We were next and the United Force made up the rest.

"Then there was the question of forming a government. At that time I refused to form a government with Cheddi; and the United Force Party which was a right-wing party refused to form the government with Cheddi. My reason for refusing to form a government with him was that he had no sense of priorities. He was not interested in getting independence for Guiana, in trying to heal the wounds. He just wanted to advertise the fact that he was a big Socialist or Communist, though I doubt whether he is more Socialist than I was or am; and also advertising his relationship with Moscow, which I thought didn't make sense at that stage. And in any case what we wanted was not friendship with one country or another but to build up our country and to introduce Socialism against our own background, our own traditions, our own history, which you cannot lift from one country to another."

The United Force Party finally left the coalition, explained Mr. Burnham. The coalition was difficult, he said. "It had been easy in the first months when it was merely a question of rehabilitating the national assets. But when it came to emphasise the co-operative, the UF did not agree. When it came to our attitude to multi-nationals, they didn't agree. In fact, the coalition fell apart in 1967-68 but we remained in office because I think two of Cheddi's men and one or two of D'Aguiar's men crossed the floor. So by the time we were ready for the elections in 1968 we already had an overall majority. And in 1973 we got a larger majority."

Asked whether the statistics of Guyanese population includes Guyanese overseas, Prime Minister said:

"No. The statistics do not include overseas Guyanese but the electoral statistics include Guyanese overseas because, under the Constitution which we got in 1965, Guyanese overseas have a vote. That was agreed to by the UF and ourselves though Cheddi Jagan himself did not attend the final Constitutional Conference in 1965. It is not similar to the United States of America's system of voting overseas. With them it is restricted to certain categories. All overseas Guyanese have a right to be registered and to vote."

Asked if he would elaborate on the difference between the Socialist policies of the governments of Guyana, Barbados and Jamaica, Comrade Prime Minister Burnham said:

"For Guyana Socialism means having the heights of the economy in the hands of the people, the main means of production and distribution, to build a society where there is equality of opportunity - we call it an egalitarian society. So far as we are concerned we have an argument, an academic or theoretical argument with many of the classical Socialists or Marxists who say that the highest form of social ownership is State ownership. We, up to now, hold that the highest form of social ownership is co-operative or community ownership. That's our argument.

"But Socialism in Guyana is, I think, difficult to achieve though, I think, less difficult than in Jamaica. We have no classical bourgeoisie. Our middle-class are really skilled persons who work for better salaries because of their skills, a few shop-keepers and so who have no political weight or clout, and a few landowners who own a lot of land, some of which they do not use, which we are now settling. Therefore, for instance, when we decided we were going to nationalise Alcan, I would say over 90% of the population said 'Yes , do it.'

Similarly with Reynolds, and as for Booker's, I would say 100% of the population agreed with it. Because we have no entrenched bourgeoisie, and perhaps the significance is historical, in that we were a ceded colony whereas Jamaica was a settled colony. That, perhaps, explains a lot.

So we orchestrated according to our programme. We took Alcan; we took Reynolds; we took one sugar company; another sugar company; a timber company. We didn't rush to take everything amid confusion."

At this I said to the Prime Minister: "You chewed and digested?" He replied: "Yes, as I said once we are like the 'Cammodi'. 'Cammodi' is one of our large boa constrictors. When it eats a meal, it doesn't eat another meal until that first meal is digested."

73

I asked Comrade Burnham about Guyana and Cuba. He willingly replied:

"Our relations with Cuba are good and I personally think we have a lot of things to learn from Cuba, especially how she has organised her educational system of work and study. It is a fantastic educational system they have. It is generally admitted that Cuba has probably the best medical facilities and health system in the Western hemisphere. These are things we can learn from Cuba.

"Cuba is also helping us in our fishing industry, in that she has acquired a great deal of experience, and that's one of our big foreign exchange earners. We don't agree with Cuba on every matter. For instance, we made it quite clear to Cuba when I was there last year and some of the fellows wanted to put it into the communique about our stand for independence of Puerto Rico, I said, 'Look, I understand your emotional attachment to this matter, but so far as we are concerned, a people are entitled to be independent when they show they want to be independent.' So we do not automatically agree with the Cubans in every matter they consider important."

Mr. Burnham added that when Guyana's position was not the same as Cuba's, the Cubans respected position.

"They have never attempted to ram anything down our throats. I think they are more sensible than that. They don't have this sort of imperialistic attitude. And certainly I think everybody knows that Guyana is small but ruggedly independent. I mean, when we opened trade with Cuba, the Americans told us: 'Well, your PL480 loan goes by the board.' We said: 'All right.' Then aid from America was reduced to a trickle and we said all right. So if the great America can't bully us so easily, we have never had any problems with the Cubans.

For instance, the Cubans and the Chinese don't get on. But we in Guyana get on very well with the Chinese and we retain good relations with the Chinese. Our most senior diplomat is in Peking. This talk about a Cuban take over to me sounds like all nonsense, because the Cubans have always behaved quite correctly. If they have a point of view they will seek to sell it to you, but when they can't sell it to you, they stop."

Back to affairs in Guyana, I asked the Prime Minister, "Will the Indians, that is the Hindus and the Moslem Indians of Guyana ever be integrated politically and socially in the national service, in the public service, in the country? And do the Amerindians have a problem? The Prime Minister replied:

"If I should start from the Amerindians, I don't think they have a problem. You see, we have now given them their lands. People were saying we didn't intend to, but that was because of shortage of surveyors and other problems. We gave them more special scholarships to accelerate their progress and we embarked upon a system of sending, highly qualified teachers to Amerindian schools. We already have one Amerindian doctor that I know of and I know another two are in training and we have a full-blooded Amerindian as one of our Ministers. I think they will be integrated. There is no problem with them."

Turning to the Indians, Moslem and Hindu, the Prime Minister said:

I think that there will be an amalgam in Guyana eventually. First of all, historically you understand how the colonialists kept Guiana. The slaves were emancipated. They did not want to work any more. So the colonialists brought various sets of immigrants and finally the East Indians. Two things they did. First of all, they allowed the East Indians to bring some of their culture and religion. Much of the Indian culture here represents the culture of the areas from which these people came in the 19th century. If you go back to these same places, you will see that their culture has moved on because culture is not a static thing.

Secondly, hitherto, geographically the Indians have been in the rural areas, particularly sugar plantations and rice fields. You will find in many dominantly Indian areas, black villages. So there is this geographical and occupational dichotomy. And thirdly, and this is where I take strong objection to the suggestion that I am racist, you cannot win an election in Guyana on the Black vote. We Blacks just aren't enough.

Traditionally there is another part of the problem. A black boy or girl with good qualifications, often opts for the Civil Service. The average Indian with the same qualifications would opt for business or proceeding to a profession or even becoming a big landed rice farmer or something of that sort.

I remember once speaking to an Indian fellow who was at that time a member of the People's Progressive Party. I said to him 'why the hell don't you all apply for the Police Service?' He said, 'Look, you think any Coolie man who can get 20 or 30 acres to grow rice will go and do that hard Police work?' Those are things one has to look at. Further, in colonial days and prior to our nationalisation of these big multi-nationals and conglomerates, the public sector was a small sector. Now that sugar has come in, sugar is part of the public sector. You will probably find, and I have told Jagan that, I said: 'You have to look at the public sector and stop talking about the Civil Service. If you want proportional employment in the public sector you may well find that you have to give up because sugar alone employs over 22,000 people of which I would say that between 70% and 80% are Indians.' Its a historical fact. I am not going to ask that Indians be put out to have Blacks in the sugar industry but that is a difficulty Jagan faces. He might be hoist on his own petard.

I think we shall all be integrated because when we go to Africa we discover that we are not Africans; when they go to India, they discover that they are not Indians. A High Commissioner of ours attended a reception in New Delhi and an Indian lady came up to him and said: 'You know, if I had not known you had come from Guyana, I would have thought that you were an Indian.' And this fellow is an Indian, totally. When bands of musicians come from India here, they are the same Indians as ours but their music, the rhythm, is so different that both of us, the Indian and African, are as much at a loss to grasp the Indian music."

Prime Minister Burnham continued:

"I went and spoke to an Indian gathering, a mixed gathering on Independence Day, the 26th May, at Rose Hall. It is the biggest crowd we have ever had at Berbice at the same time. It was over 30,000, and more than 60% were Indians. They listened, they cheered; the only thing some of them said: 'All right, we're going to work but you work the other thing and see that we get better conditions.' What is more, I grew up in a village which was half Indian, half Black. I grew up at Kitty so I know them. In the worst days of racial voting, Dr. Jagan could never beat us in Kitty. As they say, they call me 'the boy Forbes' and say, 'we go to school with Forbes, we pitch marble with Forbes.' The elder ones would tell you, 'Look, that boy been to school here, good boy.' It will take time, but the integration will come about."

Through all this discussion Prime Minister Burnham, almost ornate in an intricate embroidered shirt, sitting on the verandah of his home at Belfield, was totally relaxed.

I asked him about his home life, his personal life, hours of work and so on, the burden of being a Prime Minister of a country that is in the midst of a social revolution. Said the Prime Minister:

"Well, I suffer from the good fortune or bad fortune of having a wife who is a politician also. That means that she recognises the limitations there are upon any possibility of serious social life. She is head of the women's arm of the party, the Women's Revolutionary Socialist Movement. In any case, even before she went fully into it , she was a remarkable wife, she was a reasonable wife, for which I am grateful. As a matter of fact, one of the things that broke up my first marriage was that my other wife was not as understanding and sometimes would ask me whether I had married the people or married her. It's impossible. I have strange working hours; most mornings I am up by half-past four. Most mornings I go to bed hardly before one, two or three, and I work right through the day. You see at home here, I work. I have secretaries. I have a conference room. I have an office. I was actually handling some files before you came in. I am fortunate that I do not need a lot of sleep. My normal sleep is between two to three-and-a-half hours in the twenty-four and I am happy with that., My doctor says that I am a freak.

When I am up here, one of my forms of relaxation, especially in the rainy season, is spending about an hour inspecting the drainage in the area for the rice fields and the villages, checking sluices and seeing that they are open and suggesting new things to ease the water shortage and the water problem."

I commented that it seemed that a Guyanese had to be a hydraulic engineer. Said the Prime Minister: "Yes, or he perishes; unless God gives him fins."

Comrade Burnham added that he goes around also and looks at housing projects, trying to help them to get the material in. And then he goes swimming, he said, twice a week and when the weather is good, he rides about three times a week, horseback riding which he finds very good exercise. As a matter of fact, he says he finds horseback riding better exercise for his legs than swimming. Sometimes when he wants to think out a problem, he plays solitaire. At that time nobody disturbs him. Because solitaire is a rule of thumb and you can think while you play. "Of course," he added, "every opportunity I get to play with the children, I do so. And then when I go horseback riding I take them because they like it. When they are not at school, I take them swimming; but quite frankly I don't get to spend enough time with my family."

His handsome, six-foot two figure at 215lbs. was impressive and yet athletic. He would have a drink now and again, but normally he was on a low starch, low sugar diet , and hoped that with a diet of almost pure protein he would get back down to about 195lbs.

It was a beautiful morning when I interviewed the Prime Minister at his Belfield residence, 40 minutes drive out of the capital, Georgetown. Mr. Burnham sat stately and relaxed on a high chair with a battery of telephones by his side, in touch with his nation and the world. A strong steel grill gate with a camel's eye, easy to open for staff on foot, kept locked and guarded by sentries. But all was peace. The Prime Minister sipped coconut water slightly laced with rum - Haitian Barbancourt, fifteen-year-old in honour of his guest. As he conversed, he waved to passers-by on the main road. It was in this setting that he told me about his childhood and early years.

Prime Minister Burnham's father was the school-master at a place named Kitty. He was of Barbadian origin, both of his parents being from Barbados, from Black Rock near Bridgetown. Prime Minister Burnham's mother was his father's second wife, the first one having died. The second Mrs. Burnham came from a family up the Demerara River who had land holdings and also had what was called wood-cutting grants and they also used to burn charcoal. Says the Prime Minister:

"My father was the Headmaster of Kitty Methodist School, from what he told me, from the time he was 22 until he retired at the age of 60, which would make him Headmaster of Kitty for 38 years.

My mother was very deeply religious. I think that was due to two factors - one, that she came from a very religious family, what we used to call the Brethren; secondly, my father took seriously ill when I was four. He was asthmatic and I suppose the problems of having a family to rear with a sick husband would have made her even more deeply religious.

My recollections are that we found it hard to make ends meet. So, as the little boy in the family, I used to be responsible for minding the fowls, the ducks, the sheep and the goats. I had an elder sister by my mother and another sister and elder brother by my father's marriage, all of whom lived with us until my brother went away.

As a little boy I really wasn't interested in books and scholarship; and when I say books, I mean in learning at school. I was interested in reading books but didn't like the regimen of classes and subjects and things like that until when I was to take what used to be called the Government Scholarship. As I wasn't doing any work my father said: 'I'll let you stay home and cut grass.' So he bought me a grass knife on the Saturday. When I was dressing for school, he said, 'No. You stay home to cut grass.' Well, in cutting the grass the knife slipped. You see this mark here on my arm? From then on I decided I had better get serious and I started to take an interest in formal school work because I found the grass cutting with the grass knife a little dangerous to life and limb. It's as simple as that."

He recalled that, as a little boy with his parents in Kitty, he made it a habit, he and other youngsters, of digging out Patwa (a small fish) from the irrigation trenches. When the water is low, there is a technique of picking up a handful of mud and shying it and as you shy it the soft mud separates and you find the patwa that is in it. Prime Minister Burnham said his mother had first objected to that because she was attempting to rear me in an atmosphere of gentility even if she couldn't afford it. But I suspect that as a child I got my greatest intake of protein from the patwa."

Then young Burnham used to catch crabs during the long holidays on the beach. His mother thought it was not a proper thing to do "but that's where I also got my protein intake". The food at home, he said, was rice and ground provisions and meat.

The Prime Minister continued:

"And I remember every Thursday and Sunday we used to get soup. It could be soup with crabs or soup with pieces of beef or some kind of soup, but it always had calaloo (a local spinach) which we picked from the yard. Then I remember we had a breadfruit tree. Perhaps that is why I am not particularly keen on breadfruit today because whenever this breadfruit tree was bearing, we had breadfruit at breakfast, breadfruit at lunch, breadfruit at dinner. So I sort of vowed that when I grew to be a big man I would not be eating breadfruit again. It is only nowadays, now and again, I may take a piece of breadfruit. That sticks out in my memory."

Prime Minister Burnham said he went to the Kitty Methodist School at which his father was headmaster, next door to the church which they attended. They went to church quite often because in those days the school master of a denominational school had to be the general factotum. He used to be the lay preacher "and I had to go to morning Sunday School, then morning service, afternoon Sunday School, stay on for Class Leaders' meeting and then evening Sunday School. We also had Bible class and then Evening Service. It means that in one Sunday I was in church six times."

Young Burnham's education continued at the Central High School, a private secondary school, where after about two terms, Papa Burnham mustered up every resource he could and sent his young son, over to Queen's College which was supposed to be the premier school of the nation. There, Papa Burnham paid fees for one term and a year, and just then, says the Prime Minister:

"I remember this well, my father got a notice saying that he hadn't paid the mortgate on his house and if he didn't pay it within a certain time, they would foreclose. So the fees which he had ready to pay for my next school term had to be put together with everything he could find around the house to pay the mortgage. So my father said to me: 'Well, boy, I don't think I can keep you at Queen's College any longer.'

"But two days later, my father got a letter from the school, from the Principal of the school, saying that I had been awarded a scholarship for the good work I had done during the year before. That was called a Centenary Scholarship. And what a good fortune it was. That set me firm at Queen's College, where I had a good time and a bad time.

79

"I had a good time in view of the fact that that was the best educational institution in Guiana at the time and I got the best of what Guiana offered. I had a bad time in that I was so frightfully poor that I used to be afraid to go into the tuck shop because I used to get one cent every other day as pocket money. Now one cent could at most only buy a glass of swank (sugar and water with lime juice) so I would stay out of the tuck shop for about two weeks and save enough cents to go and buy with the other fellows. A glass of swank was one cent and a bun was one cent and I saved for it. I had to save for quite a few days before I could go and have patties or so with the other boys.

I remember very clearly there was an old lady there who used to run the tuck shop. We used to call her Cookie, but her name was Adams. She called me one day and she said she noticed that I didn't come in the tuck shop very often. She asked me what was the problem. I said to her, 'Look, to be frank, I don't have the money to come to the tuck shop every day and I feel embarrassed for the other people to be buying for me and I am never in a position to buy for them.' So she said: 'You don't worry about that. You come in and take whatever you want on credit.' I said I didn't have the money to pay. I would never have the money to pay for these things.' She said: 'You don't worry. You pay me back when you become a great man'."

Pensively the Prime Minister looked out to the sea. He said: "Well, you know, she died some years ago. She died when I was away studying. But (and the Prime Minister cheered up) she had a daughter who used to work with her at the tuck shop and the daughter became a big party member. She came in the other day asking me to help her to get a rental/purchase house but she didn't have the down-payment. Well, I was most happy to help her for the "freeness" her mother had given me as a young fellow at school."

At Queen's College, young Forbes was never very good at athletics. He says primarily not because he wasn't interested, but because even though he was on a scholarship there wasn't the money to buy football boots, cricket boots and gear, so the boys used to think of Forbes as only a book worm, which he says was not true.

"I used to go out riding and so on with the boys and when I got my scholarship allowance, so much would be put away and I would get something once a week. But we couldn't afford to buy sports togs so it was only when I was in the sixth form and things were a little easier on my parents, that I started playing some tennis, mediocre; and some cricket. But by that time, I really never became a cricketer. One of my regrets is that I never became an Austin, though I used to give the excuse to the boys when they asked me if I was not playing. I said: "No. Doctor's orders." It was not. It was only economic stringency."

Teenagers and Sixth Formers usually come into some form of romance, so I asked the Prime Minister whether any fleeting romance occurred before he left for London. Said the Prime Minister with a distant smile:

"Yes. There was one young lady I was very keen on and whom I had hoped to marry, but strangely enough, apart from the fact that I had met my first wife in London and became attached to her, when I came back to British Guiana this young lady said to me: 'I think we now live in different worlds. You have matured in one direction; I don't believe I have matured and I think we would hardly hit it off.'

A lot of people, said Mr. Burnham, thought he had decided not to marry her, but she it was who did not marry him. She it was who decided. "I was really very fond of her," he says, "but quite apart from that there was no sort of permanent romance in my life except the one with my first wife and then my second wife."

In London, Forbes Burnham found life exciting, most educative. He said it really affected his career. He had won the Guyana Scholarship in 1942 but because of the War he could not leave for England until 1945, during which time he taught at his old Queen's College and worked at other places. Then in London he soon joined the League of Coloured Peoples and the West Indian Students' Union.

"The League of Coloured Peoples was in the days of old man Harold Moody and he employed me to reorganise the system in the office. Jamaican Kenny McNeil's sister, Sylvia McNeill was there then. It was then I became interested in politics. I had read the Red Dean's 'Soviet Power'; I had read 'Das Kapital' about twice. Indeed, I had read 'Das Kapital' when I was about sixteen.

"My politics took a particular course. There was much more exposure to politics in England because it was interesting to note that in that period about 90% of those who subsequently became leaders of colonies which became independent, British colonies, were right there. You had Tafawa Balewa, Nkrumah passed through for a while, you had Michael Manley, Errol Barrow, Seretse Khama, a number of them. I think on the average, we there at that time produced about 90% of subsequent political leadership. Some of us went right, some of us went left."

Asked about George Padmore, Mr. Burnham said: "Padmore was our political mentor. And so, to a lesser extent, was C.L.R. James. We learned our politics almost at the feet of Padmore. Padmore was a great man, undoubtedly one of the great West Indians."

81

In the West Indian Students' Union where Mr. Burnham was active, he became the president, either the second or third president. "I remember clearly," he says, "the first president was Leacroft Robinson and I don't remember whether I succeeded him or someone else. But I became president and as such attended the International Union of Students conference in Europe, in Prague.

Then after these exciting years in England, Linden Forbes Burnham came back home. His first wife, a Trinadian who had been studying Optics in England, followed him back to British Guiana later the same year and they got married about two years later in Trinidad. Actually, says Mr. Burnham, he could have returned earlier from England, since he had been able to finish in two years for the reason that he had done an external degree in British Guiana, which gave certain exemptions. But the value of the scholarship was increased, so he decided to spend another year after he had taken his Bar exams, going to lectures at the London School of Economics, visiting the Trade Unions, the Printers Union, the Fire Brigade Union and so on.

Linden Forbes Burnham returned to British Guiana a changed person, with new skills and outlook to serve his country. Since then, he has experienced all the rigours of political rivalry, the stresses of Trade Union leadership and sacrifice, the embattled contest of elections and party strife and has become Prime Minister of Guyana.

In this mood, I asked him about Federation. What did he think would have happened if Guyana, British Guiana that is, had come into Federation? He replied:

"If Guyana, British Guiana, had been in it from the beginning, I think it might not have failed because I think everybody would have recognised that Guyana's resources, worked on a regional basis, offered an opportunity for viability. And I personally think that Dr. Jagan made a mistake keeping us out of Federation. Of course, the chief reason he gave was that the leaders in the Caribbean were right wing, but this kind of better-than-thou right wing and left wing doesn't decide things. I can work with Williams; I can work with Compton. You just have to find the things on which you agree. If the rest of the Caribbean came here and told me that the only direction for development in Guyana is to bring in the multi-nationals on the same old terms I would tell them: 'To hell with you.' I am not going to tell them what to do either. But we can agree on the need for exchange of technology, the need for a larger amount of trade, the need to revamp our educational system - we say a socialist education system - and I am sure we will agree on the need for an educational system which is relevant, where agriculture is not looked down upon, where a man does not consider it the apex of achievement to get a clerical job. We can agree on that. As far as Guyana is concerned, our input is Socialism. But at

82

the last conference no one objected to what Guyana said about what should be the educational system. We didn't tell them anything about the socialist content. That is for them; the socialist content is for us. But at least in the West Indies you should have a relevant educational system. Our trade, they buy our rice, we buy their oil. The other day, for instance, St. Vincent had a stock of carrots it couldn't get rid of. We only wanted 50,000lbs. but they said, could you take another 50,000? Sure. We did not really need it, but we took it. I think that if we were in Federation, it might have succeeded because you had amongst them men of vision like Norman Manley.

But, I think that eventually there will be a political union in the Caribbean. How soon it will come I don't know; but I think we will see the inevitability of it as we get real economic integration. I have been telling some of the smaller islands that Guyana has an opportunity now to go into salt manufacture. We will be prepared to help as much as we can in joint ventures for some of these islands to develop themselves as sources of salt, both industrial salt and table salt. It is a source of manufacture of caustic also which we use heavily in the bauxite industry; it can also be a source of chlorine, which as you know is the basis of many chemical industries. We are trying to encourage the regional thing. Places like Antigua must turn their dryness into value. We have turned our mud into something useful. We are going to be producing this year about 13 million clay bricks; next year we expect it to be over 20 million. All right, we have mud. Make something of the mud. And this is the view I have on our whole region, to take our circumstances as they are and turn them into assets."

THE RT. EXCELLENT AND
RT. HONOURABLE
SIR WILLIAM ALEXANDER BUSTAMANTE

G.B.E HON. LL.D
(NATIONAL HERO OF JAMAICA)
BORN BLENHEIM JAMAICA, 24TH FEBRUARY, 1884
DIED 6TH AUGUST, 1977
CHIEF MINISTER OF JAMAICA (1944-1955)
PRIME MINISTER OF JAMAICA (1962 - 1967)

6

SIR WILLIAM ALEXANDER BUSTAMANTE

MANY YEARS AGO there was a black Jamaican religious eccentric who preached and issued pamphlets saying "I will descend into Hell and set Satan free." At about the same time, a tall, spectral, white-skinned eccentric was attracting attention and challenging "I am going to drive the Governor out of King's House." The man who issued that seemingly wild challenge was to become the Rt. Excellent and Rt. Honourable Sir Alexander Bustamante, the first Prime Minister of Independent Jamaica. But at the time he was to many just a rabble-rouser whose ideas were as wild as his macabre appearance and strange attire. Nothing more has since been heard of the other eccentric, but both of them occupied the stage as national mutterings grew in Kingston, Jamaica, at a time when many voices were heard in the land, precursors of the storm which broke among the people in 1938. Since then Jamaica has never again been the same.

Whence did this Bustamante come? He was Jamaican born - though his name belies it - and he came from the same stock which produced his cousin, the brilliant barrister, Norman Washington Manley, who became an idol of society, sportsman, company director and later Premier of Jamaica. Nine years Bustamante's junior, Manley, when asked about his irrepressible cousin, remembered him well, but not altogether approvingly. "Alec", he would say apologetically, but yet with a touch of envy, "Alec was a wild fellow, rough, good for breaking in mules and horses." Then, as if dismissing the subject he would say: "But he went away and we never saw him for years."

Alexander Bustamante (his name at birth was Alexander Clarke) did go away, and did come back from time to time to Jamaica. The story - or the legend - of where Bustamante went from time to time, and why , may never be documented. Many, indeed, have tried, including the Jamaican historian on Latin America, the late W. Adolphe Roberts. The enquiries have supported many points of the variegated stories of wanderlust and adventure with which Bustamante even at the age of ninety-three still regaled his admirers and visitors. But the stories lacked consistency, though full of excitement in every version. Bustamante never minded when a guest recalled that he had previously given a different version, and laughed heartily without any sign that he felt caught out.

Norman Manley used to recall that Bustamante once came back dressed as a Spanish grandee, with broad-brimmed black hat, matador's velvet trousers, and embroidered bolero. Then, on another occasion, he came back an apostle of honey as made by the bee, started an apiary and disappeared just as suddenly as he had appeared. Then, too, there was the time when Busta (the name by which Jamaica - friend or foe - loves him and knows him best), came out and started retailing cow's milk.

These episodes may seem erratic, especially with a person of his wild and weird figure and personality - six-foot four, a gangling man topped by wild hair which he combed frequently as part of his personality act. Many were the Jamaicans who having migrated, were coming back to Jamaica to try their fortunes at one thing or other. They passed unnoticed as they came home, failed in whatever endeavour it was, and faded back into the outer world. Busta was different, he was distinctive, he came from a top-drawer family which kept a wary eye on him, and after all he became famous in later years.

At this point, a closer look at the man is needed. And here I quote from the Gleaner's archives (which at one time were also partly my concern).

> *"Born on the 24th February, 1884, at Blenheim, near Lucea in Hanover (one of the most westerly parishes) he was at birth William Alexander Clarke. He often averred that his father Robert Constantine Clarke, was an Irish immigrant. His mother has been described as a Negress. She was in fact Mary, a mixed blood daughter of one Wilson whose antecedents are somewhat obscure."*

> "Robert Clarke's mother (Alexander's grandmother) had been married first to his father and then to Alexander Shearer, a small penkeeper and farmer. Out of the latter union had come four daughters, one of whom Margaret had produced Norman Manley and another, Ellie, had produced Edna Swithenbank (later Mrs. Norman Manley)."

> "Young Alexander was therefore through his grandmother related as cousin to both Norman and Edna Manley)."

(Here it is worthy of note that the name Shearer often leads folk to believe that Jamaican Prime Minister (1969-72) who was brought into public life by Bustamante is also a cousin; not so ! The name similarity carries with it no identity of descent).

"Alexander's boyhood was passed in poverty. He often said that he had to sleep on a pile of crocus bags in a corner of the living room. He was given no formal education worth mentioning; but at picking up and applying useful facts he was phenomenally quick."

"His relatives have said that Bustamante's family, while poor, had never been really 'too poor'; that in fact the Clarkes had more money than the Manleys. Later the Clarkes were to lose their abundance with the death of Alexander's father."

"When he was about 19 (Norman Manley then being 10) Alexander left home to "work for a relative" as he used to put it. The 'relative' in question was Norman Manley's father, who had a modest property called 'Belmont' in St. Catherine. Alexander, who was a wonder at breaking in mules and horsekind, lived as a member of the family for about a year, and then left Jamaica (on his first exodus) at the age of 20."

No one is certain whether Alexander lived with his cousins as a kept hand or as a poor relation, but Norman Manley's sister, the late Mrs. Vera Moody, tells this story.

While Alex was living with them, Vera, petite and peppery, then age 15, went one afternoon on to the verandah overlooking the garden where Alex was busying himself. When Alex spotted her, he sauntered over, stepped into the flower bed which the verandah overlooked, and tall as he was, reached out for her, hugged her and kissed her.

"I drew back," said Vera "and boxed him. Then I panicked. What would big Alex do? But all he did was step back and laugh 'Ha, ha, ha!' and went back into the garden."

To follow Bustamante in his peregrinations is even harder to do by research than to follow him when he gives rambling but exciting narratives - often with improvisations - midst a circle of admirers. The Gleaner's archives compromise with the following, concerning Alex's departure from Jamaica.

"A phase of almost total confusion begins at this point. The youth, driven by a powerful urge toward adventure went to Cuba and Panama, where he worked with the tramways, Puerto Rico where he peddled Purline soap, and probably some other Latin American countries, to the United States and Canada, and also to Spain and Morocco, if we are to believe his principal story."

Indeed, I believe it because of some strange secondary evidence. Why would Morocco have so entered into Busta's subconscious that in the midst of an all out sugar workers' dispute with West Indies Sugar Company in the 1940's, he likened the arguments of Robert Kirkwood, the company spokesman, in this fashion: "Kirkwood is like a wolf baying in the Atlas Mountains." The whole atmosphere of that statement, totally irrelevant to Jamaica and the sugar plains, must have come out of some exposure in younger years to the Riff rebellion and to his stay, however brief, in the region! Busta's seemingly superficial insistence on the soft Castillian "c" connotes a short stay in Barcelona, something he picked up "on the run" so to speak. It would take many years to make a true Castillian of a West Indian migrant, but clever as he was at imitative flattery - and ridicule - he carried forever the conversational talisman of spouting about the soft "c" whenever he was persuaded to venture haltingly into Spanish conversation. These minor matters, along with others not remembered specifically, persuaded me that it was a fact that Alexander Bustamante had been to Spain and Morocco.

But, as the Gleaner's archives state it, "The voyagers trail and his ways of earning a livelihood could only be re-established now by a detective going from place to place and working on clues picked up from former associates (most of whom would have been long dead)."

Indeed, where that detective work has been done, it has revealed astonishing evidence of Bustamante's legends being fact, even if fact embellished. That he had worked on the Panama tramways is quite definitely established. Jamaican Richard Lindsay, who worked as Bell Captain in a Panama Hotel in those days assured me that Bustamante had been a ticket inspector on the tramways. And this fits in because in those days of "Gold" Panama for whites and "silver" for blacks, Busta with his Latin look and white-to-red complexion would more likely have been an inspector than a ticket collector. Busta has told several stories of his passing for white in the "Jim Crow" trains of the U.S.A. where, by speaking Spanish, he escaped transfer to the coaches for blacks.

Another instance verified by modern detection is the fact that indeed Bustamante had been in Havana in the Police Force. A Jamaican historian called at the Havana Police Headquarters in 1953, accompanied by a prominent Cuban journalist, who used his influence to obtain documentary proof of Bustamante's services, if any. A personnel card was produced. It was true. Alexander Bustamante, of Jamaica, had served as an extra, a sort of special constable, in civil-brassard. That was the official record, but it could easily have been a cover-up for more secret work.

The fact of a non-national being engaged in such sensitive work has its counterpart in many parts of the world where despotic rulers very often rely on foreigners rather than on their own nationals for sensitive protection work or investigation. For one thing, the foreigner is expendable without much domestic fuss; he knows he is taking his own risk.

In any event, whether in turbulent Cuba or in Panama (not long then seceded from Colombia to sell out the Canal to the U.S.A.) there were opportunities for a bold and brash young man. Thousands of other Jamaicans had been attracted both to Cuba and to Panama and made their fortunes if not fame. Bustamante was one of these, with special spunk added, plus his theatrical gait and manner.

So it can be accepted as fact that Bustamante did go to the land of Don Quixote at the time of the ruthless Primo de Rivera, and to Cuba during the regime of dictator Machado. The flair for the dictatorial may have rubbed off on him during these precarious times; certainly in his earlier years in public life, Jamaica became alarmed at his highly personalised form of leadership, and the Daily Gleaner which encouraged him but within limits, was forced to publish a strong denunciation of Busta's tactics under the heading "Stop Him Now!"

That was the Bustamante that came back to Jamaica in 1934 and changed it for all time. Weird, wild, monstrously lanky, eschewing the traditional middle-class paths of Jamaican life, frequenting the simpler eating places and watering holes - for his consumption of liquor was prodigious - and ladling out tales of his life whether in Spain, Cuba or Panama, and proferring advice regularly on the virtues of honey and carrot juice, backing the advice with his proclamation of dietetic experience in a New York hospital.

How did it come about that he could afford to come home and have no visible means of sustenance, living nonetheless moderately well and entertaining, as necessary, companions who were attracted to his lively chatter? Historians have thought that he made money in the Wall Street crash of 1929. I think that unlikely. As he has told me the story - with variations - it had to do with a fearsome dream he had around that time.

"I saw blood everywhere" he would say. "I woke up frightened. The next day the Wall Street crash was on us." How does one make money out of that dream, out of those circumstances? My interpretation is that he must have had most of his savings on the stock market and the dream - which may have been days before and not only the night before - providentially caused him to cash in high, before the crash. Thus, alarmed, with his money and savings intact, he fled from the perils of uncertain New York to start life anew in his homeland.

And, as they say, he really started something; something which none of the rulers in London or Jamaica could have foreseen; nor did even the ordinary people at first regard him as any potential leader. Many were the strident or querulous voices speaking at random here and there in the island - and Busta's street-corner voice tends to the querulous - and many feared (or hoped) that the serious labour disturbances in the eastern Caribbean and British Guiana would soon infect Jamaica also.

So while Bustamante patiently infiltrated an existing trades union, (the Jamaica General Trade Workers Union) and became its Treasurer-patron, he set out to make his name known in the wider world. The condition of the working classes in Jamaica was deplorable, a day's wage in rural areas being just about the cost of one loaf of bread.

Taking note that there were demonstrations by the working class against their plight, Bustamante entered the fray with letters to newspapers not only in Jamaica, but in Britain. Thus on April 15, 1935 - the year that Marcus Garvey, the tragic apostle of the world's black peoples, left Jamaica for self-imposed exile in London, Bustamante was writing thus to the Daily Gleaner:

"The Editor, Sir - In your issue of the 9th instant. it is stated that a certain gentleman said that the unemployed should not stage a demonstration and take part in a hunger march but should remain at home and send their leaders to the Corporation.

"The latter method of calling attention to conditions or grievances is a proper one as a crowd cannot speak for itself, but must do so through leaders appointed by it, but it should not be suggested that individuals have no right to form themselves into a body, and provided this is done in an orderly manner, call attention to and give practical expression to their condition and needs.

"When it was intended to give a welcome to our Royal visitors not only was this done through the people's representatives and the representatives of government by their presence and in the form of addresses, but thousands of people lined the streets of Kingston and the roads in the country to add to, and confirm the welcome given in their name by the above-named representatives.

"What is wrong is, that in spite of the question of unemployment being made the chief plank on platforms and rash promises as to its relief being made to the people when their Suffrage was being sought, when no relief is apparant or forthcoming, the people on approaching those who made the promises are told that the relief of unemployment is no business of theirs, but that measures are being taken by someone else to meet the situation.

"It cannot be denied that the demonstrators conducted themselves in an orderly manner and that the deputation that waited on the Corporation Councillors expressed themselves very nicely. . . .

". . . Hungry men and women and children have a right to call attention to their condition and to ask of people fulfilment of promises made to them, as long as they do so without using violence or being disorderly.

92

WILLIAM ALEXANDER BUSTAMANTE

"Jamaicans are patient, trustful and law-abiding, and if properly advised and treated, no one has anything to fear.

"The conditions existing today have not sprung up overnight, but they have been left to grow worse till the situation is now acute. No steps have been taken for their amelioration.

"What Jamaica needs is practical and sympathetic men interested in the country and its people and not charlatans and self-seekers making long speeches about nothing; men who by their handling of this country's affairs will make such things as hunger marches unnecessary."

Before the letter ends, Bustamante uttered one of his spicy aphorims. "Beware of the Greeks when they bring gifts and when these gifts turn out to be toads, endeavour to climb up a tree." A typical Bustamantism, going back to nature for his figures of speech.

In another letter about ten days later Bustamante wrote to the Gleaner pressing his campaign. He said in part:

"I am suggesting that a movement be started for each and everyone in a position to do so to see if we could not give employment and bread to someone, even if we have to make some sacrifice to do so. I am sure that the aggregate result would not only go a long way towards relieving the present distressing conditions, but would give us satisfaction in knowing that we are endeavouring to fulfil the prayer often said without meaning to 'Our Father ..... Give us this day our daily bread. . . .'"

"Let us start a Silver Jubilee employment campaign and let this idea be put forward in the Press and preached from the pulpit and taken up by all charitable and philanthropic institutions, and let us see what will be the result. Let us each make a pledge to employ one extra person, however small the wages might be, when we are able, and give this a try for, say, six months. Most persons could find in their business or elsewhere something one would like to have done but have never given same attention because it was not urgent. I am of the opinion that effort and money spent in this manner would not be wasted."

Later in the same year, Mr. Bustamante threw himself into a dialogue and dispute with Mr. F.H. Robertson, then a pillar of the Jamaica Banana Producers Association which had recommended a quota. During this discussion, Mr. S.W. Sharpe, also one of the spokesmen of the Banana Association, wrote critically about Bustamante's attack on Mr. Robertson. Bustamante retorted:

"Sir: One Mr. S.W. Sharpe wants to know who is Bustamante. I was born in Hanover. At a very tender age Spain became my

93

home. I served in the Spanish Army as a Cavalry Officer in Morocco, Northern Africa. Subsequently I became an Inspector in the Havana Police Force. Recently I worked as dietician in one of New York's largest hospitals."

"Bustamante is a lonely fighter! He belongs to no organisation or club. He fights on the side of fair-play. Not only that, he fights on the side of his enemy if he is on the side of justice, without fear of any consequence whatever. It is characteristic of him to always put his address with his name when writing to the Press. I have not seen Mr. Sharpe's address in his letter of today's date - makes me wonder."

To Mr. Sharpe's suggestion that he should remain silent, Bustamante said:

"Mr. Sharpe you could not keep my mouth closed even if you padlocked it."

Then he goes on:

"The great Lord might have John the Devil closed up in some pen, but He certainly has let loose a lot of devils in Jamaica, sowing the evil seeds of injustice for their own personal benefits and their friends, while the masses suffer more and more, too weak to fight for themselves, praying to Almighty God to liberate them from these angels of the devil some of whose waiting makes me feel that they could better occupy their time by becoming theatrical clowns."

The letter closes with the words:

"Good luck Mr. Sharpe! We need more gallant questioners like you, at least I do, for you seem to be comically disposed."

Writing in this style, Bustamante continued to hold the limelight with discussions on government policy, increased taxation, loan monies, slaughter houses, industrial dictatorship, promotions in the Police Force, the Water Board needing a plumber, houses without baths. On the last subject he wrote:

"Speaking of Africa, so many people believe that they are savages. We who know better must excuse them for such ignorance; but how can we excuse our own Jamaican Government for passing buildings erected as complete without baths? If this is not an action of uncivilisation, what is it?"

Later in the same letter he said:

94

WILLIAM ALEXANDER BUSTAMANTE

"I have never seen such like conditions that is existing here today in any present Republic, and yet we are always condemning the republics. Dirt and filth is what I class the sanitation of many areas of Kingston with - it is the Governor's fault."

He continues:

"Those who cannot see might be able to smell for the odour of some of these yards, as they are termed here, should be sufficient to knock them dead, as it nearly does that to me; but I suppose that some people - scentless and sightless, they cannot feel nor smell the obnoxious odour from some pits in the Corporate Area for which regulations for their periodical cleaning should be rigidly enforced."

The letter ends:

"When I visit some of these places referred to above it gives me a creepy feeling. I wonder how we escape the bubonic plague, not because of the presence of so many rats, but from the absence of cleanliness so necessary to good health."

1935 was a great letter writing year for Bustamante. He took interest in all kinds of subjects, and one of them was Mussolini who was then leading Italy into the Rape of Abyssinia. It had been suggested that the Pope could prevent Mussolini from going to war with Ethiopia. Bustamante pointed out that the Papacy "does not any longer rule government."

"I am positively certain that if the Pope could prevent Mussolini on his hell-bound determination to exterminate Ethiopians he would, just as he would prevent that lunatic Hitler from destroying a peaceful and useful race as the Jews are." In the letter, Bustamante points out that he was not a Catholic (but he did become a Catholic late in life) . He concluded with a witticism:

"I do not care for mixing a wisecrack in the matter; but to show how impossible it is for any one man to prevent Mussolini from his impending assassination of Ethiopians, I will say that any one man - holy or unholy - who can prevent Mussolini would be able to ride a grasshopper, and Mr. Editor, you know how difficult the latter would be."

During those years, Bustamante, according to the late historian, Adolphe Roberts, "was a most singular combination of money-lender, patriot, and reformer." He was talkative, incoherent sometimes, but with a passionate manner that appealed to the crowd. Clearly he was a potential leader of the masses, but he had no ready-made case. He needed a general crisis. Few Jamaicans would at that time have dared to predict that the crisis was shaping just around the next corner.

In the latter 1930's disturbances occurred in Trinidad, Barbados, Guyana and other West Indian areas, and gave Bustamante food for eloquence. He then was very often accompanied by a former Marcus Garvey aide, St. William Grant, who fancied the Garvey style of wearing semi-military uniforms and colourful robes. Indeed, when St. William Grant on Bustamante's platform would be down to speak on the Pope, he would put on religious robes. He always tried some new gimmick or costume to fit the subject about which he was to speak.

At these meetings Bustamante did not say a great deal but he interjected and made it plain that he was in fact the true leader. He had joined with ex-policeman and ex-soldier "Father" A.G. St. C. Coombs in the Jamaica Workers' Tradesmen's Union which was founded in May, 1936, and he took office in that Union and that became his first official link with a labour organisation. Coombs, of course, went on to win a seat in the Legislature and became a Minister in the Government. Bustamante went on to be the maximum leader of Jamaica. That was the range of Bustamante's life and activity in those middle years before the storm came.

The beginning of May, 1938 was when Jamaica's climacteric was reached with the massive disturbances at Frome Sugar Estate in Westmoreland. It was a totally unorganised outburst, except for the ripples that his rhetoric may have created in that far end of the island. He had nothing to do with the uprising at Frome, which was a mass reaction to bad management which permitted wretched and squalid living conditions of workers who had migrated to the area in the hope of getting a job.

The Police killed a number of rioters and wounded others with rifle fire. A Gleaner reporter, meeting Bustamante on the street, told him about it the very night, and Bustamante hastened to the far end of the island to identify himself with the riot. Later that very month, when a Commission of Enquiry had been appointed to investigate the riots at Frome, Bustamante's moment came in Kingston itself. He was credited with having incited a crowd to besiege the Legislative Council. There was restlessness in the city. A march of the unemployed took place. It is recorded that Bustamante went unheralded from the Kingston waterfront to the steps of the Ward Theatre and addressed the large audience that gathered. The Gleaner reports him as saying in regard to the Frome Commission of Enquiry on which there were Sir Charles Doorley and Sir Henry Brown, that "two Knights were propagating for his arrest," but they, not he, should be very careful. He was above them, for while they wanted to live forever, he was prepared to die today.

It was then that the crowd began to have the habit of saying "We will follow Bustamante till we die." Disorders continued in Kingston. There were strikes on the waterfront, shop-windows were broken and in some cases, shops were looted. It is recorded then that, at daybreak on the 23rd of May, Bustamante addressed a meeting at Duke and Harbour Streets at which he called the train of events "a mental revolution." Later in the day, Bustamante with St. William Grant were arrested at Parade Square, Kingston.

Bustamante's arrest led to a general strike in the capital city. Norman Manley and J.A.G. Smith, two leading Counsels sought and secured Bustamante's and St. William Grant's release and the charges against them were dropped subsequently. Thereafter, Bustamante stalked the land as the most powerful person in Jamaica. Vast meetings were addressed, emotions were high and it was clear that something new had happened to Jamaica.

Bustamante formed a number of small strike associations and was content for a moment to bask in the glory of the tumultous support which the people in the Corporate Area of the city of Kingston had given in tremendous measure as well as the labouring and working classes throughout the island. But other things were afoot. The Giovernor, Sir Edward Denham, though not a brilliant administrator, was a most humane person; (indeed, he started the first major government public housing scheme in West Kingston). He took this whole tumult under his Governorship very badly and he died very shortly after.

Upon his death the Colonial Secretary, Mr. Arthur Wooley, conceived the idea that the disturbances which were sporadic in various parts of the island might indeed get out of hand entirely. So he arranged with Bustamante, the national Labour Leader, and Manley, the National Mediator (accepted as such by the government, the workers and the influential members of society) to go to St. Mary where it was feared that bloodshed was about to break out on a large scale. The government produced, with the assistance of the Daily Gleaner, a limited edition of that newspaper for Bustamante and Mr. Manley to take to St. Mary with them on the Sunday. Denham's death had been accompanied by almost disgraceful hostility towards his funeral and things were not looking well at all nationally. I was commissioned on behalf of the Gleaner to accompany Bustamante and Manley to St. Mary taking for distribution of these papers which were announcing on behalf of the government, a new land deal for the people of Jamaica - land for the people. And so we went. All day that Sunday Bustamante and Manley addressed meetings, advocating peace, advocating a new deal for the people, recommending that no more violence should occur and so on. They met with rather dull response. I remember that late that night at a meeting in St. Mary, a vast crowd had gathered on a common, and Bustamante and Manley were speaking from a truck backed up with pumped-up lamps giving a pale glare to the place. Up to that time both Bustamante and Manley had been somewhat uncertain of their response at these meetings. Bustamante suddenly galvanized this meeting. There was a vast sweaty gathering of labouring, farm working class people glistening in the pale light. Around the truck at a distance, away separating the speakers from the crowd , was a ring of special constables, of book-keepers, headmen and the like from the estates who had been sworn in as special constables because of the general state of emergency.

Bustamante, suddenly looking at these armed men, said: "You want the people to make trouble tonight? You want them to give trouble so you can shoot them? You won't shoot them. You will have to shoot me."

A deep, great, swelling roar came up from the sweltering masses. Bustamante, tall and lanky and turbulent leapt back into the truck, signalling for silence. He said to the people: "But there will be no more trouble. You are going to get your rights." And there was a great groaning, a great groaning like a swelling of the sea, then a great ovation. The message had got across.

Bustamante, as a rabble rouser, had fully arrived with the new technique which I have called "bite and blow." A fierce remark and then a calming remark; he has used that technique most effectively up and down the country, and overseas too.

That night we slept with Manley's and Bustamante's cousins, the Purcells, in Annotto Bay. We had a late snack and retired to bed. I went into the lavatory and found a large six-shooter revolver on the seat. I realised it was the one that Bustamante had had at his hips all the while. With my own sense of mischief, I took it to my room.

Later in the night there was a great hubub and lighting of lamps, with Bustamante declaring,: "My gun has been stolen. I am going to be assassinated. I am going to be assassinated. They have stolen my gun." Manley got up; everybody got up and I got up and said: "Mr. Bustamante, you left your revolver in the toilet, sir," and handed it to him. Then there was great laughter.

From that time on, for many years, Bustamante used the threat of assassination as a call to public support and to stimulate his followers and others. It was a great stunt of his to report real or imagined attempts upon his life. No doubt there were those who would, if they could, have taken a pot shot at him, but the vigilance of crowds that surrounded him at his meetings was such that policemen and reporters and the like sometimes had short shrift because the people would not have any suspect person around their leader.

So these two great cousins, Alexander Bustamante and Norman Manley, started the great game of chess, which continued all their lives, for ultimate dominion over Jamaica.

Bustamante, the national labour leader, was worshipped by the labouring masses. Norman Manley by the intelligentsia, by the middle -class and commercial elements. How they both rivalled each other in the succeeding years is a very interesting story, but here we are concerned with Bustamante's role in it. There were a number of artisan-type unions in existence and they were mostly loyal and friendly to Manley, through Manley's attraction of people like Ken Hill, Frank

Hill, Richard Hart, who had worked closely with these unions. So the idea was proposed that all unions should get together and form a Trades Union Congress in which all unions would merge. Bustamante had formed by then his Bustamante Industrial Trade Union; the magic of his name was the magic of the Union. Charging a very low membrship fee, it had attracted and created considerable financial resources for its work and for its leader. Bustamante went along with this congress idea and attended the meetings where it was proposed that they should join together for the greater progress of the working class of all types. But when Bustamante found out or realised that his Union, which had hundreds of times more members than the other Unions put together, would be subject to one union, one vote, he jumped out of the trap and went his own way ever after. That created the notion that it was an intention to deprive Bustamante of his undoubted established mass leadership of the working class in the country and he himself, on occasion, had denounced this movement as such. Thereafter, however, it was the Bustamante Industrial Trade Union, and the others cleaved together as the Trades Union Congress (T.U.C.).

Bustamante at that time was a regular visitor to Richard Lindsay's Arlington House restaurant. At first, he used to be accompanied quite frequently by a tall, white, Latin American girl, very tall, who was way ahead of her time, in that slacks, which she habitually wore, were not then accepted general female attire in Jamaica. But later, she ceased to come along with him; then developed the romance - indeed it is a romance - between the strange, weird labour leader and a quiet solid, stolid secretary who worked with Lindsay at Arlington House. She was to become his life-long companion, his advisor, his protector, and eventually his wife. This is the same Gladys Longbridge, who is now Lady Bustamante.

A fund subscribed penny by penny by the workers bought him a large Buick motor-car. And whenever the car stopped on the street, eager groups gathered, dusting it with whatever came to hand. This was, of course, not something novel to Jamaica, for I remember in 1935 when E. Vivian Allen won the seat in St. Elizabeth. The crowds at Newmarket used their skirts and rags to clean the red dust off their new Member's car. As Adolphe Roberts put it: "Bustamante took all this seeming idolatry with a mixture of grandee gallantries, bombast, truculence and mysticism." The beginnings of a sort of political ambition came to be part of his panache in those days, and the people would sing like an anthem the chorus as each meeting ended in fervour: "We will follow Bustamante! We will follow Bustamante! We will follow Bustamante! We will follow Bustamante till we die."

An odd quirk in the relationship between Bustamante in those days and the masses was that Bustamante, no doubt taking his cue from the hard time that black Marcus Garvey had in getting anywhere with his own black people, would declare as often as possible: "I haven't got a drop of coloured blood in my veins." This was untrue, but on the face of it, he looked Spanish or Portuguese or European and he made this declaration quite often. This was to say to the people (in my interpretation) - You may not be able to trust your own coloured people but you are accustomed to accepting orders from white people and I am a white man.

Yet, many years later the same Bustamante was being interviewed in the National Press Club in Washington, U.S.A. and he was asked what was his racial admixture. Bustamante replied: "I am one third Irish, one third Negro, one third Arawak and one third white." Whereupon one of the journalists said: "But that makes you 120%, sir?" Bustamante, with a flash and a smile ,said: "That is why I am better than the other leaders." He had then come full circle from the declaration of whiteness to a declaration of total admixture of the races of Jamaica. That took a long time to work out. But he made the evolotion from one stand to the other and yet retained his influence and popularity.

The first big event for Bustamante after the 1938 uprising was giving evidence before the Royal Commission under Lord Moyne, who was sent to the British Caribbean to investigate the series of disturbances which had occurred and to make recommendations to the British Government.

When Bustamante gave evidence, the crowds flooded the place. They could not hold inside so they gathered right around the building and, though they could not hear what was going on - in those days there was no public address system - they would clap when they heard clapping from inside and they would cheer when they heard cheering from inside. In that way, remote as they were, they gave moral support and presence to their leader. It was a very long series of questionings of Mr. Bustamante by the Royal Commission, and the Gleaner's headlines at the time gave some indication of what was going on. On Thursday, November 17, the Gleaner's headline across a whole page was: "Labour Leader Gives Evidence Before Royal Commission." Then the sub-headings picked out the main points: "Mr. Bustamante wants wage minimum of a dollar a day for labour; Admits modifications in some industries; Wants old-age pension at 50; Would levy cess on bananas and raise income tax on rich to find the money."

Other headlines: "Protect Native Industry." "Jamaica merely kept as dumping ground for British goods. Declares last and present Governors fascist." (Last Governor was the late Sir Edward Denham and the present Governor was Sir Arthur Richards, later Lord Milverton). Then the headline goes on: "Elected members no good. Attributes most of troubles to semi bunch of imbeciles elected Members we have in Legislative Council." Then another statement: "Jamaicans unfriendly and cruel to each other." On another page of the evidence, the main headline was: "Mr. Bustamante Declares Majority of Industries here Can Pay Dollar a Day." Then a subsidiary headline: "Says People going about in nude condition owing to low wages. Not Out to destroy Employers."

On yet another page the main headline was: "50,000 members in his Union," says Bustamante. In subsidiary headlines: "Of these about half are regular paying members. Others pay when they get work. Trailed by Police Force. Held from Endeavours to avoid strike and how he has admonished his people for acting contrary to his advice. Aggrieved with need of law to enforce wages under certain circumstances."

Then other headlines: "Never made Seditious Speeches." "Unemployment situation more serious than low wage scale."

His reception by the various members of the Commission was uneven. Members like Sir Walter Citrine, a Trade Union representative, were more sympathetic than Mr. Assheton, financial specialist. But, altogether, the total effect of his appearance before the Royal Commission was to provide him with an opportunity to create a national manifest as it really was, of what he thought should be done for Jamaica. It was the beginning of a political concept which was only realised some five years later when he formed the Jamaica Labour Party.

It seemed natural when his cousin, Barrister, Norman Manley founded a political party in 1938, the People's National Party, that Bustamante would have regarded that as a design against his own influence with the people. So Bustamante veered away and grumbled that he had no use for "Reds." The fact is that the Party had not been formed as socialist, but Sir Stafford Cripps, who made the inaugural speech, was a hardline socialist, and that gave many people the notion that it was a socialist party. Indeed, it took many, many years to come to that declared ideology. As Adolphe Roberts put it: "The truth was that Manley's intellectuals had restricted Bustamante to the Union, taking second place to his cousin." And Bustamante would not have it. There was a period during which Bustamante was in fact a member of the People's National Party but that did not last long.

Between 1938 and 1943, Bustamante's work was cut out to consolidate his Union strength, to create the organisation and staff necessary to manage an enterprise of that size covering the whole island. He set about this in his own inimitable way. His letter writing to employers during that period gives some idea of the range of subjects and type of approach that he was wont to take. The Royal Mail Line, which was a heavy carrier of cargo to Kingston from Britain and elsewhere, was one of the companies he tangled with. Apparently, the company had ceased painting its ships in Kingston and painted them over in Britain. So Bustamante in November 1938 wrote to the Manager of Royal Mail in Kingston saying:

"With regard to the non-painting of your ship here, which is now in our harbour, on reflection I have decided that it is unfair, because when you were able to get cheaper labour in this country up to five months ago, your ship was always painted here, and now just because the unfortunate Negroes have been given a few pence raise, either you or your captain have thought it fit to have them painted on the other side. (Be it noted that the Manager of Royal Mail was an Englishman). "This is definitely unfair, it is proof of the little or no interest you have in the workers in this country, and I am not going to mince matters with you for there is going to be a fight about this.

"I do not know really to whom I must attribute this blame, but I hold you responsible as Manager of the company here, and cannot attribute the blame to the Captain, because whilst it is being said that there is no discipline in the Bustamante Union, if your Captain is the one who gives you orders, then there is no discipline in the British company either.

"According to Sir Walter Citrine's statement while sitting on the Royal Commission, he has made it very clear that if the Union in Jamaica calls a strike and the companies should suffer by it so doing, such damages may be able to be collected from the Union; but in every law there is a loophole. Nobody can prosecute workers if they call a strike themselves, and nobody can prosecute me for not putting them back to work, or extending my sympathy to where it belongs.

"It seems to me, sir, that there is a move on foot to starve out the painters of my country, and I shall not allow this without giving them that protection which I am capable of giving; and I am asking you to reply to me today whether this ship is going to be painted here or not.

"This is a matter I will get the sympathy not alone of every worker employed and unemployed, but of the entire population, and I can assure you, sir, that when I give my sympathy where it belongs all the money on earth that your company has will not be enough to induce one of my country-women or men to move one straw upon your wharf or ship.

"I am asking that the ship be painted here, and if it is not painted here, I am suggesting to you that it may be better not to bring it back with any cargo, believing that it is going to be touched by one of my country women or men.....

"I am not going to allow you or any Captain, or anybody else to deliberately starve my people out, even to the extent of risking my safety."

Most heads of departments and heads of business and industry and plantation were in those days either white Jamaican or expatriate whites who were doing fairly well in the island. A second letter is to another ex-patriate person who controlled a small factory. This one says:

"This is to inform you, Mr. Van der Porten, that all the workers in your macaroni and spaghetti factory are members of this Union. We understand that you say if you ever found out that they were members, they would all go through the gate, and so we have to inform you.

"We request that Philbertha Thomas be re-employed. She has been unjustly discharged. Secondly, that they must not lift bags weighing from 90 lbs. to sometimes hundreds of pounds; that our women are not to be used as side-men on drays (horse-drawn carts); that they are not to be used to scrub your factory. Our women are as dignified as yours from whence you came, and perhaps more ....and that you cease treating them as if they were something beneath you ..... and we request: 50% raise of pay, for 10/-, 12/- and 13/ a week only help to send women to the House of Prostitution. Heavy weight, scrubbing of floor and abuse on top of that is not consistent with the civilisation, and we want to inform you that you come under Defence projects and any victimisation may be considered a lock-out under the law. We are now giving you a chance if you think you can to discharge them 'because they belong to the Union.' If they complain of any abuse when they come to work tomorrow because I have written to you, I will send two officers up there to you. I mean our officers, not Police Officers. 'If they join the Union, you will put them through the gate!' You dare to do that. You might have been able to do that before I came back to Jamaica, not now. I have instructed them that if one hair on their head is hurt, when work is finished, come back to this office to see me. Women lifting weights, scrubbing floors, turning sidemen! Well, I tell you mister, if that's the kind of thing they do over yonder, it won't be tolerated here.

"Knowing that you do not want Unionists, there we will be watching and listening out for everything that happens there."

The next letter shows the kind of problems which arose in the rural economy. This letter is to Mr. Harry Vermont of Water Valley Estate in St. Mary and it says:

"It has been reported to me that you have discharged one Norman Facey for no other reason but because he gave information regarding prices paid by you, and the prices are a disgrace and a reflection against industrial sincerity towards labour, and that you threw him out of your hut after the man had been working for you for some six years. We are requesting his re-employment at once. Failing this, we will take such actions as we deem necessary to protect this man's interest, and , remember, Mr. Vermont, you have canes to rot and bananas to spoil and remember also that I have never agitated much in St. Mary, but owing to these abuses I will be coming over there for a month to live and to organise the workers.

"I am going to compel you and others like you to respect the rights of labour. This is also to inform you that you are to pay not less than 4 1/2d on the shilling on your cane property for all kinds of work done, by headmen and others, beginning from January 1. Some of you

103

people seem to think that Defence Regulations is for one section, but that which happens to labour can happen to employers. Failing to re-employ this man, failing to hear from you within four days from the date of this letter, I will take such actions as I think necessary to compel you to respect labour.

"It seems to me that most of you overseers who hand out your hands to get money to live in St. Mary seem to believe that you are capitalists and today you are there, and tomorrow you are gone. You are all just labourers like any other labourer. Furthermore, you have instructed my secretary, Mr. Johnson, that he is not to come on your property. I have instructed him to come as long as he has business there, and it is for you to have him arrested and I will defend him. I cannot write you people in St. Mary a courteous letter for the most of you are against Trade Union, and against labour, and so I must fight you, beat you, and then we will become friends.

"I have sent a copy of this letter to your Cane Farmers' Association, and remember that all the workers are to be paid not less than 4 1/2d. on the shilling bonus from January 1 this year. I will be over there soon and I will be coming with my tent. In 1938, when I came over there, nearly all the employers had vacated their premises, even the dogs and cats. Owing to this same bad treatment of the workers, the St. Mary planters are going to love the Bustamante Industrial Trade Union, and I will read this letter at your door when I come over. I want to co-operate with every employer in this country, but also want to fight everyone who is not co-operative and you can't beat me, Mr. Vermont.

"We are asking for the re-employment of William Shaw who was employed as assistant cattle-man, and who was sent to lead cows, which was not his job, and which he refused to do. You people come under Defence Regulations as labourers come. You can be dragged before the Defence Board. More than that, you can be prosecuted if you violate the Defence Regulations. Perhaps you did not know that Mr. Vermont. It looks to me that the Cane Farmers' Association has very little control over their members. If that is so, we will bring the agreement to an end and no work will be done."

The reference to Defence Regulations arises from the fact that World War II was then in progress and Jamaica, like much of the British Commonwealth, was brought under the Defence Regulations which inhibited any action that was likely to prejudice the war effort such as the non-production of cane and the like and withholding of labour on essential things.

As a final sample of that era, this last letter deals with a government department. It is written to an expatriate, E.G. Whitbred, who was then acting

Commissioner of Commerce and Industries in the Government's Marketing Department. Says the letter:

"Replying to your letter No. 4455/44 dated 26th June, 1944, in connection with coffee workers employed at the Coffee Clearing House in Harbour Street, Kingston, I would like to point out to you this fact, that repeatedly the Secretary of State for the Colonies has publicly stated that it is the desire of the Imperial Government that the living conditions of the colonials should be raised....

"We feel that it is your duty whether you were born here or not to endeavour to improve the conditions of those who work for government under you. There is not one coffee planter in this country who is paying their workers enbough for them to exist upon, and government has less rights to commit this unpardonable sin. It is government's duty to endeavour always to improve the conditions of labour. It is more so government's duty to see that their employees are paid more than private employees , so that there should be no reflection against government, and that government shall be in a position to critiise others, and to make laws to compel them to do the right thing, but it is a known fact in this country, that whilst government servants are paid big wages, the lower workers who are called labourers and subordinate staff are not paid enough for them to exist upon.....

"We talk so much of democracy, not alone here in Jamaica, but in England, and whilst this is practised in England, it is not practised here. Even those who come from abroad, and who talk of democracy, when they come to the colonies, they obviously feel that we are colonials, that we are just coloured people, and we can live on that which only a mongrel dog can live upon. The wages you give them, I think they should have tossed it away in the sea, for it is an insult to call it a raise. I cannot see why you and I need a thousand pounds to live on, and other government servants need so much, and the labourers need very little. When Lincoln says, 'We might not all be equal in everything, but we are all equal in putting food in our mouths.'

"No wonder that there is so much prostitution in this country, so much people in the Poor House, so many people in the Prisons, and so many people in the Asylum, through the pauperised pay not only paid by private employers but by government.

"It always angers me when men who are getting a big salary, which I don't grudge nor criticise, feel that others who are working under them are worth nothing: that is the sole point in my mind always.....

105

"We are not a political union fighting for self-government, but we are going to fight until the Heavens fall, until government servants who act as employers, and private employers realise that the workers have a right to eat, and to send their children to school."

These letters of course bridge a period during which Bustamante was finding his way into the stream of political thought. Note his reference to self-government which was the slogan of the party founded by his cousin, Norman Manley, in 1938. But in between these years many strident and vioent occurrences had accompanied Bustamante's path as he struggled to hold a political line in reserve and to build his Union against what seemed to be the philosophy of the Jamaican Government at the time to use the Defence Regulations as a lever. Thus it was that early in 1940 Bustamante called a strike in the banana and waterfront industries and the Shipping Agencies used non-Union labour to break his strike. According to the Gleaner archives, Bustamante announced that he would retaliate with a general strike. Declaring that the war effort was menaced, Governor Richards stopped all leave for soldiers for a week and armed the Police. The likelihood of a sojourn in Interment Camp loomed for Bustamante and other agitators. But that did not happen until September of the same year, 1940, when Bustamante was taken into Preventive Custody for alleged violations of the Defence of the Realm Act. The Gleaner archives say official accounts of his stay at Up Park Camp are lacking, but several persons report that during that period of internment, Bustamante's attitude was philosophical. He seemed to regard the situation as being one of the hazards of the game and allowed no personal bitterness to develop because of it. The offer his cousin, Norman Manley made to him, to hold the labour movement together while he was a prisoner, was gratefully accepted.

The interpretations of that offer of help and its acceptance differ. The fact is, however, that the T.U.C., which was the Manley link of the labour movement did go into the Bustamante Industrial Trade Union (B.I.T.U.) to assist it in its myriad problems of that period. Bustamante gained by having his Union managed in his absence, and the T.U.C. benefitted by gaining a wider range of influence. But the story goes that an attempt was about to be made in 1942, whilst Bustamante was still in preventive custody, to have the Constitution of the B.I.T.U. altered. This Constitution is unique in that at that time, at any rate, resolutions for alteration of the Constitution had first to be approved by the Executive Committee and the Executive Committee consisted of Mr. Bustamante himself and others of his most faithful supporters and officers. The story was that the intention was to get a resolution democratising the Constitution of the B.I.T.U. (which made Bustamante president for life) and then have the resolution taken before the annual meeting. Somehow, Bustamante was made aware of this contingent problem, which seemed about to arise and information was taken to Sir Arthur Richards, the Governor, who perhaps determined not to make either Party too strong, did not wish to see Manley's T.U.C. gain too total an ascendancy. Whatever may have passed through Sir Arthur Richards' mind, the fact is that on February 8, 1942, Bustamante was released and the Gleaner archives says that the release was "timed

106

by Sir Arthur Richards to prevent P.N.P. helpers who gained influence in the B.I.T.U. from amending the B.I.T.U. Constitution to remove Bustamante's controller power."

Bustamante took this favourable turn of events with composure, and for a while he was fairly dormant. Then, all of a sudden, he launched vigorous attacks, violent attacks, upon his erstwhile helpers and the People's National Party for being false to his trust. But opportunity knocked once again, because just then a new Constitution for Jamaica came into the offing. There were discussions in the Legislature and throughout the nation as to the form the Constitution would take, and eventually it was agreed that this new Constitution should be based on Adult Suffrage and that elections should be held in 1944. The People's National Party already existed, well organised all over the island. Bustamante was starting late in this sense but he started with a large, ready-made following from one end of the island to the other. And so it was that, to take the advantage of Adult Suffrage to gain political power, Bustamante formed the Jamaica Labour Party, (J.L.P.) based on his Union strength and his popularity with the whole labour force. He took complete charge of his new Party, he named the candidates and it is alleged that he had said: "If I put up a yellow dog, the people will vote for him," which was as near the truth as made little difference.

In the general election of December 14, 1944, Bustamante's Labour Party won 22 seats out of 32 seats to the House of Representatives. Norman Manley's People National Party won only 5 seats and he himself failed to gain a seat; Independent candidates gained 5 seats. The People's National Party polled only 23.5% of the votes whereas the Jamaica Labour Party polled 41.4% and Independent candidates, 30%. Thus did William Alexander Bustamante become, in 1944, the first Chief Minister of Jamaica. As history has since shown, he became, in 1962 also, the first Prime Minister of independent Jamaica.

The foregoing history may seem extensive in relation to the lateness at which political emergence occurs in this recollection. But the foregoing is analytical of the society in which Bustamante rose, as well as of the kind of man he was under different kinds of circumstances. He now became Chief Minister of Jamaica to sit on the Executive Council with the Governor, who retained Chairmanship of "the principal instrument of policy." Bustamante elected to take the portfolio of Comunications and Works, but he never surrendered his Union leadership. Indeed, even well past 90 years of age, and partly invalid at his mountain home at Irish Town, Bustamante remained nominally and de facto Leader of the Bustamante Industrial Trade Union, having completed 23 years of service in Jamaica's legislature and Parliament.

How did he adjust himself to the responsibilities of a Chief Minister in running the whole government of Jamaica? At first he did not. Early in his own regime as Chief Minister, he was involved in an outbreak in relation to violence at the Mental Hospital in Kingston which led to his arrest for manslaughter. In

February 1946, the Mental Hospital Union of Employees (allied to the P.N.P.) struck for better conditions and the Governor (Sir John Huggins) agreed to see a deputation. It appears that Bustamante was incensed that he had been ignored. He was ill at the time, but he telegraphed the Governor: "Have no dealings with the strikers. This is not a strike; it is a rebellion. It must be crushed."

Thereafter he and his colleagues collected a squad and marched to the Mental Hospital. In the ensuing fracas, a number of persons were wounded and two persons died. Bustamante and his fellow Member of the Executive Council, Frank Pixley, then responsible for Finance, were charged with manslaughter. Because of the fact that Kingston was one of the few areas of Jamaica that was strongly supporting the People's National Party, (indeed the events occurred in the constituency of Florizel Glasspole who was first elected in that area, an area in which the Jamaica Labour Party had never won a seat until 1980), there was a change of venue for the trial and it was sent to the St. Mary Circuit for trial in Port Maria.

Bustamante and Pixley were acquitted. And during the trial, the Kingston dock workers went on strike so that they could go with their Chief to Port Maria for his trial.

Over the years, the joint responsibilities of Chief Minister and Labour Leader continued to create difficulties for Bustamante, such as when ruffians pretending to be supporters kept loafing in the Union headquarters premises. Bustamante (though this has never been admitted publicly) caused the Police to raid his own headquarters and remove a lot of the ruffians and loafers. Bustamante's secretary (who became his wife) Gladys Longbridge, took common cause with the arrested workers and resisted the Police and entered the Police waggon, although she was not arrested. This, no doubt, was to show common cause with the workers whether they were ruffians or not. Bustamante, however, made a demonstraton throughout Kingston, got crowds to surround the Central Police Station where the men had been held. He wept. He bewailed and declared he wanted to go to prison and sleep in jail with his people. He took advice that day from his cousin Norman Manley and all day he continued with his personal rampage.

I remember very well at night after this day of widespread demonstration, Bustamante telephoned me at my desk as Editor of the Gleaner and asked if he could hear how the report for tomorrow dealt with the matter. I read the whole report to him, whereupon he said: "Fine, fine son! Fine son! But take out that part about my false teeth falling out as I shouted at the Police."

I promised him that I would - and I did. Imagine! on a day during which he had been so fiercely rampant, he was composed enough to be sensitive over such minor details. He came out of the episode without serious compromise of his role as Chief Minister, yet redoubling his reputation as a Labour Leader who stood up for his people. And ruffians no longer crowded his headquarters after that.

It would seem strange that in the position in which the Chief Minister was in trouble, he shoud have called Norman Manley, Leader of the Opposition Party, to help him. One of my trade union and politicial friends says: "Alexander Bustamante had what could be described as an obsessive loyalty to his relatives, particularly to his cousin, Norman Manley, for whom he had a special 'soft spot' and for whom he repeatedly expressed love and admiration." On one occasion he is reported to have told Ken Hill when the latter was Mayor of Kingston: "I love my cousin. Norman is as weak as shredded oats; he may even be a sneak - willing to wound but afraid to strike. But he is so innocent, he could be a saint and if he were to die now he would go straight to Heaven." The same source said that Bustamante also appeared to be fond of Michael Manley (who subsequently became Prime Minister). Indeed, Bustamante compared Michael Manley to himself and Michael's brother, Douglas Manley to their father, Norman Manley. He would say: "Michael takes after me.... Douglas is like his father, Norman."

While heading the government Bustamante ruled his own Party with total self-centred confidence. To be one of his Party did not necessarily give anyone total freedom. Indeed, one of his Executive Council Members, E. Dudley Evans, an attorney who held the portfolio for Agriculture in the first Labour Government, came to fall out with Bustamante and Bustamante called a meeting near to Evans' home on Maxfield Avenue where he declared to the large crowd: "Dudley Evans resembles a rat-bat in a cave." His imagery seemed so intimate to the crowd that the people in the audience kept roaring with laughter even after the meeting was over.

Sir Hugh Foot (later Lord Caradon) had this to say of Bustamante in his book on his own career: "Politically he is an opportunist, unpredictable but brilliant. He sometimes appears reckless and irresponsible - or rather he used to be in his earlier days - but always he shrewdly calculates the effect of his actions."

When the elections of 1949 came around, Bustamante's Labour Party again defeated the People's National Party but by a narrower margin . He thus remained political leader of Jamaica until 1955, when for the first time the People's National Party won a general election. During that long period of the 11 years, Bustamante made many trips to England, during one of which visits the London Times wrote this about him:

"Mr. Bustamante is as remarkable as the circumstances in which he came to prominence. Uneducated in the strict scholastic sense of the word, he makes up for this deficiency with an apparent limitless store of common sense, shrewd intelligence, and an uncanny way of making friends and influencing people........He has sharp wit, an amazing memory, a daring imagination and tremendous physical capacity."

So Bustamante was soundly defeated in the 1955 electionand to many it might have seemed at the time that his career was at an end; indeed his Party became quite moribund and depressed, despite the fact that at the end of his term of service Bustamante was knighted by the Sovereign.

As a Leader of the Opposition Bustamante was quarrelsome rather than controvesial, although there were moments when he went back to his old time love of strange expressions. One one occasion from the Opposition Bench he said of the then Premier, Mr. Manley, "You are like a peacock without feathers. I have had enough of all of you. I am going to clean you all up."

Altogether his years in Opposition gave him the limelight only when matters of West Indies Federation came to the fore. And as this same matter of Federation was crucial to his return to power, it is interesting to look back at the start of that matter when Bustamante was Chief Minister in 1947. The then Secretary of State for the Colonies, Mr. CreechJones, came to Jamaica and presided over a conference in Montego Bay to see what were the possibilities of closer association of the Commonwealth Caribbean. Norman Manley, though not even a member of the Legislature at that time, attended, as did Bustamante as head of the Government. Manley and most of the others from the Caribbean were federationists at heart but Bustamante was against it in a strange way, saying that if Federation were to be, the British Government would have to provide millions of pounds to finance it. So he did not take a totally negative position but based it on the financial implications, claiming that if Britain wished to get rid of the colonies and put them in a Federation, Britain should put up millions and millions to finance it. And that remained, with variations, his theme while he was out of office and in the Opposition. The germs of that Federal idea rankled.

The first elections to Federation when it did come about were in 1958 and it gave Bustamante a platform upon which to conduct a campaign against Manley's People's National Party who were determinedly in favour of the Federation. Strangely enough, although the Manley Party had won decisively in the local Jamaican elections in 1955, they lost the 1958 elections for the Federal Parliament. Bustamante's Party gained more seats in it than the Manley Party. But the Federal reality was nothing near what had been expected of its leadership. This gave Bustamante continuing opportunity to attack it and criticise it and sneer at it. Bustamante on that account had hoped that since his party had won the Federal elections it would have a better chance in the next Jamaican general elections in 1959. But it wasn't to be and Bustamante's Party was again defeated in 1959. The surprise nature of that election, no doubt also helped to defeat Mr. Bustamante because Mr. Manley called it prematurely and it seems, took the Labour Party by surprise.

Says the record at the Gleaner: "Sir Alexander took the defeat badly. He said the voters would rue it. The implied slur was on the voters for what he regarded as their folly in rejecting his Party and free enterprise. It certainly looked that, as of 1959, he could sit back as an elder statesman with little or no expectation that at 75 1/2 years old, he would become Prime Minister of Jamaica."

Sir Alexander resumed his letter writing to the Gleaner; altogether his party seemed to have been in the doldrums., Then came a very strange episode. Sir John Mordecai has written about it interestingly in his book "The West Indies - The Federal Negotiations." The strange episode not yet totally explained was the resignation of one of Mr. Bustamante's members in the Federal Parliament, Mr. Robert Lightbourne, one of his favourites. Mr. Lightbourne resigned his Federal seat to undertake certain business operations in Trinidad, and so there was to be a bye-election for Mr. Lightbourne's seat. A meeting was called by Bustamante and his senior colleagues to decide on who should contest the seat. Mr. Edwin Allen was the person who had lined up himself to do battle there. There are many versions of this episode as will be seen from the Mordecai book, but on my information, what transpired was that Bustamante who normally ridiculed Mr. Edwin Allen, did that to the point where he suddenly announced that he was not taking part in the contest at all and they would not put up a member to contest the seat. My information is that some senior political legal associates of Mr. Bustamante coined the idea then, that very night, to make it a bigger thing and make it a total rejection of the whole Federal concept.

This was the ruse or device or gimmick or accident that led eventually to Norman Manley deciding upon a Referendum whereby the people of Jamaica would vote whether they wished to continue in Federation or to be independent. It was an ill-fated decision for Manley and a windfall for Bustamante. In the Referendum in September 1961 (when it would have seemed that Bustamante had little chance of ever leading Jamaica's government again) the people voted against Federation by some 40,000 votes. This raised the hackles on Bustamante, his fighting attitude returned and he saw - as his Party did - the prospects of victory in the next elections.

Both Parties sent representatives to London after this to settle the Constitution for an independent Jamaica. A very interesting thing occurred which perhaps holds the key to the reason why the British Government allowed Jamaica to secede from Federation when in fact it was already federated. This incident concerned a luncheon at Buckingham Palace to which the Queen had invited both Party Leaders. As it turned out, Bustamante had been invited as Leader of the Opposition. He sent a note with due protocol to the Palace to state that he was not able to attend as thus invited, because he was not in England as Leader of the Opposition, nor was Mr. Manley there as Prime Minister. They were both there, he said, as Party Leaders of their respective Parties come to negotiate a constitutional Independence. The Queen then altered the nature of the invitation. This made Manley furious but, as the grounds on which Bustamante had taken the point were real, there was nothing to do about it; they both attended the luncheon in good fettle. At the conference in London, the details of Jamaica's new Constitution were settled and, strangely enough, it was not disputed that Manley was required to have an election when Independence was granted, unlike any other Commonwealth Caribbean territory, all of which continued under their existing leadership when they became Independent. My theory is - and I have dealt with it elsewhere - that Norman Manley agreed to face an election as the only way that Britain would agree that Jamaica could have the right to come out of Federation.

When the Independence elections were finally called in April 1962, Bustamante was returned to power with a seven seat majority in the 45-seat House of Representatives, becoming Jamaica's first Prime Minister, just as he had been Jamaica's first Chief Minister.

In moments of elation and excitement, he would revert often to his old rambunctious nature and, on one of these occasions, he quipped to a crowd of friends: "So my cousin Norman is a Q.C., Douglas (Manley) is a Doctor of Psychology and Michael (Manley) is a Bachelor of what, Science? All University graduates eh! And poor Busta? But I beat all three of them. Ha! ha! ha! Busta eat all of them for breakfast and hungry for lunch. Ha! ha! ha!"

His career as Prime Minister in the administrative sense was coloured by the fact that the middle class and P.N.P. elements generally were most depressed that they were out of office; co-operation with him wasn't easily given. He retained some of his livelier habits, but in a sense the responsibilities of a Self-governing Independent country modified his behaviour on many an occasion. Sir Kenneth Blackburne, who had to deal with him as Governor General, says that he appeared to govern by hunch, though his hunches had a quite remarkable habit of being right. There was no more warm support of the British monarchy, but his principal bogeys were socialism, atheism and, for some time, birth control. Says Blackburne: "He was the most generous and honest of men, but his ways were difficult for a dyed-in-the-wool Civil Servant to understand."

Blackburne's book relates that early in 1962 Sir Alexander was present at a dinner party given by the Governor General for Princess Alice and Lord Mountbatten, both of whom were staying at King's House. He relates "When the ladies had left the dining room, Bustamante leaned across the table to Mountbatten and pointing to Blackburne, said: 'That's the man we want as our Governor General.' It was my first intimation and it came true on Bustamante's choice." But even in those days, recalls Blackburne: "Bustamante delighted in giving visitors a demonstration of the past. Leaping to his feet he would bare his chest and point to the place where, so he said, the British bayonets had threatened him."

At all times Bustamante remained anti-Federation and anti-socialist. Sir John Mordecai recalls that when entertaining Prime Minister MacMillan in Jamaica, Sir Alexander had told him: "Prime Minister, you are trying to use a Federation to get England out of her responsibilities. It won't work." He said all this in great amity.

But when Oliver Lyttleton sent troops to British Guiana on the basis that Her Majesty's Government was not willing to allow a Communist State to be organised within the British Commonwealth, Bustamante cabled the Secretary of

State for the Colonies: "If British Guiana were fighting for complete self-government within the democratic nations, I would have stood behind British Guiana, but British Guiana today can get no sympathy from me - can get no sympathy from the free thinking world. I am sorry for the people there. I am not sorry for the leaders. They are not leaders at all. They do not know what they are doing." This was quoted in Dr. Jagan's autobiography, discussing some of his darkest moments when the Constitution of his country was removed while he was Chief Minister.

I had a great deal to do with Sir Alexander during the preparations for Independence and at Independence. He, as Prime Minister-to-be and Mr. Manley, had agreed that I should be made Chairman of Jamaica's Independence Celebrations, an ardous honour which I shall always remember. The demands of the United States missions for space and accommodation and facilities required by the United States chosen representative, Vice President Lyndon Johnson, continually brought me into conflict as it were with all the other demands. Normally the Governor General (rather he still was the Governor), Sir Kenneth Blackburne, tended to be conservative, but Prime Minister Bustamante would say "whatever the Americans want, let them have it." This might relate to his long sojourn in the United States, but it is also evidence of his general liberal attitude in such matters. A crisis came when seating was being arranged for the Royal Box at the Independence Flag-raising Ceremony. It had been decided by the Protocol Advisers that Vice-President Lyndon Johnson and his wife, Lady Bird, would not sit in the Royal Box but in seats close beside the Royal Box, in which Princess Margaret and her husband would be seated. The American Protocol Officers disputed this decision. Governor Blackburne more or less stood his ground, but Bustamante instructed me to put them in the Royal Box. He had been convinced by the American argument that if the Queen herself had been present, they would accept that the Vice-President would not be entitled to be in the Royal Box; but as the Queen was being represented by someone else, the United States representative could also sit in that box. And so, not altogether amicably, it was decided.

Another matter relating to Independence concerned the programme and the cost of it, which had been published widespread by the Minister of Finance, the late Donald Sangster, after meetings with the Independence Committee. Bustamante felt that it wasn't doing his governmnent that much good to seem to be wasteful and he summoned a meeting of the Cabinet, and I was ordered to be present. Sir Alexander slashed the whole programme to ribbon, without consulting anybody for that matter, and indeed when he was slashing the vote for school children's festivities, the Minister of Education, Mr. Allen, ventured to put a word in and the Prime Minister silenced him with: "You know about education; you don't know about economics."

Fortunately I understood the Prime Minister's mood and I was able to get him to undertake that most of the things would still be done, including the fireworks, but that he would get money for these things separately, from the oil companies and other big organisations in Jamaica so as not to burden the taxpayer with the cost of it. He kept true to his word. Indeed, eventually the celebrations cost quite a bit more than was originally projected because the very Parliamentary Members who were critical of the expense caused it to be increased; they demanded that fireworks be not only in the capital towns of each parish but in the principal towns of every constituency. Such is politics.

Jamaica's colourful, swash-buckling politician, known in his earlier days for having revolvers at his sides, had been tamed by 1962 into a Prime Minister, responsible for the conduct of his nation. But age will tell, and three years after he became Prime Minister, he was stricken with a cerebral occlusion which led to loss of sight to a tragic degree. The rest of his term was spent running the country by remote control through his deputy Prime Minister Donald Sangster. But even as an invalid he retained a sense of mischief. I do remember one day visiting him. He related that an Anglican Minister, a Canon of the Church of England, had come to pray for him. By this time, Sir Alexander had definitely become a member of the Roman Catholic faith and so he had got out of the seeming denominational difficulty by telling the Canon to go and say the prayers in the drawing room, thus not apparently feeling that he had committed any heresy by forsaking his Church. "I told him" Busta said "to go and pray in the drawing room." On the same occasion, a prominent P.N.P. was present with him in the bedroom and he said to this P.N.P. person: "Teacher, I know, you only come to see if I am dying, because you P.N.P. don't like me at all. But I am glad to see you and I know you are my friend."

Gradually Bustamante's condition deteriorated into one of considerable blindness and he moved to his mountain resort on the road to Newcastle where he lived with Lady Bustamante, continually sought out as a senior citizen, as a National Hero, to be consulted, for his advice and the comfort of his pleasant company up to the time of his death in 1977.

It may well be that in his retirement, he had not wished to be succeeded by Mr. Donald Sangster and so had notified the Press only that he had appointed Donald Burns Sangster "to lead the Party into the election." But that is another story. He lived to see his Party run a further full term of office, giving him and his Party really ten years of rule in Independent Jamaica.

In summary, perhaps to give the unusual legend of this man's life, I think I will make two quotations. One is from a letter which in November, 1976, appeared in the Daily Gleaner from a reader:

> "He was born a long time ago. He formed the Jamaica Labour Party in 1943 when he was 59. He was the first Prime Minister of Jamaica. He celebrated his 83rd birthday as Prime Minister of Jamaica. He is the only surviving National Hero. He has outlived most of his contemporaries. His is a uniquely pre-eminent personage. Now, old warrior, you are 92 and on the eve of your great victory - what a life you have had! We salute you - Sir Alexander Bustamante - you are super."

The other quotation is from the columnist in the Gleaner. Thomas Wright, one of the most assiduous writers who generally tortured people with his wicked wit. He wrote this about Bustamante:

> "When people have no constitutional means of changing their government, there is no other way of protesting or of expressing dissatisfaction than by a process of harassment, civil commotion, and general bloody-mindedness. For this process, Sir Alexander's temperament was ideally suited, and he and his people took to one another like ducks to water."

> "He might have been a communist agitator, concerned not with Jamaica, but with Russian imperialism. He might have been a Marxist bent upon the destruction of the only economic system which, at this point in history at least, is appropriate to our continued development. He might have been a Latin American type of Fascist, bent upon setting up a personally profitable dictatorship."

> "That he was none of these things, and that he brought, or helped to bring, Self-Government and a new life to his country without at the same time disturbing unduly our historical or economic continuity is something that should stand to the everlasting credit of Sir Alexander and to the good sense of our people."

THE RIGHT HONOURABLE
SIR ERIC MATTHEW GAIRY
F.R.S.A.

BORN ST. ANDREWS, GRENADA, 18TH FEBRUARY, 1922

CHIEF MINISTER OF GRENADA (1961-1962, 1962-1967)
PREMIER OF GRENADA (1967-1972)
PRIME MINISTER OF GRENADA (1972-1979)

7

ERIC MATTHEW GAIRY

GRENADA CERTAINLY HAD A swinging Prime Minister, especially at week-ends. My last week-end with Eric Matthew Gairy was certainly like that. On the Friday afternoon he was at tennis, lobbing and serving and smashing effectively against a civil servant opponent on the green hard-court of a community centre just next to the Holiday Inn complex in Grenada's capital, St. Georges.

And when his chauffeur-driven Cadillac failed to start, he had the driver - a police corporal - open the bonnet and tighten the battery terminals with a spanner while the Prime Minister himself went behind the wheel and got the Cadillac off to a roaring start.

The following night, Saturday, he joined the Governor General, chartered accountant Sir Leo deGale - one of Grenada's historically rich planter class - and Lady deGale on the receiving line at Government House for a reception for two large groups of visitors. One was a party of English folk invited to the island by the Grenada Tourist Board and the other some 100 white and coloured Americans from the Fun Club of Denver, Colorado. Prime Minister Gairy stood beside the Governor General immaculate in all-white outfit, shoes and all. (Mrs. Gairy was not present).

The Prime Minister later presented each visitor with a package of the spices of Grenada, nutmeg, mace, cinnamon, tonga beans, cardamom, coriander, cloves and turmeric. Attached to each package was an ornate card printed in gold - "Dr. E.M. Gairy, R.L., K.G.C., F.R.S.A., J.P." The visitors loved it.

At the party a boys' steel band - the Black and White Steel Band - banged out lively tunes and had the honour of the Prime Minister passing by to chat with them.

The party ended with the Grenada National Anthem at 8.30 p.m. and by 10 o'clock the Prime Minister was at his Morne Rouge night club overlooking the western horn of the magnificent five mile white sand beach named Grand Anse by the early French.

At his "Evening Palace", as the night club is named, the Prime Minister wined and danced till well into the morning, mixing conversation with his political cronies and critics, while entertaining a large contingent of the tourist groups he had met earlier at Government House. He put on for them a special dinner of local dishes, curries of chicken and beef and mutton. They all danced to the lively playing of the Defence Force Band and sampled the hot beat of Jamaican reggae and Barbadian spouge as made famous by Jackie Opel of Barbados, Bob Marley and Jimmy Cliff of Jamaica, and it was champagne all the way for the Prime Minister. Some of his white American friends, who were at the centre of controversy in Grenada, and political executives of his Party, were helping to run the place.

This zestful Prime Minister put away at least five bottles of champagne. "I never have less than four bottles in all on a Saturday night," he told me, "for I share in at least 32 bottles." There he was, dancing in his all-white outfit, this time open-necked shirt with a white scarf, informal but natty, showing off his velvet black complexion and lighting up his flashing smiles which came on and off like a bright lighthouse.

That is how I have always known Eric Gariy to be wherever he is, in the West Indies or overseas - intense, sharp. When he is at play, he is at play. As soon as a break comes, it is "fete for so" with wine, women, and who knows, wrong.

Some of the girls from Denver kicked off their shoes and came into barefoot revelry. He danced with as many as time would permit, whether they were Grenadians or Americans or English. Many of them were in lovely and lavish evening gowns and the whole dance floor jumped with the kaleidoscopic mix of blacks, whites and in-betweens.

I gave up at midnight, but at 8 a.m., the Prime Minister telephoned me saying, "Well, pal, I have just got in and I am going to take a nap. Will call you when I wake up." Which he did sharp as a needle to talk political business with me. But don't take Eric Gairy just for fun. It is merely how he relaxed between his sometimes grim decisions and actions as head of his beautiful but sometimes turbulent island, with ugly problems shared in good measure with the other black West Indian islands.

How did this controversial, colourful and rather maverick character come to take over the political scene in his home country, Grenada?

A generation before, the honey-toned, middle-class dominant elements of Grenada would never have thought that any such person could take over leadership from their moderate isolated types that had dominated the country for so long. It had been an elegant middle-class; it had also been clever; it had dispensed with Europeans in the government service by the simple device of legislative prohibition on two posts being held by any one person. At that time, there was a widespread habit in the British Caribbean of having two offices like Postmaster General, or Collector of Customs, Collector of Taxes or the like being combined. Though each salary was relatively small, the combined salaries made the post attractive to persons from the United Kingdom or elsewhere, to take the job. But having prohibited these combinations, of course, the white man disappeared in general from Grenada and the middle-classes were very proud of the way they were running the Spice Island. But other thoughts were afoot.

In 1950, sly and rambunctious Alexander Bustamante from Jamaica visited Grenada to attend a sugar conference. The honey-toned folk of the middle class sniggered at him and thought how could Jamaica have produced a leader of that rather rugged, rough and unpolished type. Bustamante spoke one night in the square in St. Georges, and so moved the crowd that I subsequently wrote that although the elite in Grenada were sure of themselves, the day a Grenadian emerged who had the ruggedness of Bustamante they would be thrown aside, and the island would be taken over by this new dynamic kind of leadership.

It was not many months later that Eric Matthew Gairy, who had come home from working in Aruba, proved the prediction right. The story of how Eric Gairy took power has all the hallmarks of the charismatic demagogue. Years later there was still reservation towards him, but on the surface enough of them backed him or remained neutral, so as to give him a fair chance against the extreme power left and others. Hence, after 22 years in office, he won the 1976 elections, though with a reduced majority.

Eric Matthew Gairy was born in St. Andrews in Grenada on February 18, 1922, the son of Douglas and Theresa Gairy. He received his early education at St. Mary's Roman Catholic School, LaFillette, and St. Andrew's Roman Catholic School, Grenville.

As a pupil at school, the record states he achieved very high standards in academic work and took a keen interest in church activities, scouting, school gardening and sports. At the age of 12, this talented lad was selected to deliver a sermon at the Grenville Roman Catholic Church on the Feast of the Holy Family. We see there the beginnings of a life rooted in the Catholic Church and the capacity to communicate. Eventually he worked as a teacher at his old school, St. Mary's Roman Catholic, before migrating to Aruba at the end of 1943 at age 21.

During his stay in the Dutch Island he did a correspondence course with a view to studying law, but abandoned these studies when he returned to Grenada.

Gairy was in Aruba at the time when there was a need for workers at the oil refinery. It was wartime, and some 3,000 West Indians - Grenadians, Jamaicans and other immigrant workers from 22 different nationalities - were recruited.

Eric Gairy soon worked his way into a position of leadership on the Employees' Committee which represented all the workers. He became President of the West Indian organisation among the workers and excelled in the many sporting activities in which the workers were involved and was also outspoken in his leadership.

The Grenadian workers including Gairy returned home when the people of Aruba started to clamour for the best positions at the oil refinery to go to the native people of Aruba and Curacao.

Prime Minister Gairy says that when he came back to Grenada, he was struck by the deplorable conditions of the workers. Then he started to campaign relentlessly and successfully for all workers to secure better wages and improved working conditions. According to his biographical study, he established the Grenada Manual and Mental Workers Union and introduced the system of political parties with the formation of the Grenada United Labour Party which he led to victory in five out of six general elections, the last of these in 1972 when his Party won 13 out of the 15 seats, all except Carriacou and old man Marryshow's seat, St. Georges.

The Grenada Independence Secretariat records that, on February 21, 1951, Mr. Gairy held his famous demonstration outside the Legislative Council Chamber. Cheers went up when he arrived at the market square to lead the huge crowd to the top of St. John's Street. There they were halted by a cordon of Police guarding the entrance down to Church Street. Throughout the day, he kept demanding a meeting with the acting Governor, G.C. Green. There was much commotion Gascoigne Blaize, the secretary of the Grenada Manual and Mental Workers Union, was arrested. When Gairy learned of the arrest, he went to the Police Station that afternoon to see the officer in command, whereupon he also was arrested.

About midnight, he was taken under Police escort to H.M.S. Blackwatch, a British warship, then in harbour. Up to that time the Labour leader was unaware of his destination. Next morning he awoke to find himself in Carriacou and he was driven to Top Hill, the Government Rest House, where he remained for eleven days

On his return to St. George's at 2 a.m. on March 3, he was escorted to

122

Government House and later that day met with the Acting Governor and representatives of the plantocracy and the commercial sector. In this regard, Premier Bradshaw of St. Kitts relates that in the negotiations which followed, he (Bradshaw) played a conciliatory role. After Gairy's release from Carriacou, the Union had gone on strike and there were disturbances. Mr. Gairy sent a telegram to Bradshaw asking for his assistance and eventually Bradshaw arrived and found that the situation was that the Governor and the employers wanted the local Labour Commissioner to arbitrate the dispute, whereas Gairy felt that Mr. Balthrop, labour adviser to the Secretary of State for the Colonies, should arbitrate. Bradshaw spoke with the Governor and the employers and ultimately got them to agree to arbitration by the Chief Justice, Sir Clement Malone. With this Gairy also agreed and thereafter matters settled down to a successful outcome for Mr. Gairy's labour demands.

The discussion lasted for two days, and Gairy succeeded in securing better wages for his workers. On April 9th, 1951, the agreement was signed, and in addition he obtained back pay for the workers and fringe benefits such as paid holiday leave for those working 200 days or more a year.

Incidentally, the amicable relationship of 1951 between Mr. Bradshaw and Mr. Gairy came to a tight test during Federation when, as Federal Minister of Finance, Mr. Bradshaw put Mr. Gairy on the mat about the management of grants-in-aid from the Federal Government; but even so that ended also amicably.

Prime Minister Gairy's administrative record as head of the government of Grenada had many ruptures and crises. He lost his seat in the Legislature due to proof against him of an election offence - marching to and fro at his opponent's meeting at the head of a Steel Band. And so he was out of office. But here again this novel, indomitable politician put a bold face on it. He purchased the Governor's discarded official car, got himself a chauffeur and drove around quite proudly to show that while he may be not in the Legislature, he, somehow, was in power.

However, during Mr. Gairy's exclusion from Parliament, his Party retained power with a slim majority. This happened at a time when the Constitution had been amended to provide for the appointment of a Speaker and the removal of the Administrator as President of the Council. The then Administrator, Mr. Jimmy Lloyd, took steps with the Colonial Office to get Mr. Gairy back in Parliament, and this was eventually done. But beaver-like Mr. Gairy gave scant courtesy to the member who had been holding his seat in Parliament and harassed him so much that the Member fell into tears and handed in his formal resignation. It is said that Mr. Gairy did not even tell him thanks.

All through these years Eric Gairy had been dramatic and intolerant of any form of seeming rivalry. Once, the wife of the Administrator was invited to cut the ribbon at the opening of a small plaza by the Minister of Trade and Production. Prime Minister Gairy was invited but did not attend because he felt that his wife should have been asked to cut the ribbon.

He adopted at all times the role of leader of the broad masses, and this led him into considerable confrontation with the law and with authority. Indeed, a Commission of Enquiry had to be set up on his administration (when Premier) following activities in relation to an unofficial Police Force and to atrocities alleged to have been committed by these men who became known as the Mongoose Gang. Later, Mr. Gairy, as Prime Minister, had confrontation with his own Attorney General, a Guyanese, whom he expelled from the country. The disagreement arose over the Attorney General's differences with the government concerning prosecution of two illegal American immigrants who had been given asylum by Mr. Gairy in Grenada.

Of course, here the parallel of Bustamante and his own genius for unpredictable action can be recalled because, in Jamaica, while Bustamante was head of the government, the legal apparatus sought to appoint as Chief Justice, a jurist from the Eastern Caribbean. Mr. Bustamante said he would not have it. But, he was powerless to prevent it. He then stated that as Minister in charge of Immigration he would forbid the entry of the jurist. So the legal authorities had to back down and choose somebody already in Jamaica. But different people have different methods.

The Enquiry into the conduct of Premier Gairy arose out of his conduct when he sought to prepare Grenada against insurrection of a black power nature. A mutiny occurred in Trinidad on April 21, 1970 in the First Battalion of the Trinidad and Tobago Regiment. A few days later Premier Gairy delivered a radio broadcast on "Black power in Grenada." In this broadcast, Mr. Gairy said:

"There are no significant threats in Grenada today. However, being aware of what has been happening to some of our neighbouring islands - Trinidad and Tobago in particular, one cannot be too cautious, and consequently, as Premier of Grenada, Carriacou and Petit Martinique, I feel myself in duty bound, to address you at this time......There has been quite some talk recently throughout the region about 'black power', about acts of violence and talks about threats.....I have absolutely no doubt that 'black power', as manifested in Trinidad and Tobago can do a tremendous amount of harm to any country......I cannot speak on the merits or demerits of Trinidad and Tobago's case........I cannot boast of having the patience of Dr. Eric Williams. It is said that when your neighbour's house is on fire, keep on wetting your own house. We are now doubling the strength of our Police Force. We are getting in almost unlimited supplies of new and modern equipment........The Opposition referred to my recruiting criminals in a Reserve Force. To this I shall not say yea or nay. Does it not take steel to cut steel? I am proud of the ready response to my call on Grenadians, regardless of their record, to come and join in the defence of my Government and in the maintenance of law and order in their country. Indeed, hundreds have come and some of the toughest and roughest rough-necks have been recruited......I know that I would have a ready response from the very responsible people of this country who would be dedicated to protecting themselves and their families, their properties and estates and the good name of Grenada as a whole, and if and when the call is made for the formation of the VIUPP - Voluntary Intelligence Unit for Property Protection - men, intelligent young men and old men - and perhaps women will be called upon to join.

"Our Police Force is being doubled to meet the situation. The Force are aware of the diligence exercised by the Trinidad Police. Grenada's Police Force is certainly not on a lower level than the Trinidadian Police Force in any respect. Today, the Grenadian Policeman knows that by his efforts in stamping out the attempts of those involved in black power or any other subversive movement, he can win the award of "Policeman of the Year" and climb the ladder of promotion or receive monetary awards. The Police are geared to keep this country clean and in an atmosphere of peace and quiet at all times."

The Commission of Enquiry that investigated this matter found that "the strength of the Police was not doubled; although any Grenadian hearing the speech of the Premier would have been justified in believing that any increases in the strength of the Police Force would necessarily have been done under the provisions of the law. That speech set the stage for the recruitment of a force of men by the Premier without any legal authority or statutory control and this state of affairs was fully disclosed in the totality of the evidence of Mr. Gairy himself and that of several other witnesses."

That was how the infamous Mongoose Gang came about, similar in many ways to the Ton-Ton Macoute who were set up by Papa Doc Duvalier in Haiti. Many were the atrocities charged against this secret Police Mongoose Gang and the Commission of Enquiry said it included many persons of vicious criminal record. The Commission described this episode as "an unhappy chapter in the history of Grenada. They were an unlawfully constituted body of men, albeit paid from public funds, whose qualification for service in many cases, particularly among the leaders, was their known disposition for violence and lawlessness. They committed acts of violence and brutality and....they effectively caused a break-down of law and order in the State."

The Commission further found that the responsibility for their establishment, recruitment and control was peculiarly that of Mr. Gairy in his personal capacity and not as he stated in his capacity as Minister for National Security, for the reason that the Minister of National Security has no legal authority to establish law enforcement agencies outside the provisions of the law of the State.

At the hearing of the Enquiry, Mr. Gairy gave to the Commission the assurance that the Police aides would never again be recalled for service similar to that which they hitherto performed.

125

The Commission reported that this assurance was "gratifying" and that they were satisfied that Mr. Gairy believed that the demonstrations by the black power and other subsersives were aimed at preventing or delaying Independence for Grenada, and that his commitment to lead Grenada into Independence in February 1974 was an objective so desirable that the possibility of delay by recurring demonstrations was not to be countenanced.

"The reputation of the Police aides for violence was a matter of common knowledge. It was the excesses of brutality to which they indulged that was responsible for the appointment of the Commission. Mr. Gairy was aware of their records and of their propensities. He had personally supervised their selection. He assumed the sole responsibility for recalling them, notwithstanding a promise to disband them."

The Commission said that Mr. Gairy's belief that all these demonstratons were being done to delay Independence was a belief well founded and genuine, but, said the Commission, "we cannot commend the measures to which he resorted in order to arrest its development."

And so Grenada, after these turbulences, moved into Independence and became an independent member of the Commonwealth in 1974.

Said Gairy to me: "Looking forward, I see an independent Grenada, Carriacou and Petit Martinique. projecting a friendly attitude to large and small nations, attracting big investors to establish industries to help solve the unemployment problem, also a proper sense of values and variety of skills which will win acclaim at Caribbean and international levels."

He said his main driving force was his philosophy of life which, in sum, is a great belief in the Supreme Godhead and the importance of continuing development of the inner man, the spiritual self. He is a student of Yoga and is keenly interested in the Mystics.

Anyone observing Eric Gairy at work or at play can well believe this. All through his political career he has mixed the mystic with the political. Indeed, on one occasion he lost considerable status among Catholics particularly by appearing in the Harbour of St. Georges in a boat illuminated to give the appearance of Christ on the Sea of Galilee. Many of his election tactics and techniques have related to quasi-religious manifestations. His early commitment to the church still lives vigorously with him. But perhaps in another sense, as in Haiti, it is a church that is not strictly limited to the Saints of the Catholic Calendar. Little wonder that Mr. Gairy's addresses to the United Nations were so strongly based on the Mystic.

DR. CHEDDI JAGAN,
D.D.S.,

BORN ALBION, BRITISH GUIANA, 22 MARCH 1918

CHIEF MINISTER-PREMIER OF GUYANA (1957-1961)
PREMIER OF GUYANA (1961-1964)

8

DR. CHEDDI JAGAN

EARLY IN 1963, I visited British Guiana (now Guyana) and had interesting talks with the two rival political leaders, Premier Cheddi Jagan and Opposition Leader Forbes Burnham, both of them Socialists, the former wishing to have straight elections; the other, analysing the racial spectrum of dominant Indian majority, wishing proportional representation.

Reviewing now the views that they then expressed, each of them separately, one sees that they have both behaved consistently with their announced policies.

Dr. Jagan had said then that he was prepared to agree to have an election before Independence; that he was opposed to proportional representation; that he wanted to create a Guyanese consciousness in terms of art and culture (later on a Burnham policy); that he recognised that his party suffered from the fact that they were the most "left" party, and this did not please some people outside who tended to take the side of the Opposition (later the Government); that undeveloped countries have no chance of fighting back against adverse conditions whereas the big international fellows are always integrated (a major world problem even today).

Still, in 1976, Jagan was the Marxist-Leninist and Burnham the Fabian Socialist, both left of centre, but Dr. Jagan after a while ceased to be totally opposed to the Government of his rival and re-entered Parliament on the basis that critical support was what the country required from the Opposition Party.

When I sat with Cheddi Jagan in 1963, we discussed many things - government policy, development programmes and the like, and at a sentimental point in his reflections on the past, he pulled out of a drawer a photograph of himself looking at some records in the Immigration Office. He showed me the picture. It was one of him as he researched the details of his grand parents; how they were indentured and how they were brought to British Guiana. It was a moment of pathos and of pride to think how far Cheddi Jagan had come to be sitting in the seat of Head of Government of British Guiana.

When I revisited Guyana in 1976 he was then in Opposition. We sat down again and he told me his life story. He said:

"My grand-parents came as indentured immigrants to work on the plantations at Port Morant, a sugar estate."

"As you know," he said, "this was part of a scheme in this country after slavery was abolished in 1838, to bring Indians from India. This immigration ceased in 1917. My parents came with their parents."

Dr. Jagan went on to explain that his father and mother had very little education. In fact, he said, his mother was illiterate. She couldn't read and write, but she gave valuable service to the Party.

"My father worked on the sugar estate in what was called the Creole Gang. He was at first a cane cutter working on the estate, and then became what they called champion cane cutter, and then became a 'driver.' In those days the drivers were used to get the workers out of the barracks to work, driving them out as it were, sometimes with a whip. One of my father's problems was that he tended to have a split loyalty. Having reached that position, he had a feeling of sympathy for the working class, having come up from the ranks of the workers, but he also felt that he had to carry on the job as part of management, although being aggrieved as part of that management, because he could not rise to a higher position. For at that time local people could only rise to where he was. Above him the next category was called an overseer and all the jobs as overseers were either reserved for Englishmen or Scotsmen. That was the background of my father; that was his dilemma."

Cheddi was the eldest of twelve children, eleven of whom survived. At home in Berbice, life was simple if not hard for his family growing up in the conditions of those years.

"We had the same things all the time, rice and dhall (split peas) and sometimes fish. As Hindus we never ate beef or pork. My mother was more religious than my father and that note is very important to see how she developed politically.

"For when my wife and I were in jail in 1954, my mother took upon herself to go all over the country doing political work, raising money and so on. And our political work increased greatly in that period because she felt not only the Christians but some of the Hindus, were collaborating with the colonial regime. She did not so much lose faith in her religion as in the religious establishment - seeing religion in the sense of a political organisation she lost interest in religious formalities as such."

But to go back to the way of life in those days, Dr. Jagan remembers with warmth the Saturday night treats which his father would provide. Papa Jagan, after work, would go to the shops and meet the others at the Poor Man's Club, and he would eventually come home bringing sardines and bread and biscuits and sometimes a piece of cheese. It was wonderful. Food was very, very simple. They lived in a very small house but life was warm in the love and affection of the family.

It struck me at this stage of our conversation that Dr. Jagan's father seemed to have very good relations not only with Indians but with Africans at the estate. "Yes", says Dr. Cheddi, "my father was very friendly with another black 'driver' and a dispenser as they worked together. So I never grew up in an environment where I saw or considered that Indians were at a higher or different social level from the African."

Cheddi's parents made sacrifices for him to get an education as the eldest of the children.

"Basically, my father did not want me to go through the kind of experience he went through, the hardships and sufferings. He was anxious to let me have an education because he thought this was the means by which to break out of the sugar estate environment. So he sent me to a private school and to other schools and eventually to Queen's College in Georgetown, a Grammar School, the foremost Boys School for British Guiana. Well, having graduated with what was then called the Cambridge Examination, equivalent of the present G.C.E., I was out of school for a year, couldn't get a job. There were offers made to me to work as a teacher but the pay was very, very small; and then also you had to become a Christian in order to get a teaching job because most of the schools were run by the Christian denominations. This is why, subsequently, our Party in 1950 called for an end to dual control of schools, whereby the State paid the teachers but the denominations employed the teachers.

"Having finished at Queen's College, I couldn't get work and I didn't want to go back to the sugar plantation where I may have got a job in the office or something. Fortunately, two of my friends from Queen's College were the sons of dentists and they were going abroad to study. In conversations with them I gathered that it wasn't going to be very costly to go to Howard University. However, my father didn't want me to do that because he said he wanted me to do law; the law course was only three years and dentistry was about six years. I then persuaded my father that I did not think at that time that I was so vocal as to be a lawyer, as I thought a lawyer had to be able to talk. Perhaps another thing influenced me. When I was a boy and used to go to the sugar estate hospital, I was very impressed with the local district doctors.

Cheddi Jagan went to Howard University in Washington. However, he said that he found that in terms of gradations of colour, unlike British Guiana, the black people were always at the lowest rung.

"So I began to see this and made common cause with the African peoples, and I could understand how a black person felt in the United States. I stayed in a room with one of my Guianese black colleagues and I never felt any difference, and I felt, however, the suffering that the black person in America was feeling.

"You see, my education in the United States was not just formal going to University and all that. I was working my way through and did all kinds of odd jobs. I was a salesman, and when I was in Chicago at NorthWestern University, I lived on the borderline between what they call the Gold Coast and the slums. There you found a lot of people who were derelict and broken down, alcoholics and others. I was going to school not far away and working at nights in the Gold Coast at a residential hotel there. So I was able to see both sides, which normally students are not able to see. This helped my whole orientation towards politics. At that time India was fighting for independence and America, under Roosevelt, was in favour. I identified not only as a Guyanese but as an Indian. A combination of all those factors helped me to orient myself not merely to politics but to independence for my country.

"Looking back, I would say that in my youth on the sugar plantation, the oppression of it, not only physically but sociologically, and then my experience in the States, and seeing the debasement and how working black people lived there, these were the main things which influenced my whole outlook in life. Thus my role in going into politics."

At this point I put to Dr. Jagan that in the Caribbean generally among socialist politicians it is common to regard the plantation system as a blot on the region's history, and even Castro at one time thought it was a bad thing to have. Yet so many people are turning round and saying you have to produce sugar to survive. We are all now trying to make more sugar than we made in the past. But the plantation system as such is not the same any more, I queried.

He replied: "While we do not object to the fact that you have to produce surgar, neither do we object to the fact that it has to be run on a large scale; Cuba has found out. What we object to - and this has to be seen dialectically - is that in the old relationship of colony and Mother Country, the colony on the periphery was made into a raw material source, with the Mother Country the source of manufactured items. And what we find is that the price of the raw materials is constantly declining or advancing very slowly, whereas manufactured goods are advancing in price far more rapidly. This causes great loss to Third World countries. And because the Third World depends only on its main products, when the price falls, it can have disastrous consequences. In other words the mono-culture can lead to disaster.

"In fact it was worse in India where Lancashire cotton took over. India had a more advanced textile industry than England and England destroyed it; Indian development was arrested leading to violence. Because of the general background Caribbean leaders have felt it was necessary to diversify and so the Cubans themselves were in a great hurry and they have made some mistakes. They went into some industries which were not properly checked out and found out the problems of having to buy the raw materials outside and what you pay for them. Those are the economic questions. So they went back to sugar."

Dr. Jagan added, however, that that kind of problem has to be seen now in a new kind of relationship, for instance, the Caribbean arrangements, COMECON, where having a mono-culture need not necessarily be a disadvantage any more. Because you have guaranteed prices, you have guaranteed markets, you do not have the fluctuations and so on. For instance, he said, "take oil, you see how the price of oil has practically ruined the economies of some Third World countries, yet within a socialist economy although the Soviet oil prices increase to Poland, for instance, still the price to them was two-thirds of the world price. In other words, in COMECON you have a new kind of relationship and you don't have the instability of the whole free enterprise world".

He continued: "So in that sense, to come back to your question, we are not opposed to the plantation system as a large scale productive unit; they are advantages in that as compared with small scale. What we were complaining of was: one, that the money which is earned here is exported out of the country; two, you may say that very often the most intelligent people in the country, in the sense of imperialism, are paid the highest salaries so that they do not defend the national interest here but defend foreign interests, and three, they stultify the development of the country. You can see that if you compare the Cuban industry today with sugar in Guyana and in the free enterprise days. You can see that: we do not even make our own refined sugar in Guyana. We have been stultified. So it is not that we do not recognise the importance of sugar, but one cannot have an overnight change; it has to be changed over a period of time. This has to be done in terms of the national interest."

After this exposition of the dialectical position, I asked Dr. Jagan to come back to his United States stay where he was married in 1943 - he had married Janet Rosenberg. He referred me to his autobiography, The West on Trial

Says Dr. Jagan in his book: "We did not have the consent of parents on either side. Janet's father had threatened to shoot me. My parents too were unhappy. Since I had long been absent from home, my marriage aggravated their unhappiness. They were anxious for me to return and now they wondered if I would."

Around that time Cheddi Jagan had been having trouble with the United States with politics and legislation. Although he had qualified, to practise as a dentist reequired not only the Doctor of Dental Surgery degree but also a State Board Examination certificate and he could not take the examination, because he was not a citizen. He could not become a citizen, because although he was not from India, he had been put into the categories of Orientals and so came within the ORIENTAL EXCLUSION ACT. So the field of dentistry was closed to him and he had to work as a dental technician for about six months. Then he received his military draft card and, after he passed his physical fitness test, the authorities, while unwilling to let him become a citizen, were quite ready to draft him as a private in the Army.

Says Dr. Jagan in his book: "I had mixed feelings about the war, torn between President Roosevelt's internationalism on the one hand and pre-war American isolationism, plus the attitude of the Indian National Congress Leaders on the other. Roosevelt was to me a fighter for the underdog. I sided with him as I always had whenever there was a confrontation between those in power and the suppressed and the oppressed. At home I always sided with my father against the planters; in a family dispute, with my mother against my father. Roosevelt's fight against big business in the United States and his New Deal Programme in Puerto Rico had greatly impressed me. But I was equally influenced by the stand taken by the Indian National Congress Leaders, who, while not taking any positive steps to obstruct the war effort, did not actively participate . . . . .

"At that time my perspective was not as broad as it is today. I saw Hitler and Fascism through the eyes of the Indian National Congress and I identified the struggle for freedom in India as part and parcel of the struggle for freedom at home. I did not then clearly understand that freedom was indivisible, that it was necessary to oppose fascism anywhere and everywhere in the world.

"Faced with this dilemma, torn between isolationism and internationalism, I sought a way out in a protest to the Draft Board authorities. If they were not going to commission me a lieutenant on the basis of my D.D.S. degree, I was determined, I told them, not to join the Army as a private even if it meant going to prison. Eventually, they gave me six months to get my State Board Examination certificate; though I do not know how they expected me to do this . . . . .

"But before the moment for decision came I decided to return home, in October 1943. A few months earlier Janet Rosenberg and I had been married at a simple ceremony at the Chicago City Hall. Having bought some ancient dentistry equipment fairly cheap, I was now ready to go home. I kissed my wife good-bye and joined a Greyhound bus for Miami. Janet was to remain for a few months in

Chicago for the time being to continue her job as proof-reader at the American Medical Association, while I was to woo my parents into accepting her and finding the money to pay for her passage. She arrived shortly after, just before Christmas.

"I had had mixed feelings about returning home. I left the U.S.A. with feelings of sadness compounded with suspense. Since most of my formative years from 18 to 25 had been spent there, I had become completely adjusted. I grew to like the people with whom I came in contact, so generous and warm-hearted and I was greatly impressed by their traditional values, their efficiency and their material achievements. And I too, in spite of difficult experiences and shocking observations, had imbibed the propaganda that the United States of America was a land of unlimited opportunity, that with hard work success was always assured. After all, mine was also an Horatio Alger success story, from rags to potential riches.

"Disillusionment was to come later when I read more widely and pored over statistics, facts , interpretations and analyses. I saw then how superficial my observations and conclusions had been, how I had conformed like so many millions of Americans to automatically accepted ideas. It was then that I began to think again about all that I had seen and to question seriously whether the United States was really, really 'the land of the free'."

And so Cheddi Jagan came back home a much wiser man to face his own country and its problems. He says:

"When I came back in 1943, there were no political parties in British Guiana but the Critchlow movement had brought into the legislature local people who had, call it, a nationalist outlook. The legislature had very little power because way back in 1928 when the planters feared that with a legislature which really had power they could lose their control of the country, they caused the British Government to revert British Guiana to a Crown Colony so that the legislature since then had become a very weak medium for political reform. On my return, I joined the British Guiana East Indian Association where the influence of persons such as C.R. Jacob and Ayube Edun was felt. Our representatives were hammering away in the legislature for constitutional changes including Adult Suffrage. However, I soon found that we were not getting anywhere. We lost one of our leaders who defected and I as treasurer found I could do nothing. Edun was running the Union personally as if it was his personal property. Then I also saw they were collaborating with the planters. So I got into difficulties with them. Then in 1947 I got elected to the legislature as an independent under limited suffrage - with no adult suffrage yet. In that year a Labour Party was formed between all the old politicians and comprising the people in the labour movement who wanted to get into Parliament. They did not want me in it because they were the old forces, some of whom I was challenging. But we had started in 1946 the Political Affairs Committee; it was a Marxist study group and we were putting out a bulletin and so on.

135

"When I was in the United States as a student, naturally, I was trying to improve my political and ideological education. So when I was in dental school I realised that my education was very limited. In my pre-medical course I took natural sciences and things like that and no social sciences. So in my last two years at dental school I began going to Y.M.C.A. College right in Chicago and did Political Science, Economics and Philosophy. But while in school I had never been exposed to Marxist-Leninist teachings and philosophy. Some of our professors were radical but not Marxist-Leninist.

"Now, towards the end of that period in 1945 that was when the Soviet Union was making its glorious contribution towards the War. So we found a lot of people beginning to praise the Soviet Union for its role in the world and so on. I would think that in that period when I came back socialism was very much in the air, and Marxist-Leninism was not something that was looked at as a bogey as it was when the Cold War had started after 1947 and into the '50's. My wife also was associated with Marxist-Leninist groupings in the United States as a student at the University, and I remember she gave me some of these little Lenin Library books and I read them - I am a very avid reader - and it opened up a whole new world of understanding to me. In other words I could then understand all of my background and what I had seen in the United States and I could relate it all into a coherent whole.

"In 1946 we formed this Study Group for ourselves to study more about Marxism and to relate it to the British Guiana situation and to the Caribbean and expand our work. Four of us started it, my wife, myself, a chap named Ashton Chase who grew up as a protegè of Critchlow and worked in Critchlow's office, and a fellow named Jocelyn Hubbard who was secretary of the T.U.C. And just to show that there was no horror about Marxism, Hubbard went to the Founding Conference of the World Federation of Trade Unions in Paris in 1945. The whole West Indian movement and Jamaica were part of that then; the Hills and all of them were part of this though they were later expelled from the P.N.P. in 1952, when Norman Manley brought back his son to take over the Union and all that."

Referring to an earlier visit to Jamaica, Dr. Jagan said:

"That's what I said when I was in Jamaica, that anti-Communism in the long run doesn't pay. Because although in British Guiana we suffered for it, in Guyana today you don't have any right wing who can come out in the streets and cause trouble. But in Jamaica you have it because of that anti-Communism of Norman Manley; and so that Party has a strong right wing inside it and outside. I commented on that in my University speech at Mona.

"So it was against that background that we started. With the Cold War abating, that period was much like now. Socialism is now becoming more and more attractive. Remember that the Socialist British Labour Party won a landslide victory in the 1945 elections and it was against that kind of atmosphere that we

136

began to work here. So I got elected as an independent fighting against the Labour Party candidate but, immediately after the elections in 1947, I joined the British Guiana Labour Party in the hope of working for unity which is always our goal - unity and struggle. We struggle against reactionary tendencies but we are always trying for unity. So I united with them. Their life was to be short. Within two years the Party was virtually extinct in that two of the members were brought into the Executive Council and the others did not have a coherent voting pattern in the legislature. So in less than two years the thing broke up and this created the basis for our Party which was formed in 1950.

"Burnham left in 1944 for England as a student, having won a Guiana Scholarship. He was expected to return in 1949. We had heard that Burnham was playing an active role in student politics in England and was also associated, I think, with the London branch of the Caribbean Labour Congress, so we arranged for him to come home via Jamaica. We go back to our outlook towards Jamaica as the leader of the Revolution. He did go to Jamaica and when he came home eventually, he joined us. It was a tussle for a while, a little bit of wavering whether to join what was called the League of Coloured Peoples or to join with us. Eventually, Burnham came with us because in the League there were already places on top which were filled and it was not easy to displace people like Carter and Denbow, whereas in our set-up we created immediately a post of Chairman and Leader and he became Chairman of the Party and I became Leader. So we were able to get Burnham in at the beginning of our Party's formation. That is more or less the background of that."

I asked Dr. Jagan: "How did you two come to split?" His answer:

"I think one has to see this in terms of Burnham's own personality, I suppose his own background and upbringing, the fact that he was a Guiana scholar. His sister wrote a book called, Beware of my brother, Forbes. She was with us in the sixties and she explains the whole background of how he grew up, how he wanted to be on top and things like that. There were manouevrings before we won the '53 elections, Burnham wanting to become the Leader of the Party, but that failed. Then when we won the elections and we were selecting the Ministers, he issued an ultimatum - leader or nothing. But he had to give in when the Georgetown people whom he and his group were hoping to use as a force against us, found out what was really causing the crisis. They went against him and he had to back down.

"It was not just a personality split, it was also a right wing opportunistic split, a personality question withBurnham and, secondly, the pragmatic approach of the traditional socialists as against the Marxist-Leninists.

"The pragmatic approach says politics is the art of making deals, but for us Marxist-Leninists it is a matter of principle, so in the course of our political career, our party's career, we have suffered. We had this set-back in 1953, Friday,

137

October 9, when it was announced that the British Government had decided that the Constitution of British Guiana must be suspended to prevent Communist subversion of the government and a dangerous crisis both in public order and in economic affairs. Armed forces, it was announced, had landed to support the Police and to prevent any public disorder which might be fomented by Communist supporters."

In Jamaica, I recall that at that time there was great military activity combined with the British Navy in the Jamaican area. The Jamaican Press were told that they were only undertaking exercises. Later it was realised that the truth was that they were on a serious mission to land in British Guiana. At that time, I was told personally by a senior military officer that the reason why the press were being deceived by the Army was because they did not wish to have bloodshed on arrival in British Guiana, where, if their arrival were pre-notified, they might have to fight their way into the city. It seems, however, that the British Government had anticipated that Dr. Jagan would make a unilateral declaration of independence and wished the Army to get there before any such thing could be done. This Dr. Jagan denied.

He said he and his party and his supporters were in grave danger from the hostilities that were being generated against them.

"There are those who didn't like us for what they knew that we intended to do. That is, that we just didn't want independence, but we wanted independence and economic transformation and social justice. Therefore they removed us using all kinds of political means.

"So, what happened basically is that those forces, including the British Government, installed the PNC and the United Force at the next election. They dictated the policies, they changed the whole ideological framework of Guiana and that bred dissatisfaction in the country. The fact is that after we were put out, Guiana was told what to do in domestic and foreign policy. This inevitably led to the worsening conditions of the people; therefore, they had to build up an apparatus of propaganda to suppress us, which was reflected in trying to close down our paper and so on. They used suppression, physical suppression. A part of this was coercion, part of it was to bribe and corrupt some of the people in our leadership to break away; others who did not want to move suffered physical harassment and victimization; they could not get jobs and all that sort of thing. And, finally, the use of the Police and the Army not only as strike breakers as they have been used from time to time, but also to keep them in power as in the last elections when they just went in and seized the ballot boxes.

The fact is that after the military occupation and the suspension of the Constitution, a new Constitution came into effect in July, 1961 with internal self-government. In those elections held on the "first past the post system", Dr. Jagan's party gained a majority and he became the country's first Premier with internal self-government. The history books record that having succeeded and got back into the seat of power, great turbulence came about in Guiana with the introduction of the Kaldor budget which was followed by a general strike, and by continued labour disorder. By that time arrangements were being made for the new election of 1962 under proportional representation. And although Dr. Jagan's party got 24 seats as compared to Burnham's 22 seats and the newly formed Conservative Party, the United Force, seven seats, Burnham and D'Aguiar made a coalition which enabled them to install Forbes Burnham as Prime Minister, an historic step leading to May 26, 1966, when the country became independent.

As to the Army invasion of 1963, Dr. Jagan says that, despite what the British announced, the Army really came to Guiana because of his own request.

"You see, we were caught in a dilemma. The Police were in sympathy with the PNC. The composition was such from colonial days that in the racial context there was great danger for us. But our vindication came when we won 18 out of 24 seats; that was the biggest achievement to our credit. What was happening was really this: there was a Commissioner of Police, a white Englishmen, who was taking orders from the Governor. The Governor, who was in charge of the Army, was taking orders from the Colonial Office. The Colonial Office was taking orders from the Foreign Office and the Foreign Office was taking orders from the American State Department. So they blocked us in every possible way. When I got offers of aid from Cuba and other places, I could not sign an Aid Agreement. I could sign a trade agreement with Cuba to sell rice, to sell timber and other products, but I could not sign an Aid Agreement although I negotiated it. When it was referred to the Governor here, he referred it to the Colonial Office and everything got stalled. The Security Forces and the Police were being used in '63 not to maintain law and order in the country but to allow the thing to blow up. The British Government could then have an excuse to say that Guiana was not ready to go into independence. You see, when the American Government pressed the British Government not to grant independence to Guiana after the 1960 elections the British Government was embarrassed, because in 1960 at a conference in London, they had promised that whoever won that election would take the country into independence. So something had to be done. That is how the CIA came in and the British, who had control of the Army and the Police, allowed it. You see, the British Government doesn't act on the basis of consistency. For instance, Ian Smith declared U.D.I. and the British Government did nothing. But Ian Smith was a protector of Imperialist interests therefore they wouldn't move against him. But in Guyana, if we declared independence they would suspend the Constitution immediately as in 1953, because they wanted us out, they and the Americans who were pushing them, wanted us out. In fact, from all that happened, it would seem that the British were prepared to go along with us hoping that they could turn people like me and succeed with us as they had done in India and Kenya and different places. But the Americans were more hysterical based on what was happening in Cuba. They thought Guiana was becoming a second Cuba."

Dr. Jagan's view is somewhat supported by Nigel Fisher's biography of the late Ian MacLeod, at that time British Secretary of State for the Colonies. Says Fisher:

"Although the West Indies were within the American sphere of influence, the United States Government never sought to influence British policy in our attempt to establish a workable island Federation. But in the aftermath of the Bay of Pigs, the Americans were naturally interested in British Guiana and did not care for the prospect of an independent, Jagan-led, Castro-type government on the South American mainland.

"President Kennedy told MacLeod of his anxieties during a long talk in the Oval Room at the White House. He said he understood our policy, but he hoped we would not move too quickly towards independence. MacLeod replied 'Do I understand, Mr. President, that you want us to de-colonise as fast as possible all over the world except on your own doorstep?' President Kennedy laughed and said 'Well that's probably just about it.' MacLeod answered that he appreciated the President's point of view, but that our policy to bring Guiana to independence would continue. The American attitude did not slow down his (MacLeod's) approach, although the serious racial strife between the African and Indian communities in the colony a year or two later, and the difficulty of getting any agreement on the Constitution between Cheddi Jagan and Forbes Burnham did impose an inevitable delay."

As I sat talking with Dr. Jagan in his busy office, with lieutenants moving in and out with various administrative requests, I wondered what was his future. At 58 he had been three times his country's elected leader but now, though controlling perhaps the largest party numerically, he was an almost ineffectual leader of the Opposition. Indeed, for a long time he would not take his place as an Opposition member, but later rejoined Parliament to fulfil a policy of critical support. What of his future? Said he:

"We have put out recently a 17-point proposal which we are saying must be implemented if Guyana is to be able successfully to defend its sovereignty and also to go on to socialism. We have five major aspects. One is the need for creating national unity. We are telling the government that it is not enough just to make declarations on this point; they have to remove all the obstacles to national unity. By that we mean ending political and racial discrimination, harassment, which goes on against our members and supporters; the ending of bureaucratic administrative methods of rule, and police/military methods of rule; and applying normal democratic political methods of struggle for political struggle.

"We are calling also in this sense for the separation of party and state, the mass organisations. Here, the PNC is getting all mass organisations to affiliate with it; the army is affiliated with the party and everything. We are asking for separation of these. They may all work towards the same objective of socialism but they must have their independent functions; and Guyana must have a multi-party system as you have in some socialist countries which are not one-party states...Bulgaria with two parties, Czechoslovakia....Germany and East Germany. And we say national unity is necessary not only for defence. In that case we will be calling for a People's Militia to train and arm all the people as Cuba has done; and also important for the development of the economy. If people are dissatisfied at the bottom they are not going to produce and you have low productivity.

"Another point we have made is democracy. Democracy is essentially the building of socialism. If you have rule from above autocratically, if coercive methods are used then there will be dissatisfaction and the peopple will not produce and the bureaucrats will be put in different levels of authority. They have really no contact with the people; the people are not involved in the decision-making process or in management what is called workers' control in factories; as a result you cannot increase production or productivity. We have said socialism means giving people more, developing them materially and culturally, and you cannot do it from the thin air or expect that some other country can give you; you have to produce it. The two things are inter-related.

"Then we are calling for an end to extravagance and corruption. There must be an Integrity Law. I am trying to get this Law, incidentally, and there must be firm action against all cases of corrruption. Leaders must set an example and we must have firm action, disciplinary action to stop this kind of thing because the man at the bottom is not going to tighten his belt and work hard if he sees that all of it is squandered.

"Then we say that socialism cannot be built without socialists which means that we must go in consciously for the training of adults, who will be imbued with the tenets of Marxism-Leninism, its theory and practice. Because if you don't know the theory, if you don't know the practice, even though you may intend to go there, you will not get there. We have examples in the socialist system where there are right and left deviations of Marxism and Leninism, where you have different models. You have, for instance, the Yugoslav model as distinct from the Soviet model. Marxists themselves are now arguing what is really Marxism and Leninism.

"Then we feel that firm relations must be established with the socialist states......Mossadeq succumbed in 1953 because he nationalised the oil company in 1951. He failed largely because he was anti-Communist. He was a nationalist but anti-Communist. The Soviet Union was willing to buy the oil but he refused to sell because of his anti-Communism and eventually the CIA and the imperialists created a shipping blockade. Dissatisfaction arose among the workers, the factories had to close down, they couldn't sell the oil or ship it out and so Mossadeq collapsed. Similarly, experience in Vietnam and Angola has shown that socialist countries' support is absolutely necessary to win the battle for national liberation. Cuba has shown that even after you take over, you face military attack, economic blockade, aggression and so on and as a result, socialist aid is necessary.

141

"I made a radio broadcast this morning and I was saying it is not enough just to say we are non-aligned, and we have to depend on what is called self-reliance. During the Angolan crisis the Organisation of African Unity was split right down the middle; they were powerless to help. This applies to the whole non-aligned movement; they didn't play any decisive role in that situation as a body. We are making the point that the experience in Cuba, in Angola, in Vietnam has shown that to win power, to hold power, to build socialism, it is absolutely decisive to have the help of the socialist world, to work closely with the world's socialist community. Our objective is not just to fight imperialism, but to satisfy the people of Guyana, to solve their problems of unemployment, raise their standards of living."

Referring to Mao's China, said Dr. Jagan:

"They have a personality cult. This is a principle that was in the Soviet Union in the Stalin period but now they don't go infor that at all. They go in for what they call collective leadership. That was Stalinism which was an aberration. They admit this now, and that's why they have down-graded Stalin. Things like we fight against here in Guyana also - Burnhamism and the cult of the personality.

"In the matter of South Africa, for instance, if Southern Africa and then the other states become liberated, then the whole balance of world forces shifts against imperialism in favour of socialism. If that happens, the Soviet union can cut down its military expenditure, can cut down on its military and they can go and work in factories. The Soviets have a shortage of labour. In that way, they will be able to give the people more. They will be able to turn the production of war goods into production of domestic goods, utility goods. In that sense in the long run it serves the patriotism of the Soviet Union.....Maoism is violating the principle of patriotism and internationalism."

Said Opposition Leader Dr. Jagan finally:

"When I started out in politics, I had no dream that I was going to become a Prime Minister. The Party wasn't even formed then. People ask me sometimes: If this thing keeps going like this, how do you get back in power; 'how do you see yourself?' I say it is not a question of myself. I say you have to see this dialectically too, in that when the PNC was working with imperialism, they saw their duty to hold us down; but now that imperialism is attacking them, they will have to see the need to see us as an ally and not only as an ally but as friends."

And so, in 1976 Jaunty, perky, bright, almost volubly articulate, Cheddi Jagan at 58, again looked forward to a new role in the future of his land - Guyana.

THE RIGHT EXCELLENT
NORMAN WASHINGTON MANLEY
M.M., Q.C.

(NATIONAL HERO OF JAMAICA)
BORN ROXBOROUGH, JAMAICA 4TH JULY 1893
DIED 2ND SEPTEMBER, 1969

CHIEF MINISTER OF JAMAICA (1955-1957)
PREMIER OF JAMAICA (1957-1962)

9

NORMAN WASHINGTON MANLEY

Gᴀᴍɪɴ ᴀɴᴅ ɢᴇɴɪᴜꜱ, shy yet arrogant, coldly analytical yet given to much emotion, these were mixed up traits in Norman Washington Manley. As a student in school, rebellious - rebellion with a touch of mischief - as a soldier with artillery in the trenches in World War I, much of that rebelliousness remained midst horrible human sacrifice. He was of a generation that was not allowed to live peaceful, simple lives between their teens and manhood. His were years of gore and stress. Perhaps this made him the greater man because, with his natural intellect, his studies should not have been a trouble, but he had to work very hard in those embattled circumstances to achieve the academic success he did before returning to Jamaica.

In the late 'twenties one would see him in the precincts of the Supreme Court of Jamaica looking like no other barrister-at-law. Most other barristers affected fairly formal dress, with woolen suits and the like. All wore waistcoats, as did Norman Manley. But he contrived to affect cheaper suitings with the gun mouth trousers hitched high up under the waistcoat exposing an expanse of white socks between the cuff and the shoe. I thought at the time - and others of us did - that it was an affectation to attract notice to himself. It probably was. Every so often streaks of those early years would suddenly emerge as he strode the public scene either as brilliant counsel, or as politician, or as elder statesman.

He was in a sense the product of many crises. Losing his father when he was of very tender years and his mother just at the critical period of his high school life, losing his brother in action in the War, he had been through more crises by the time he was adult than most people have the chance to encounter. And the dramatic nature of his character and his many changing patterns in later life also derive considerably from the almost neurotic courtship between himself and his first cousin, Edna, whom he married, and who is, in her own right, almost as distinguished in her own sphere.

Norman Manley has described his early years; "Do not imagine it to be like life even in rural areas these days. We had no friends except family. I never met a girl, except a working class girl, on social terms till I was 19 years old. I never went to a 'party' till after I returned to Jamaica in 1922. I grew up as a 'bush' man. I earned my pocket money cleaning pastures and chipping logwood at standard rates. I would go out in the morning and share lunch with the workers, or if we were looking out for stray cattle, walk the day and get home late at night, after 12 to 14 hours on the constant move. The result was that I was tough as hell and developed a stamina that I have never seen surpassed. Maybe that is why I have a record in championship sports that will never be beaten in these days of specialisation, a record of seven wins at one single sport meeting."

Hard and humble were the beginnings and circumstances of this great man who first introduced modern political parties to his country, who fought most to give the people, all the people, the vote, who helped to put trade unionism on a modern and organised scale, who led his people into self-government, who took the nation into federation with the islands of the Commonwealth Caribbean, then withdrew it back to itself and to independence on its own. Such is the man who after all those years had to see his rival and cousin, Alexander Bustamante, become the first Prime Minister of independent Jamaica, a goal for which Norman Manley had striven all his life.

Son of Thomas Albert Samuel Manley, a planter and produce dealer of Porus, and Margaret Ann, daughter of a small pen-keeper named Alexander Shearer of Blenheim, Hanover, Norman Manley was born at Roxbourgh in Manchester on the 4th of July, 1893 (Independence Day of the United States and for that reason affording him the middle name Washington). Norman was the first son, one of four children.

As the Gleaner's historian said when Norman Manley died in 1969:

".......... full of honour but too soon to see his second son, Michael, become Prime Minister of Jamaica.

"If we seek a unifying link in the various branches of that famous Jamaican family, which included so many prominent Jamaicans, it is to be found in 'old man Shearer', as he was called, a vigorous and highly original character.

"The future Premier grew up on the soil in the most literal sense of that term, and he never lost a profound attachment to it. His father had made himself a citrus grower of some consequence while Norman was still a boy, and Norman took the keenest interest in this phase of his outdoor life. Then the father died rather suddenly. The mother could not carry on successfully with the property alone. But old man Shearer's wife also died and he, having gone totally blind, concluded that he would give up his Blenheim home and join forces with his daughter. A half-ruinate property called Belmont, in St. Catherine, was bought for a modest sum, and the rest of the two families settled down there to live from the land."

At times they were joined by Manley's cousin, Alexander Clarke, also a Shearer grandson, who was some nine years older than Norman (and was destined to become the first Prime Minister of Jamaica). The Clarke name would be altered in due course to Bustamante. The cousins drove cattle, chipped logwood and shared whatever pot luck was boiled. Norman and Alex do not appear to have been very close. Indeed, in later years, Norman, while expressing affection for Alex, remembered him as a rough, rambunctious, bullying type as a boy, when, of course, Alex was so much older than Norman. As a child, as throughout life, they were separated by more than their ages, for Norman's inclinations were markedly studious, relieved by a passion for organised sports, while Alexander preferred the outdoors.

After attending elementary school, young Norman went on to Beckford and Smith's High School in Spanish Town. He used to ride horseback between his home and school. For a short time before that, he had gone to Wolmer's, but when he was nine and the family fortunes collapsed, his mother could only afford to send him to the elementary school at Guanaboa Vale, very near home. Then he went on to Beckford and Smith's where he was a weekly boarder with the Headmaster.

He says:

"I rode to school every Monday morning and rode home on Fridays. In the week I got into all sorts of trouble with my horse which the Police thought should not be galloping through the town."

In his Linstead recklessness on horseback was foreshadowed his adult propensity for hard driving as a motorist. Few of his friends or colleagues would willingly travel with him at the wheel; for he held nearly all the rumoured records for point-to-point journeys over the rugged marl roads of Jamaica in those days. He was not so much reckless - he was extremely skilled at judgment of road surface and hairpin curve - as he was daring; he seemed to revel in the narrowness of the margin by which he had avoided the other vehicle. His life nearly paid for it in 1946 when his car went off the road and catapulted into the valley on the Gordon Town Road. Yet, on the last evening I met him before his death he was whimsically telling me that he planned to drive his family in his Benz at 105 miles an hour on the Boulevard (Kingston's fastest motorway at the time).

147

So far as he was a motorist, he was fatalistic and daring all his life. The Linstead days on horseback were to be as characteristic of the man as of the boy.

Norman got a half-scholarship to one of the leading secondary schools in Jamaica at that time, Jamaica College, where he went from 1906 to 1913. He spent the last year as a pupil teacher.

Of these days at Jamaica College Norman Manley wrote:

"It was a tough school in those days with 100 boarders and 50 day boys. Bullying was rampant and there was a good deal of homosexuality, for the most part not carried to extremes. I suffered a lot from bullying and was the target of one lout who made life a burden. I had fully made up my mind in my second term to run away and go home.

"Then one morning I tried to fight it out, and by great good luck, the headmaster's son, a fine man of about 40, was passing by just as the fight started. He prevented the crowd from interfering, as they surely would have done in favour of the older boy and against the comparative newcomer. So it was a straight fight and I won, I suppose largely through desperation. I regret to say that for the rest of that term I turned the tables quite remorselessly. But it was an isolated case. I devoted a large part of my time trying to suppress bullying - not without success where I had the physical advantage."

But Norman Manley was not merely a champion of the oppressed. As he puts it himself:

"I was not a supporter of law and order at school, and by the middle of 1907 became the ring-leader of a group of boys who deplored discipline and set out to undermine the authority of any Master we thought showed signs of weakness. This went on till I was 16 years old, and then, greatly influenced by my mother's ambitions for me and by her death, I decided to turn over a new leaf by going to the Headmaster and announcing I intended to try for the Rhodes. To say that the Headmaster was shocked is to put it mildly. I had done little work and showed no special promise at anything. In those days, a Rhodes scholar took the same paper as a Jamaica scholar and that was strictly based on two or three years' specialisation in a particular subject like languages or mathematics or science. I was reminded by the Headmaster that not only was I far behind in studies, but also had a thoroughly disreputable reputation, which would make it almost impossible for him and the other Masters to make the report on leadership and good character which was basic in the scholarship award.

"However, I insisted, almost out of stubbornness but largely because it had been my mother's wish, and she, shortly before her death, had actually engaged Mr. R.M. Murray, of blessed memory, to take me on as a private pupil and see if by coaching he could discover any hope for me in mathematics, the only subject in which I had up till then showed any aptitude."

148

How Norman turned over a new leaf was not as simple as it might have seemed. He said he did so, but with such complete ruthlessness, breaking with the rebels of whom he had been ringleader, that the Headmaster had to remonstrate with him for not remembering that mercy should always temper justice.

Norman Manley was certain that but for the fact that the Headmaster knew what a gallant fight his mother had been making with the four children, he Norman, might never have been saved from the disorders into which some of his school life led him. And he is certain that R.M. Murray's belief that there was some hope for him and Murray's tremendous skill as a teacher made all the difference.

During these school years, Norman established a formidable reputation in sports. He not only won seven events and set five records at the school championships at Sabina Park, he became outstanding in cricket, football, rifle shooting and boxing. His record for 220 yards in 22.9 seconds was not bettered for 24 years. His 100 yards dash in 10 seconds, in 1912, stood unbeaten until his own son, Douglas, equalled it in 1941. In 1912, Norman's fast deliveries topped the bowling averages at school in cricket, while he scored the largest number of goals in the football season and led the rifle team as captain. Truly, he was an all-round sportsman of great talent, guts and endurance. At a most critical stage of his education Norman was on his own. The family decided to lease Belmont out. Norman's eldest sister, Vera, was already established in England as a music teacher and she got the rest of the family to join her in England, that is, her younger sister, Dr. Muriel Manley, and Norman's young brother, Douglas, who died in 1917 in the Battle of Ypres in Flanders, leaving Norman to work for the Rhodes in Jamaica and to spend his holidays with friends of the family or at Jamaica College itself. So, here he was now, all on his own.

About this he says:

"To be frank, I enjoyed being on my own. I was a tough and unsentimental youngster, I worked - and I worked very hard - I did a bit of everything - track athletics, cricket, football, rifle shooting - filled my life. I also taught at Farm School at Papine and in 1913 for six months at Titchfield School in Port Antonio."

He admits that when teaching maths, he never failed to end every maths class with half the girls in tears. "I suffered from a quick, flaring tempe,r" he says, "which it took me half a lifetime to learn to control. Indeed, I doubt if I ever learnt. Constant, inhibiting violent efforts at control gradually wore it down till it seemed to disappear, with its place being taken by a sort of arrogant indifference which was eventually mistaken for the real me."

It is interesting that this great man, in the autumn of his life, could write these words abut himself. He was truly a self-analytical person, but he was just as

149

ruthless in analysing anybody else, family, friend or foe. As he was at 16 in basic nature, so he was through all those magnificent careers in law, politics and life.

Norman Manley won the Rhodes scholarship for Jamaica in 1914, and while still waiting to go off to England, he finished the teaching term at Titchfield. But while spending time with a life-long friend in Falmouth, Mr. Leslie Clerk, he picked up a very bad attack of typhoid fever. As he recalls, those were not the days of antibiotics and, anyway, he had been going around with his iron strength for four days with a temperature of 104 degrees before he was finally diagnosed and sent off to Nuttall Hospital. He recalls that this illness, which nearly killed him, had a great effect on his life and character. He says he had the fever for seven weeks and for four of the seven weeks he was delirious and at death's door. When he was well enough to leave hospital he was just a wreck of his old self.

"I doubt if I ever did recover all that I lost, and certainly one result was that, years after, I discovered that I had lost that extra muscular snap that makes you a good runner or jumper. These were physical effects. I do not think my powers to do long hours of mental work were affected, for, well beyond middle age, in fact, till I was 70, I did not regard a 15-hour day of concentrated work as excessive Before, I must have been one of the hardest and most ruthless young men in the world."

Norman Manley, however, considered that that grave illness changed him to a person "with a new range of emotional understandings that at first I hardly knew how to cope with. It is not that you become soft so much as that the world you live in expands and your awareness of it is enormously enlarged." He regarded his life as profoundly affected by the illness.

When he arrived in England and went to the home of the Swithenbanks with Edna and her brothers and her sisters. It was to be the start of a remarkable romance between Edna Swithenbank and Norman Manley, which endured all their lives.

Norman Manley entered Jesus College, Oxford, to read law, and it is recorded that at once he attracted the notice of the tutors. But the outbreak of World War I in 1914 interrupted his studies, as it did those of so many other young, gifted aspirants. After attempts to join one or other kind of military unit, eventually Norman enlisted as a private in the Royal Field Artillery and became a first-rate gunner. A historian, who has commented on this period of Norman's life, says "stories have been told to the effect that he encountered race discrimination in the British Army which caused him to refuse a commission and sowed in him the seeds of a certain anti-English prejudice. These may be dismissed as gossip. The best contradition of them is to be found in the fact that at no stage of his career was he anti-English."

Of this period Norman says himself:

"I joined in East Deptford, a centre of East End London. Seventy percent of these men were Cockneys with a view of life all their own. I got to know them very well and a great affection developed between us. They were first-class thieves and would rob your last farthing if you gave them the chance, but for kindness and generosity I have never met their equal.

"If you were broke and did not have a cigarette to smoke they would not hesitate to give you one if they had two. They came to look on "Bill", as they called me, as a great oracle and I was to settle a thousand arguments about everything under the sun. When deadlock occurred, the watchword was, "Let's ask Bill." I was careful to plead ignorance unless I really knew and could explain and so preserved respect and confidence.

"They showed an innate courtesy, I suppose, because we liked each other. They soon found out that I did not like being called 'Darkie' as came natural to them, and I have heard a real tough guy get hold of a new arrival, a casual replacement who automatically called me 'Darkie', and take him aside and say 'Don't call him that; he doesn't like it. We call him Bill and we like him.'

"I remember once when I was ill for about a week with fever how they looked after me. If I was on guard duty a friend would take it on for me and when I was real bad they nursed me in a simple way so that I could avoid reporting "sick" and leaving my unit by being sent off to hospital. I did not want that to happen as I liked where I was.

"As I say, more than half of our men were East Enders and my own Sergeant was a Covent Garden market porter. And I shared with another Covent Garden market youngster the honour of being reported to be the best gunlayer (that was my job) in the Division with its six batteries of 4.5 howitzers. . . . .

". . . . .I had made up my mind to accept no form of promotion - I was a gunner and a gunner I would remain. So I was not worried about promotion. Nothing in the future gave you concern. Your job was to do your job as a soldier and stay alive if you could. You blessed each day, you prayed to be spared some hair-raising experience, like being caught in a severe German artillery barrage or a gas attack with gas shells; but that aside, to be alive was to have a future, and worry about the future had no place."

When he was promoted corporal, that created problems. He says: "Here I came up against violent colour prejudice. The rank and file disliked taking orders from a coloured NCO, and their attitude was mild by comparison with that of my fellow NCOs; corporals and sergeants resented my sharing status with them. They were more spiteful and later conspired to get me into trouble. It was only the Officer class that I could expect to behave with ordinary decency, and both aspects of this phenomenon I fully understood. To be frank, I had the greatest contempt for my fellow NCOs and I was later to discover that a sense of superiority was a good protection from the obsessions that colour feeling can create."

151

A sergeant, however, booked Norman Manley on a charge arising out of a long journey to locate each battery in the division on the move and map their positions. The sergeant would not accept Norman Manley's explanation of the long time it took to do this and so put Corporal Manley on a charge before the Commanding Officer.

"I explained to the Commanding Officer that the NCO's resented my status because of my colour and that there would never be a peaceful relationship and I offered to throw in my corporal's stripes if he would transfer my brother and myself to a battery of guns. The Commanding Officer jumped at this and put through a transfer whereupon I resigned as Corporal and reverted to the rank of Gunner and went off to the D Battery of the 39th Division. I remained as a gun-layer until I left the Army in 1919."

As Norman Manley was awarded the Military Medal for bravery and gallantry during the war, it should be interesting to read some of his descriptions of that kind of artillery and trench warfare in which he was involved 24 hours a day.

"In preparation for an attack by the artillery it meant building dug-outs for six guns, about 1,000 rounds of ammunition for the guns, each shell weighing 45 lbs and they came up in boxes in pairs, about 100 lbs to the box. For about one month, about thirty of us used to leave our camp at about 5 p.m. to walk ten miles to where the shells had been dumped by lorry. Then, arriving by 9 p.m., we kept on till 4 a.m. carrying boxes of shells about two miles to where gun-pits had been prepared. Then we broke up and got home to camp as best we could. It was 20 miles walking and seven hours carrying a heavy load half the time."

They had been spotted by the Germans and Norman describes how his brother, Roy, who was in the same gun-crew met his death.

"I was not there when the Germans struck but my brother, just then 21 years old, was. It was just at dusk when they opened a terrific artillery fire on the wood (where the guns were). In five minutes half our men were dead or wounded. Those who could, ran out, and among those running was my brother Roy, carrying on his back a man thought to be wounded - it turned out he was dead - and then he too fell, killed by a shell that burst a little distance off and sent a small fragment of its casing straight into his heart." In memory of Roy, he wrote, "He had a fine mind and a large and generous love of life and people."

Norman had some close shaves in the War but he says:

"I bore a charmed life. Two incidents stand out. Once we were being shelled - it was about a daily occurrence - and a great run for safety ensued. I was running north at top speed when I heard the roar of a coming shell - they came with an awesome sound as their velocity was just a little less than sound. I knew from the increasing horror of the noise that I was in for a near shave and at the last split second dived for the ground and felt the shake of the air as it passed so near to me.

"As I fell I heard a shout from a runner behind me. 'Bill is gone, they've got him.' Then I felt myself covered with earth and the noise of an exploding shell and came to realise that I was actually at the bottom of the crater made by the shell say 6 feet by 10 feet wide. My escape was miraculous.

"But the very next night I had an equally miraculous escape. It happened that I was on guard for the night. We had found it best to abolish guard duty with four men on, one NCO and three men each doing four hours' duty. We took a chance with one man for 12 hours, well understanding that if the single man on duty was ever caught sleeping, we would be forced to undertake the proper system. It never happened in three years although there was always an officer doing the rounds and himself on duty for the full 12 hours.

"Well, I was on duty that night and a sudden shower of gas shells fell on us. Those were high velocity. You did not hear them coming. The shell casing was light, as they exploded on touching the ground with an instantaneous fuse, and you knew you were under gas attack because the noise of the explosion was different from that of a high explosive shell.

"My duty was to wake up everyone and see that they ran out of danger and this was easily done. Next morning I found my little lean-to upset and my rolled up blankets and things riddled with fragments of a shell which had exploded right beside the shelter. If I had been there and not on duty I would have been as riddled as my blankets were."

Those days of trench warfare must have had a deep impression on this young man anxious to go and study at Oxford and caught up in one of the most disastrous wars that has ever occurred; but he lived throughout it and even found time to do some philandering and to make himself a crown and anchor gambling cloth which he used profitably when the opportunity arose. All this goes to show that his sense of mischief and fun was always with him, even where death was the pervading thing.

Norman Manley was on a study course in England when the war actually ended. He had been sent to take this special course. He says:

"I was on leave in London when Armistice Day came. I was in Hyde Park that night with an estimated crowd of one million. It was over, but I could get no sense of joy. Long anticipation of some events leaves you cold and practical when they arrive. Here was the war ended. Over a million families faced the future without the stimulus of an unfinished war and with the intuition that the future would engage everybody's minds, and less and less would the sacrifice of the past be remembered.

153

"Then I thought of myself, my family and my future. My brother was gone, my sisters were reasonably set on their careers. There was hope of selling Belmont, but our share would hardly leave each of us more than about three hundred pounds. Enough for me for one extra year to make up for the scholarship year I had lost."

Of his time at Oxford, the <u>Gleaner's</u> obituary says:

"Returning to Oxford in 1919, Manley took his Law finals with first class honours. He was the Prize Man for his essay at Gray's Inn before being called to the Bar on the 20th April, 1921. He then spent almost a year in the London Chambers of S.C.N. Goodman. It was a formative, happy year for him both professionally and personally.

"In 1921 he married his cousin, Edna Swithenbank, whose mother, Ellie, also had been a daughter of Alexander Shearer. She was born in England, her father being a Yorkshire man. They remained in England where Norman Manley was doing the rounds of the courts following famous advocates and observing how the profession to which he belonged was functioning at its highest level. During that time Edna gave birth to Douglas on May 30, 1922. When that baby was eleven weeks old, on August 18, 1922, the father, mother and infant sailed for Jamaica."

Norman Manley then began carefully, patiently, thoroughly to feel his way into the practice of his profession in his homeland. His long and brilliant career at the Bar which he eventually surrendered for political dedication to his work as Party Leader, would have been more than sufficient to gain him a very honoured place in the annals of his country and of his profession. But, as it turned out, his legal pre-eminence and success were to be only the beginnings of his accomplishments. He triumphed finally in national service to his people and to his country.

H.O.A. Dayes, one of the most pre-eminent of the legal men in Jamaica, said of Norman Manley as a lawyer:

"He was incomparably the greatest advocate Jamaica ever had; and the best lawyer too. The cases he conducted were of every class and category. The victories were legion. To have him on your side was a passport to success. He became a legend in his lifetime.

"From the beginning of his practice he was a success. He fairly rocketed into prominence, won most of his cases, was appointed a King's Counsel within ten years of starting to practise, and was acknowledged to be the leader not only of the Jamaica Bar but of that of the British West Indies. Before the question of his participation in politics arose, he had figured in thousands of big civil and criminal actions. This is no collective term used for effect; the number was actually thousands."

154

Norman Manley's biography in the Gleaner lists the Spaulding murder trial in 1924, the Walker trial 1927, and the Alexander trial 1931 as among the boldest of the cases. All were murder cases involving notably complicated evidence and motives. The Alexander case, however, is probably the best remembered. Feeling was running so high in Kingston that the venue had to be changed to Mandeville. The trial broke all records by lasting twenty-three days.

The Gleaner says: "A prime sensation at the Alexander case was the offering in Court of an exhibit consisting of a plaster cast by Mrs. Manley of the head of the victim," (who had been shot through the brain allegedly by his wife, who was charged with the murder).

I was at the Alexander murder case, which I attended as a Reporter. It is interesting to see the major tactic that Norman Manley used as leading Counsel for the defence. The Government Chemist had produced a photograph of the periphery of the fatal bullet and sought to establish by his ballistic expertise that it exactly proved that it came from the pistol which had been alleged to have been used by the accused. Now this bullet was under handling in the two levels of Court, Police and Counsel, Jurors inspecting it and the like for some two months. Then at the end of this 23-day-old trial, as the evidence was coming to a close, Norman Manley on behalf of the accused required that the Government Chemist repeat the procedure, re-photograph the bullet and let the Court see if in fact it would produce the kind of periphery photograph that was in evidence. This was done and it exploded the case for the prosecution, because it was not much like unto the previous photograph. As I reported the case, I concluded that Norman Manley had taken a long shot and suspected that in fact the bullet could not, at that distance of time, be re-photographed to get the exact result of the first photograph.

In that marathon trial, Norman Manley had the assistance of a whole series of pathologists and other specialists. Indeed, before the trial, he had undertaken, himself, a great range of ballistic experiments - shooting into sheep's skulls at varying distances and the like, to establish the kind of penetration made by the bullets at various distances, depending upon various types of weapons used. Indeed, an Armourer Sergeant had to be brought into Court to give evidence on much the same kind of problems and probabilities.

Great advocates tend to defend their cases on a multiple of bases simultaneously, while in fact having the real defence put in simply as part of the rest, only at the last phases making it emerge as the crucial defence.

I remember a case I reported in Port Maria where Norman Manley appeared for a grocer who had shot and killed a man who had run away with something from the shop. The case was conducted on the basis ostensibly that, under Common Law, a citizen is entitled to use whatever force is necessary to apprehend a felon who is fleeing. The deceased in this case had stolen some groceries and the grocer was pursuing him, shot at him and killed him. But quietly during the medi-

155

cal evidence, one noticed that the doctor giving evidence of the post-mortem had said that the bullet penetrated the lungs. Manley in just a few questions asked the doctor and obtained the information that the bullet in passing through the body had hit no bone or hard tissue.

At the close of the case for the prosecution, Manley said he was calling no witnesses. This gave him the last speech as against the Crown. And when the Crown had dealt with the case on the basis that it had been contested, Manley, in commencing his address, asked for the bullet to be produced and to be shown to the Jurors. They all looked at it as it was passed round. Then Manley, addressing the Court, said:

"Your Honour, this bullet is immutable testimony to the innocence of the prisoner at the Bar. The bullet hit the ground, ricocheted and hit the deceased. Any examination of that bullet will show that it hit some hard substance to deform it and the doctor has told us that it hit no hard tissue inside the deceased, therefore it must have ricocheted which caused it thus to be distorted and the prisoner, therefore, is not guilty at all. He was merely making an attempt to apprehend the criminal but did not kill him directly. "

Verdict: Not Guilty.

Norman Manley's legal successes were not confined to the morbidly popular mark of murder trials. Indeed, he more than once told me that if Jamaica had been a large enough country in which he could have specialised, he would have specialised in matrimonial causes because, he said, it is in these disputes and litigations that one gets to understand the deepest wells of human nature.

Two of his great cases were in England, one in which he successfully defended a Jamaican charged with murder in Manchester. The other is the famous Trade Marks litigation between Vicks Chemical Company and the manufacturers of Creosote Vaporub. Manley represented Vicks arguing the case in all the hearings which went right up to the Judicial Committee of the Privy Council. He established that the name Vaporub was identified in Jamaica with the Vicks product to a point that made its use by any other firm a commercial steal. The presiding Judge in London, who afterwards became Lord Chancellor, later remarked in a public speech that a colonial barrister, meaning Manley, had recently presented before him the best argument he had ever heard in a trade mark case.

Manley, back in Jamaica, awaiting the result of that case, showed extreme acceptance of fate when, by an error, I received information that he had lost and so told him. He said: "Well, you know, I thought we had it in the bag." But when a few moments later I was able to phone him the correct information that he had won, he blasted me for putting him through the agony of thinking he had lost. Later, Manley told me that on his first day arguing the case before the Privy Council, he found he was making no headway with the Court and then intuition told him to alter his mode of address and be less histrionic and more low key. Which he did and immediately got the attention of the Court in a way which he had not had before. He was warmly gratified that the Court had commended him on the presentaton of this most complicated trade mark litigation.

As the Gleaner commented after Norman Manley's death: "Yet Manley's success at the Bar was not enough to satisfy a broader form of ambition for service which was second nature to him." Edna Manley has told that one day in 1936 she found her husband brooding, and when she questioned him, he brought his aspiration to the surface. "Law in my life is an emotionally and intellectually bankrupting thing," he said. "I will have to find a way into a wider life."

One could say that his welfare period of life commenced with the formation of Jamaica Welfare Limited in the creation of which his influence had been great. The programme of Jamaica Welfare consisted largely of adult education along practical lines, training in co-operation, cottage industries, group activity in agriculture and manufacturing. The purpose was to enable people to live better lives, have better homes, to feed themselves better and to turn to account their production in creating a fuller life.

As a lawyer representing one of the major banana exporting companies, Manley became involved in various discussions which led to Murray of United Fruit Company and d'Antoni of Standard Fruit agreeing to an export cess on bananas which would be available for the work which Jamaica Welfare was to do. Manley is widely credited with the idea of the cess but he himself has declared that it arose as an offer from the banana giants during these various discussions which were held. However, the Banana Industry and all concerned knew that Manley was the person who made a success of it.

Jamaica Welfare was a pace setter because it became the model adopted by the British Government after the 1938 riots and the subsequent 1938 Royal Commission, to start, in the troubled West Indies area, movements for the improvement of the welfare of the people.

In these years of his pre-eminence as a legal luminary, as an advisor on major industrial matters, Norman Manley continued to live a life in which his work, culture, sport and everything were a part. No concert failed to have his support and attendance. He raced horses, he was a patron of boxing, and indeed, he was visible and interested in everything that was going on. In manner he remained a person who preferred a somewhat tattered look. The Gleaner's obituary says: "He was a lean ascetic looking man with bushy hair, disreputable legal robes and clothing."

I remember him in 1935 appearing in an Election Petition case in Falmouth. He stayed overnight in Brown's Town, a few miles away, and came to court in the morning wrapping his black robe round his trouser front, which when he came to speak in Court was revealed to be buttonless except for the top button. He seemed to delight in letting people think that he was a threadbare person.

At musical affairs which he attended regularly (and indeed in which he was for a time the music critic of the Gleaner newspaper) he was no brooding musicologist, but he participated with zest. One of his successors as Gleaner music critic said that "music was what he often turned to when he sought release from the demands of public service. But he was not a man to whom music was a mere opiate. He brought to it the same intelligence and concentration, the same single-mindedness and enthusiasm he brought to everything he did; and while his musical intellect might have been the envy of many a trained professional, his sensibility and innate gentleness allowed him often to be moved to tears."

At the other end of the emotional scale, on occasion I would hear him shout "Ole" standing and clapping when any high peak of musical performance brought him to that pitch of fervent approval. His library at Drumblair, his residence, was a true introduction to music for anyone minded to have a broad experience of recorded music. Art was a parallel in the libraries which his wife and himself maintained, all of which were open within limits to those they considered would benefit by the educational input of these records, books, illustrations, works of art and the like. His home indeed became a centre of culture in Jamaica.

During those years, there were several of us who would suggest that he should enter politics, enter the legislature and contribute to the wider leadership of the country. But he was committed to the improvement of the people's lot in another way, by the Jamaica Welfare way, and would say "Our problems are economic, politics is another matter. Our problems are economic." He kept his hand to that plough of leadership in the people's welfare at the organised level of village centres, community centres, and such matters.

Just about this time, Norman Manley's first cousin, Alexander Bustamante, was getting into the news as a flamboyant spokesman for the workers. Having fortuitously identified himself with riots which had occurred at Frome, Bustamante grew in stature as a person who spoke for the dock worker and labourers generally. Following upon the riots at Frome, at the western of the Island, the government appointed a Commission of Enquiry and the enquiry was sitting near to Frome on the 23rd of May, the very day when the riots in Kingston closed down all business and commercial life in the capital. I was at the enquiry in Frome, where Norman Manley was holding brief for the West Indies Sugar Company, a subsidiary of Tate & Lyle of the United Kingdom, owners of Frome which was then being constructed as a major sugar factory and sugar estate. So, while Bustamante was actually being jailed in Kingston on behalf of the workers, Norman Manley was in Savanna-la-Mar holding a watching brief for one of the major employers. Suddenly, during the enquiry, I saw Manley go to the Commissioners of Enquiry, speak to them, then he came to my desk - the reporters' desk - and showed me a telegram from his wife reading, "Hell Broke Loose in Kingston You

Must Come." Manley said to me then (because perhaps I was one of the persons who had tried to persuade him to go into active politics) he said to me then, "the Commission has adjourned. I must go into Kingston and see what I can do for the people." With that he left; he remained in work for the people at every level for the rest of his life.

When he arrived in Kingston it was a great turmoil although blodshed wasn't involved except where the police had to fire occasionally. Manley made a pact with the Governor and with the Courts by means of which Bustamante would be released on bail. And Manley also went and held a vast meeting with the striking workers on the waterfront, thousands and thousands of them.

The fact is that Bustamante was never further charged. He was released and, in the confusion and danger of the situation, Norman Manley undertook to be public mediator in all these matters. For the rest of his life, he was continuing the public work of leadership which he started that day. When Manley addressed the workers on the waterfront, he was tremendously impressed by their zest and spirit and determination and by their uproarious response of acceptance for his advice to them to be patient, to be steadfast and to be assured that their problems would receive attention, and that he would see that Bustamante would be freed.

Manley told me afterwards, bearing in mind that he had never been a public speaker in that sense, that never before had he so moved a vast concourse of people and be so moved by them. It may be that he naturally accepted that some of the approbation of this vast crowd was for him personally, and did not realise totally that he was there as an adjutant speaking for the accepted Labour Leader. This became clear as he started to make speeches to groups and at street corners as the problems of settling the industrial dislocation of the island continued. And he would be very puzzled on occasions by the lack of response that his speeches received from the very same type of people who had so effusively cheered him. That was to stay with him for the rest of his life. Even his best friends and his most ardent supporters will say that Norman Manley spoke best at public political meetings when he was speaking on behalf of someone else, defending one of his colleagues or supporters, but hardly effectively, as in Federation Referendum when he was, so to speak, calling for support for his own ideas, his own principles and his own policies. It is probably the art of the advocate to be able to speak for others, but not always to be able to speak as effectively on his own personal behalf.

Fairly widespread turmoil continued in the island and, by tragic coincidence, the Governor, Sir Edward Denham, was stricken with diverticulitis, underwent surgery at the Kingston Public Hospital and died. The demonstrating worker-type public naturally regarded this as some sort of spiritual victory for them in their protest; they became even more demonstrative especially in the city and in some of the rural parishes like St. Mary and St. James.

The acting Governor, Arthur Woolley, consulted with Manley and Bustamante - Manley as National Mediator and Bustamante as National Labour Leader. A plan was devised to announce land for the people and a new deal. The Gleaner, at the government's request brought all this out on a Sunday (the first Sunday Gleaner in history). And I was ordered to go along with Manley and Bustamante to St. Mary to distribute these newspapers to the crowds which were to be addressed by Manley and Bustamante to persuade them to moderate their anger and to be patient, that better things were ahead.

This was done without incident one whole Sunday until late at night, and Manley would on occasion say to me and to others, "How did my speech go?" He was quite uncertain of the effect his public advocacy was having on these people in turmoil. For most of the day Bustamante was equally uncertain because Manley and himself were, in a sense, playing with fire since St. Mary was in an angry mood. However, Bustamante achieved a break-through at the last meeting of the night we spent at Manley's and Bustamante's cousins, the Purcells in Annotto Bay. It was a good day's work because in fact very little disturbance occurred subsequently in St. Mary, and a High Court Judge was appointed to hold Sessions and hearings from the people as to what was in fact happening in that parish. This served to restore confidence and to abate hostility.

The details of how Manley set up a Public Committee, negotiated with some of the employers and eventually got Governor Denham round to giving agreement to Bustamante's release is set out patiently and clearly in Manley's Autobiography. This was an unfinished work and his writing ended just at the point where these negotiations and crises were being analysed in retrospect.

The fact is that from then on Manley was in public life. Arising out of the national crisis, a number of left wing persons, notably N.N. Nethersole and Ken Hill, who were among those who had sought previously to persuade Norman Manley to form a political party and to come out in public life, got closer to Manley now, along with left winger, Vernon Arnett and centrists William Seivright and O.T. Fairclough. With others, the idea was confirmed that a political party should be formed. So, on September 18, 1938, the People's National Party was founded publicly at a large meeting at the Ward Theatre in Kingston. It was a party which had everything in it. O.T. Fairclough who had lived in Haiti for many years had a concept, though not spoken, of an elitist party and he, as founding secretary, recruited a great number of upper class, planter class, business class persons to rally to Manley and save Jamaica. The leftists had quite different ideas and were the prevailing influence because, even without their knowledge, Norman Manley had invited the austere socialist, Sir Stafford Cripps of the British Labour Party (also a relative of Edna Manley) to make the keynote speech.

There was the picture of a very staid, influential Jamaican audience packing the Ward Theatre coming away staggered by a socialist spokesman's announcements. Although the party did not formally declare itself socialist for some years, there were the beginnings of schism, for some people who believed in

Norman Manley and wished to come under his leadership, wondered whether the party was not in fact to be an extremist party. Indeed, in Norman Manley's own speech at the opening of the party, he said: "I take the view that no amount of benevolent administration will ever produce a people with a national spirit unless they possess a political organisation in which they share and which marches with the destiny of the people as a whole."

After the launching of the party, Manley was everywhere at the same time. He did his legal work and yet he was everywhere in the island organising, building groups, helping to create the realism and the potential structure of a national political party. In all this Manley remained "unshaken in his socialism, albeit it was of a mild brand, and nothing could budge him from his belief that voting in a democracy must be on the basis of adult manhood suffrage without a literacy test." This was to be one of the crucial problems that lay ahead; but Manley never flinched from his belief in adult suffrage without a literacy test.

Manley had committed himself to Universal Adult Suffrage. It was the basis upon which Jamaica has made its political progress and was the factor that worked so strongly against Manley and his Party when they came to face the electorate in 1944 under Adult Suffrage, defeated severely by the Jamaica Labour Party under Alexander Bustamante.

Having committed himself to the philosophy of adult suffrage, Manley went on to give his party a practical basis, namely a trade union movement. Bustamante gave no intimation then of political ambition. In fact he had sat on the platform at the foundation meeting of the People's National Party. Manley made the attempt to copy British institutions and weld all the existing unions, including the Bustamante Industrial Trade Union, into one Trade Union Congress. There then existed a number of craft unions, clerks, tobacco workers and the like and these, Manley suggested, might merge with Bustamante's union into a Trade Union Congress. Bustamante suspected, resented and eventually rejected this form of combination because, under that, he would be outnumbered in voting by a vote for each union, when in fact he had the large majority of the working class organised. And so, the Trade Union Council was formed as a conglomerate of all the former existing craft unions; leaders like Florizel Glasspole, a centrist, came into the picture of party and union. The union of these craft groups grew from strength to strength but in no way approximated the numbers of the BITU. But it was a basis, and upon that basis the People's National Party and the TUC as affiliate body moved forward and prospered.

Manley regarded Bustamante's rejection of the proferred Union grouping as "selfish" and "treacherous". He spoke often of how he had saved Bustamante; he called Bustamante a mountebank. The Gleaner obituary says however "Manley never failed to check his anger and remind his listeners that circumstances had given Bustamante an important role to play in the island's struggle, and that there would be occasions when it would serve the general cause to support him, if only for the greater political good."

The Gleaner's obituary continues "With the outbreak of World War II in September 1939, Manley's career entered a third phase. He had already turned down the post of Attorney General, later a Chief Justiceship and a Knighthood."

Leaders and factions had been unanimous in pledging themselves to support the war effort. Manley made it clear that he would continue to work for Jamaican self-government and the building of labour unionism along sound lines. He said that, if properly conducted, there was nothing in either activity that should alarm the authorities. Whether he believed at the start that others would be as moderate as he, is an open question.

The fact is that Bustamante did not play that game and carried his trade union tensions to the point where in fact he was interned under Defence Regulations by the Governor, Sir Arthur Richards. Manley, true to his general philosophy and no doubt because it was also in the interest of his Union, carried on the Bustamante Union through the T.U.C. officers during the period of Bustamante's internment.

It was around that time also that Manley and the People's National Party declared themselves formally to be socialists. The party had been a general party including all elements, right, left and centre, but after Sir Stafford Cripps had given it a socialist tint in his inaugural speech, the left wingers gained more and more ground inside the Party.

I remember speaking to Norman Manley on his way from court one day and asking him whether he did not think that to try and sell self-government was a big enough task to achieve successfully, and if he did not think that to add another massive purpose - socialism - to that programme was probably biting off more than could be chewed.

His reply was very, very cold, distant and thoughtful. He stopped walking and said, "You know, this war that is on, after this war, the world is going to be a socialist world, so we might as well be prepared for it."

The fact that subsequently the party abandoned socialism as a doctrine for many years doesn't alter the assessment that Manley, from the start, was a socialist. And ultimately his party was to become fairly extreme socialist after he had passed away.

Norman Manley was one of the spear-heads in the negotiation for a new constitution for Jamaica although his party held no representation in the legislature of those days. And eventually he won out on the basis that the new constitution and the new Legislature should be based on adult suffrage. Thus were the first elections of December 1944 to come about. He lost those elections disastrously, gaining only five of the 32 seats.

He himself failed to gain a seat in the legislature largely because he had
162

changed his image as the rational mediator and had become brash and almost reckless in his support of the more rabid left wing elements of the party. Indeed, on the day the constitution was first proclaimed with a great parade in the main square of the city, Norman Manley, through friendship with a member of the Kingston Parish Church, which stands on one corner of the square, got himself into the church and up into the clock tower where he was seen during this great parade waving a clenched fist from high on top of this bell tower.

This created shock waves throughout the upper and middle classes, to think that Norman Manley was now a rabid political personality. And so he lost the seat he contested in that 1944 election and only succeeded five years later when again, however, his Party was defeated. But during those long years in the wilderness, opportunity was taken to strengthen the Union side of the political movement and the TUC grew much stronger, though it had internal stresses between the left-wingers such as Richard Hart, Frank Hill, Ken Hill and centerists like Florizel Glasspole. But the left wingers seemed to have over-shot their arrow. They grew so arrogant in the power they exercised in the political movement as well as in the Union that they seemed to have had ambitions of unseating Norman Manley. And he sensed that. The result was that the press and other interests were clamouring for Manley to declare whether it was a party of the philosophy of its leader and its moderates, or was it a party of the left wing who seemed to have bigger public image than the leaders in the party. Manley bore with this for quite a while and then suddenly he announced a purge, a trial. This led to the ousting of extreme left wingers Richard Hart, Ken Hill, Frank Hill and Arthur Henry - the four H's - from the Party.

The basis upon which they were expelled was that they had Marxist aims for the party which was not a Marxist Party. In a sense the charge was one merely of convenience because the party was a Fabian Socialist party in its main leadership. But a great politicain takes no decisions that are critical unless there are at least three sound reasons for it. In this case, Norman Manley had at least three sound reasons. Firstly, his own leadership of the party was being threatened by this group. Secondly, it seemed expedient for the party to be free of these left wingers for the next election which would be in 1955. Thirdly, he knew that his son, Michael, who had been at London School of Economics, another Fabian centre, was shortly to come out to Jamaica. So that Norman Manley knew then that he could free himself of these street-corner demagogues and re-equip himself with a new popular front through his son, Michael. And so said, so done.

The description of the Red Purge as given in the Gleaner's obituary of Norman Manley is that a major problem loomed behind the scenes at that time. Manley had held from the start that all types of leftists were welcome in the PNP, provided that they undertook to give complete loyalty to the programme and policy of the party, which was socialist along moderate lines, while flatly declaring that it opposed communism. Even before the election there had been rumours that exremists were plotting to disrupt the T.U.C. and then to form "red" cells aiming at control of the party. If this became generally known and steps were not taken against it, the PNP could never expect to win the next elections in '54-'55.

"Those close to Manley were aware that he hesitated for a long time, reluctant to go counter to his theories about the freedom of ideas. At last he approved the setting up of a Commission of Enquiry by the Executive of the Party. The hearing commenced on December 27, 1951, and continued from week-end to week-end until February 3, 1952. The taking of evidence occupied sixteen full days.

"The charges were to the effect that Ken Hill, Frank Hill, Richard Hart and Arthur Henry of the T.U.C. had been engaged with others in the dissemination of communist doctrine. It was also shown that the leftists had received a contribution of £500 as recently as December 1951, from the 'satellite' state of Czechoslovakia. The four leading figures, Ken Hill, Frank Hill, Richard Hart and Arthur Henry were found culpable as charged and forced to resign from the PNP. Six others were censored. Following this act, a new Union, the National Workers' Union, was formed to take the place of the disrupted T.U.C. as the voice of labour sympathetic to the People's National Party. This Union, the National Workers' Union, today dominates the industrial scene alongside the Bustamante Trade Union."

When Michael Manley came home to Jamaica, he became for a time a member of the staff of the Party newspaper Public Opinion. Then he became a supervisor of the new trade union, the National Workers' Union, where in fact he physically replaced the four H's who were the dominant figures previous to this in the National Workers' Union.

Having lost two General Elections in a row, those of 1944 and 1949, Manley and his party, with a new look went into the elections of 1955 and won. The People's National Party won 18 of the 32 seats and the Jamaica Labour Party, which had been reigning from 1944, gained 14 seats. So Norman Manley became at last Chief Minister of Jamaica and, in 1959, he won an even more sweeping victory. The Gleaner's obituary states that Manley's administration placed heavy emphasis upon agriculture and education, with the encouragement of new industries also a priority. Livestock, poultry and all standard crops were assisted. Products were increased and new markets opened. The public library system was widely expanded and the Jamaica Broadcasting Corporation was founded to be operated partly on commercial lines and partly as a State Corporation for the provision of entertainment, instruction and the fostering of local talent. New incentive laws were passed which resulted in the opening of more factories, most of them financed by overseas capital. A notable contribution to the increase in national revenue was made by the deal with the Bauxite Companies which raised the amount Jamaica got for every ton of bauxite mined from 2/8d to 14/-. Projects on a grand scale included the work of the Palisadoes Recreation Development Committee, the plan to develop Negril Beach, which has been called the finest beach land in the world, then lying unused, and various housing schemes in Kingston and suburban St. Andrew.

Manley made several trips to London in the interest of the Federation of the West Indies and in February, 1958 it was formally established.

This is the crucial point in the history of Norman Washington Manley and not only of himself, but of Jamaica itself. Norman Manley, the chief proponent of a Federation of the West Indies, having joined in accomplishing the foundation of the federation himself, had early doubts and declined to seek election to the Federal Parliament. Manley for some time reserved the announcement of his decision as to whether he would seek federal election or not. I was not deceived by this delay for his wife, Edna, had told me while the Capital Site Conference was on in Jamaica that if Jamaica did not get the capital site, Norman could not go to Federation. I asked her why and she said "I will not have him living in a suitcase between two capitals a thousand miles apart." I said, "Well, I am sorry, it seems therefore that Norman will not be going to Federation because it was quite clear Jamaica will not be getting the Federal capital site." And so it came about that the Leader of the Federal movement in Jamaica declined to serve in the Federal Government and did not seek election, which brought about the choice of Grantley Adams as Prime Minister; and the eventual break-up of Federation.

In the event, Federation did not gain popular support in Jamaica. Indeed, Norman Manley's party, the Federal Labour Party, lost the Federal Elections and Bustamante's Jamaica Labour Party, which had been critical at all times of the Federation, got the majority in that election. It was an ominous sign. As the Federation proceeded with ham-handed administration by the Governor-General, Lord Hayles, and by the Prime Minister, Sir Grantley Adams, Jamaica cooled more and more towards the Federation.

Manley shifted his positions adroitly. He wished to save the Federation he had done so much to foster, but he realised that its opponents had two powerful arguments. The plans for the economic development of Jamaica - his own plans after all - must not be hampered by Federal customs regulations and taxation. Jamaica's majority position must be protected by proportional representation in Parliament so that Jamaica would be more strongly represented. All this was bruited about, all the while Manley becoming more disillusioned and Jamaica more discontented with Federation. This festered over the years until 1960 when, largely because of intransigence by the Eastern Caribbean towards Jamaica (and especially so by Dr. Eric Williams), Manley had to take a critical decision and he took it. He called a referendum to decide whether Jamaica would remain in Federation or would become an independent sovereign country.

I said in a speech to the University in 1974:

"Had Manley called an election he could have disciplined all his Ministers and Members of the House to fight for victory - just as he had done in 1959. But he chose a referendum. A referendum did not imperil his colleagues' seats or cost them money, but also it did not force them to fight to win the referendum. I

165

am sure that Norman Manley knew that if he lost that referendum he would lose all; he fought that fight almost single-handed - and lost. . . . .

" . . . . .There was more to it than that. My knowledge of the events of those times is that the only way the British Government (whose agent was the late Iain MacLeod, one of the cleverest Ministers Britain had), the only way that Britain would let Jamaica out was that it should vote "no" at a referendum, not at an election. MacLeod had looked at the picture, and so declared that Manley having lost the 1958 Federal Election and having won the 1959 General Election, should not be allowed to have a General Election about secession from Federation but should be required to leave it wholly to a referendum response by the people. . . .

" . . . . .MacLeod exacted the price that Jamaica would be let out of Federation only if the referendum so said; the further price would be that independence for Jamaica, if it came, would require a new election. The dictate was that Norman Manley and his Party would need a new mandate from the people since the last time they went to the polls they were committed to a Federation and not to solitary independence for Jamaica.

"Indeed, the Independence Conference in London was most unusual. At the conference, presided over by MacLeod's successor, Reginald Maudling, few realised - not even Buckingham Palace it seems - that Manley was not there as Premier but as joint leader along with Alexander Bustamante. When they were both bidden to lunch at Buckingham Palace, the truth came out. Bustamante objected to being invited as Leader of the Opposition. The Queen then issued new invitations to them as joint leaders. No surprise, then, that Jamaica had to have pre-Independence elections. That was the sacrifice, the price paid by National Hero, Norman Washington Manley, to obtain Jamaica's secession from the federation he had helped to create.

"As I pointed out, no other Commonwealth West Indian leader had been required to have an election before the Independence of his country. Jamaica paid that price: Norman Manley's sacrifice."

From this it would seem that Ian MacLeod had been most severe on Norman Manley. But it was MacLeod who helped to find the formula by which Manley got the chance of taking Jamaica out of Federation. The Federation was a legal entity and Jamaica belonged to it and was part of it and had no legal right to secede. The Federation was going on towards full independence as a sovereign nation, as Dr. Eric Williams so often insisted it should. But there was very little hope for it to continue, though it was legal; a way was found by MacLeod for Norman Manley by a referendum followed by an election if the referendum declared for independence. MacLeod was very, very much a supporter of Norman Manley. Indeed, it has been stated - and the statement has gained some credence - that Ian MacLeod offered Sir Grantley Adams a peerage if he would resign as

Federal Prime Minister in order to bring Norman Manley in to see if the Federation could then be saved. Grantley Adams did not acept any such offer and the Federation went on tottering, forcing Manley to have a referendum. Whether Manley ever hoped to win the referendum or not is uncertain. My hunch is that he played it two ways: if he won the referendum then all well and good. If he lost it, he would have achieved independence for Jamaica, which was one of his earliest ambitions.

So having lost the referendum, he and Bustamante and their groups went to London and, in February 1962, finalised the new Constitution for an independent Jamaica to come into existence on the first Monday in August 1962, as it did. In London at the time when as Leader of his party's delegation at the Howard Hotel he announced to the Jamaican press the April date of the General Election, I said to him quietly afterwards: "You have called an election that you cannot win." He said: "Why can't I?" I said: "You can't win Cornwall."

He looked far away and said softly: "Well, that's where the fight is."

As I said at the University occasion:

"I know that he knew that for him disaster lay ahead. He paid the sacrifice of not being the first Prime Minister of the country for which he had fought unswervingly for independence and sovereignty.

Norman Manley took his defeat in the 1962 Independence Election with calm. He plunged into his new role of Opposition Leader with energy and determination. Meantime, he and his party made plans to woo the countryside and to win back the support which they had previously enjoyed.

In 196p, says the Gleaner's obituary, Mr. Manley decided that his party needed a new look. Its policies he averred, were too close to those of the Jamaica Labour Party. He took the matter to the PNP Executive and they appointed a Committee headed by Mr. David Coore, Q.C. and including left-wingers, Mr. Allan Isaacs and Mr. Vernon Arnett.

"The result of the committee was a return to the socialist programme of the PNP, declared in the 1940's. This nearly wrecked the party again. At the annual meeting of the party held in November 1964, Mr. Manley had to use his own personal influence to keep the party together when both sides clashed boisterously. He postponed further consideration of the programme and got the executive, the National Executive Council, and eventually the party to agree to new proposals which represented a compromise between the left wing and the moderates in the party. Socialism was still the policy, but it had been watered down to include private enterprise and private enterprise in co-operation with the government, as well as co-operatives."

As the Gleaner said at the time of Norman Washington Manley's death, although privately deploring the compromise, Norman Manley proved himself again the ideal party leader by accepting the decision of the majority and backing it in all respects. So that when Norman Washington Manley died, the PNP was once again an avowed socialist party, dedicated to social reform which had been the central motif of his long and distinguished public career.

It is now a matter of history that Norman Manley's son, Michael, adopting this philosophy won the 1972 elections and then proceeded to harden this combined policy into "Democratic Socialism" on which basis he conducted the 1976 elections which he won by a landslide.

On the day after his death I wrote this summation of the great man:

"Norman Manley was in every sense a great man. His stamp of greatness was no mere insular magnificence; he had the mind and the measure of the truly great anywhere. Whether in things of the intellect, in the skills of the law, in the arts of life, in public dedication or in family devotion, his was the genius of total and unselfish commitment. Indeed, his faults lay mostly in his very virtues - his righteous sense of consistency; an almost fanatic loyalty to those who marched the rugged course of life beside him; a commitment to principle even when in political terms the practical course was sharply different on the nation's compass. And through all this, be it victory or vicissitude, he loved with unquesting fidelity the magic circle of those who, by birth, sacrament or mutual patriotic intimacy, became his large and loyal family.

"Such was the man, a marvel among men yet so simple as a person. He was father, prophet, leader, fighter, but having all those external roles, within him when in the hours of quiet he shed his public armour, he was tender, even shy; solicitous in deep silences, rustic with the folk and moods of high mountains; steeped silently in communion with the graphic arts; transported with the romance of music or intrigued with its abstractions; living a shared creative life with his gifted partner. In these retreats from the arena, his soul and spirit were re-charged and nourished for the drain and drama of his public life."

All in all, Norman Washington Manley achieved all the heights and suffered all the despondencies of a career in public life, devoted at all times to his people, his nation and to fulfilment of the great talents given to him.

THE RIGHT HONOURABLE
GEORGE CABLE PRICE

BORN BELIZE CITY, BELIZE, 15TH JANUARY, 1919

CHIEF MINISTER OF BELIZE (1961-1963)
PREMIER OF BELIZE (1964-1981)
PRIME MINISTER OF BELIZE (1981-1984, 1989)

10

GEORGE CABLE PRICE

GEORGE CABLE PRICE, on becoming first Premier of Belize at age 57, in 1976, faced a most critical problem, a problem unlike that of any other Caribbean country. His country, Belize (formerly British Honduras) was almost beleaguered by the acquisitive aggresssiveness of Guatemala, its southern and western neighbour. Belize became an associate member of the United Nations and although the U.N. General Assembly endorsed a resolution which re-affirmed "the inalienable right of the people of Belize to self-determination and independence" and declared that "the inviolability and territorial integrity of Belize must be preserved", Guatemala persists in its claim to nearly one-half of Belize.

Indeed on 4th February, 1976, Guatemala had organised a march of a million of its people to its capital and then to the borders of Belize in a threatening, menacing action. Providentially for Belize, on that day Guatemala City was stricken by a vast, disastrous earthquake and so that act of terror did not come off. Premier Price's problem was that Britain was still responsible for the security of Belize and therefore had the duty of repelling any Guatemalan attacks on the territory. The United Kingdom had military forces of various sizes in the area intended to discourage Guatemala from taking aggressive action against a small people. But Mr. Price, if he opted for independence, had at once to find his own armaments to cope with the threat on his borders, which could only mean impoverishing the country to provide weapons instead of pushing ahead with economic development.

In the political international sphere, Belize had good support from individual leaders of the Organisation of American States. It had strong support from the Commonwealth Heads of Governments meeting in Jamaica in 1974, but Guatemala has not renounced its intention. The position of Guatemala at all talks had been rigid and inflexible. Guatemala had demanded, as the price for settlement of the dispute and for the secure independence of Belize, the cession of one-quarter of the territory of Belize to Guatemala.

"This preposterous and contemptuous proposal," stated a Belize official document "has been rejected out of hand, and Belize now faces the prospect of an indefinite prolongation of its colonial status, a status which is an affront to the dignity and an obstacle to the development of the Belizean people." The official stand of the Government of Belize was that neither Guatemala nor Spain nor any other country settled or exercised at any time effective jurisdiction over the territory. There were occasions when the right of settlement was militarily challenged by Spain, but the last such challenge in 1798 was repulsed, and the people of Belize have remained completely undisturbed since then.

Who are the people of Belize? A land of 8,600 square miles on the Central American mainland which also has dominion over 266 square miles of islands. The territory was settled by Britishers in the first half of the 17th century. By the first quarter of the 18th century, Africans were imported into the settlement as slaves, and they soon greatly outnumbered the whites. During the 19th century, there was an influx of Maya, Mestizo (Spanish/Maya) and also Carib refugees from the Eastern Caribbean. The population has been augmented at various times by immigrants from Asia, the Caribbean, Central America and from the Middle East. Europeans account for only about 3% of the population, whilst the rest is made up of persons of Maya, African and Asian descent. More than 95% of the people living in Belize today were born in Belize and regard themselves as Belizeans, a distinct people. But Belize is a land, large thouugh it is, of only 140,000 people, compared to Guatemala, a larger country with six million people.

Premier Price was indefatigable in seeking international support of every kind for the perpetuation of the independence or the guarantee of the independence of the nation and people of Belize. The first press interview I had with Mr. Price was way back in 1963 when the country was still British Honduras. He made it clear that they would not surrender even one square centimeter of their national territory; that every citizen could be assured that they did not intend to be integrated, reincorporated, assimilated or taken over by any country. It was clearly stated then that the new nation would be the nation of Belize (which derives from the Maya words "be" which means a road and "likin" which means towards the east. Hence Belikin - Belize - the road to the east. In 1976 Guatemala was still insisting on rights and claims whch history cannot support, even though Spain at one time claimed territorial rights in ancient Belize.

In conversations with Premier Price in 1976 he said, that looking back say to 1957, the British at that time never gave British Honduras any encouragement that the country would ever become independent or ever have a self-governing constitution. It was just a colony as far as they were concerned, with no future. And so Premier Price thought that, as they were not independent, they could not get into international organisations where their voice could be heard. "So we were very much opposed to the British colonial system. We used to say the iniquitous British colonial system. It was like a war cry."

Mr. Price related that they thought that they would look for help elsewhere. They went to Mexico. They went to the United States. They went to other Republics. The one which showed an interest then was Guatemala, which was interested in getting rid of the colonial system in Central America. So, for a time, Guatemala and Belize went parallel roads fighting the colonial system. But there came a time when it became very clear that while Belize - represented by Price's People's United Party - saw the final objective as independence, Guatemala saw their final objective as incorporating Belize. "At that time then we found we could no longer travel the parallel roads", says Mr. Price, "we were then opposed, and we told Guatemala so. We cannot get along any more with the British colonial system because we in Belize want not only the British colonial system to be dissolved, but to go for ourselves on to independence."

Premier Price related that in 1957 they went to London to discuss economic aid for Belize. They took with them an economic plan. Looking back at it later, he said: "It might have been an elementary plan, but nevertheless it was a plan, the cost of which, if I remember rightly, might have been $16 million. And all the British were willing to offer to help finance the plan was no more than $2 million."

It was during that visit to London that he met the Guatemalan Ambassador to Britain. The Ambassador invited him to listen to a proposal where there would be an associate state Belize, with economic aid to develop the territory of Belize.

"I listened to the Guatemalan Ambassador's proposals and said, 'well, let's think it over.' I didn't say yes, I didn't say no, but in my mind that was a lever to use in negotiations with the British Colonial Office: You only give us $2 million when we need $16 million, and here is somebody offering us $16 million and more. Can't you do better? But evidently I was not allowed to think that way in those days. I was a colonial subject with no free mind. I was not supposed to do that, but I think what made it worse was that two of my colleagues, Mr. Glenbigh Jeffrey and Mr. Henry Bowman, were terrified at the very fact that there was such a concept. They were alarmed that I even said let us use it as a lever, and one of them or both of them told the Governor, Governor Colin Thornley, that I was negotiating with the Guatemalans. They didn't put it the way it was, they just exaggerated it.

"While that was going on, we had an understanding among the four delegates, Mr. Katoose, Mr. Bowman, Mr. Jeffrey and myself that we would keep this quiet. And so it came as a surprise to me when the then Secretary of State for the Colonies, Mr. Lennox Boyd, called us in, put us at a large table with all his advisers on the Colonies - the whole Colonial Office . Governor Thornley sat there and accused me right away of having talks with Guatemala. I straightaway denied this, having made a previous arrangement with my colleagues that we would say no to anybody. So I said no. And I said no to them to the very end. It was then that Lennox Boyd said he would adjourn the meeting, we would meet again, and I was to tell him what had happened.

"We adjourned and I said we keep the same arrangement, keep it to ourselves.

"I then went to Germany, went to Cologne to try and interest some firm there in timber projects in plywood and wallboard. On my return to London, we agreed that the arrangement to say no still stood. So when we went for the second meeting, I said no, we had no such encounter with Guatemala. Lennox Boyd said then he would send us all back home; he would discontinue the talks because he knew - even though I said we did not have such talks - that we did have talks with the Guatemalans. Governor Thornley said he would go and tell the people what I was doing and the people would all turn against me. It was then that I said: 'I will fight you to the bitter end on that.' "

Premier Price continued the story:
"We broke up the meeting and that same night I was able to get out of London. We were to get on a ship; it wasn't air-plane. I went to the Colonial Treasurer, Mr. Oates, to get an advance. He would not give us an advance, but fortunately we knew some oil people from Shell Oil Company and they advanced us the money. We bought tickets on the Pan American plane, and Mr. Katoose and I beat the Governor to Miami and arrived on the same plane in Belize City. But I made sure that I got out the plane first that day. We told our story to the people. We told of the events. I don't like the word story, because it has a connotation. I related the incidents and the debate in the Legislative Council was broadcast.

"The Colonial Secretary was the prosecutor. The Governor himself got on the radio first and practically condemned me, saying that I was selling the country to Guatemala, lock, stock and barrel. In the debate on radio, the Colonial Secretary was like the prosecuting attorney. Mr. Jeffrey and Mr. Bowman spoke against me. I was called a swine. But Mr. Katoose stood up in my defence and I defended myself. And in all humility, I must say that after I was finished there was a loud applause in the Legislative Council and its surroundings and I could see how the officials blanched, turned white as a sheet, surprised. Here was someone they called a traitor being acclaimed by his own people as having stood up to the Colonial Office.

"That was in 1957, and I was turned out of the Executive Council. That was the crisis. The British themselves and some of their spokesmen had termed those incidents as an unpardonable crime against the Belizean people, creating a phobia in the minds of the people, a psychosis of fear, that even to talk to Guatemala about Belize was treacherous. The British Government have made any settlement very difficult because they have never come outright and told the Belizean people:

'We cannot sustain you any longer as a colony; we cannot give you a defence guarantee because we are cutting down our defence budget.' They have not done so and what is being done today, in 1976, is we are trying to reach a settlement, a just settlement preserving our rights and achieving our independence and preserving our territorial integrity. This has been made doubly difficult because of the happenings of the past created by the British Colonial Office."

Of those days in 1957 when he was turned out of the Executive Council, Mr. Price says:

"I was in the doghouse. I was out of the Executive, but I was still in the Legislature. They could not expel me from the Legislative Assembly because the people put me there, but they could put me out of the Executive Council. And so in 1958, '59 and 1960, we carried on our agitation even though I was outside of the Executive Council. I travelled the country; I worked up the party with the help of loyal party workers. I couldn't have done it alone. And it was then in 1960, I think, they sent Sir Clifford Blood, a Constitutional Commissioner, who recommended for Belize the Ministerial system and self-government; the Constitution we have today.

"We went to elections in 1961 and my party won all 18 seats. And when I was called in by Sir Colin Thornley to form the new government, he said: 'It's incredible, incredible.' He couldn't believe what had happened, the same man who kicked me out, he had to meet us again. Then out of that system came full self-government when the Governor was no longer, and is no longer Chairman of the Cabinet. But even when the Governor was Chairman of the Cabinet, we were practising self-government all those years by having our own Cabinet meeting, say on Monday, and then I met as Chairman on Tuesday with the Governor with everything already cut and dried.

"It was in those years that it became more clear to us and we became more convinced that we could not go into independence unless either the Guatemalans withdrew their claim to Belize or we had a Defence Guarantee. At that time in 1964 when we moved into self-government, the Guatemalans protested and broke off diplomatic relations with London because they complained that the British Government had not cleared with them the decision to grant full, internal self-government to Belize.

"So, at that stage we knew we had either to get the Guatemalans to remove their claim or have a Defence Guarantee. We tried again through mediation. There were several meetings with the Guatemalans, the British and the Belizeans and it was decided to ask the United States to mediate. The United States set up a mediator, Mr. Bethuel Webster, a New York lawyer. He gave his mediation in April or May of 1968. Then another curious thing happened. During the mediation we had invited the Opposition to take part. By this time in '65 there had been another election. We had won 18 seats in 1961 and in 1965 we won 16 of the 18 seats and the other party the N.I.P., the National Independence Party, won two - Mr. Goldson and Mr. Murray. We had a written agreement between Mr. Goldson and me that on the release of the mediator's report we would do nothing about it without consulting each other and together we would reach a decision on what we would do. I worked by the agreement, trusting he would do so, but he broke the agreement. A few minutes after the mediator's report was made public, he called a mid-day meeting near the National Assembly building in Belize City. He frightened the people. He spread alarm that we in government, the People's United Party, were going to accept the Webster Report."

Mr. Price explained that the Webster Report was apparently pro-independence, saying there should be an independent Belize, that was in the first paragraph.

"But every paragraph thereafter was to hinder th way to independence - that we would have to consult Guatemala on foreign affairs, that we would have to do this and the other. In carrying out the agreement, I thought we would at least put it to the country and hear their views, knowing that it was not suitable but we would go through the motions of consultation with the people. But Mr. Goldson didn't wait for that. He stirred up civil unrest. There was stoning of buildings; people running through the streets setting fire to dirt boxes, vandalism.

"We maintained the situation for eight days after consulting the country, and then we finally decided after the eight days that we would reject it. I would like to make the point here that it is not that we did not make up our minds from the very start that it was not suitable, but we had an agreement to consult each other and we had an agreement, an undertaking, to consult the people. So it could not be said that we did it on our own. We talked to the people.

"We got over that in 1968. Now, Belize is a Central American country geographically and to that extent it has a Central American destiny. But the world does not stand still. The Caribbean Sea is so wide that it takes in Mexico, it washes Mexico, it washes Central America, it washes South America and the island countries. So there came about an evolution of thinking, an evolution of regional development. There was this Caribbean Community, a new concept of the old West Indian Federation. Belize is Caribbean. So we said 'well, Central America, anytime we try to make some advances or to try to get into the Central American regional development, we are blocked by Guatemala.' Belize cannot live alone in this world; we have to join with someone. So we joined CARIFTA first, then CARICOM. And it was arranged very well.

"The name Belize is Caribbean; it's not West Indian; it's Caribbean. CARICOM is an organisation of independent countries as well as non-independent; but the very fact that there are independent countries in it makes way for the non-independent to become independent some day. There is a clause that if you don't like it, you can come out. There is unanimity of voting, not majority and minority. And I think CARICOM has helped us very well. But for the Regional

Bank, Caribbean Development Bank, we would not have been able to finance many of our projects today-electrification, agriculture, industry, tourism, housing."

But, the Premier said, other things were happening. The sub-regions were merging into one big region. There were groupings in the area such as CARICOM, the Central American Community of Common Market, Andean countries, and the Latin American Free Trade Association.

"And you see where they are merging together in a shipping line - Jamaica, Costa Rica, Trinidad and Guyana. We see it in sugar; we see it in bauxite. So, as I see it, the Caribbean Community will be expanded to take in some of Central America and Belize will then form the chain link that can bring both groups together. We are Central American and we are Caribbean. Today the future is in this kind of thinking.

"What we have done is try - failing a Defence Guarantee from the British - to win friends in the world today. We have been trying very hard to win friends for Belize and in the last three years this is what we have done. We have attended the Panama Conference of the Security Council where Guyana spearheaded the cause of Belize, urging that the Guatemalan claim to Belize is a potential threat to the peace of the Americas. It was then that Mr. Salim Salim of Tanzania said: 'Price, you should internationalise Belize.' We took him at his word and we worked on it. Our Minister of Home Affairs, the Deputy Premier, Mr. Lindberg Rogers - a pillar of strength, visited some African countries, Egypt, Tanzania, Sudan, Kenya, and so on, winning support for Belize for the day when we went to the United Nations.

"Then Prime Minister Manley of Jamaica raised this Belize question in Algiers at the Third World Conference. Then there was the Commonwealth Heads of Government Conference at which we got full support for an independent Belize. A few months afterwards, Mr. Rogers and our Attorney General, Mr. Shoman, went to Lima, Peru, and also got support from the Third World. After that it was United Nations and the vote that made history, one of the motions that got the highest number of votes in the United Nations. The vote asked the Guatemalans and the British to get together, settle their differences over Belize so that Belize could emerge as an independent country with its territorial integrity; and for a report to be brought back to the next sitting of the United Nations this year (1976).

"Then another curious thing happened. The first series of talks under the umbrella of the United Nations motion was to have been on February 9, in New Orleans this year; and the Guatemalan Government was organising a big demonstration for federalcy. They counted they could have got a million people to march on the capital and some to march into our country from the border. Providentially that was stopped by the earthquake of February, so all that was stopped. Now, they are talking; proposals are being exchanged. The time has not come to make some of it public yet because nothing definite has been reached to tell the people. But the future I hope is that we will go back to the United Nations and out of that I hope the Guatemalans will change their attitude towards Belize."

177

Who is this George Cable Price? He was born on 15 January, 1919 in Belize City, right after World War I, when Spanish influenza in severe epidemic form was a scourge in Belize City. George says that he has been told that at the time of his birth he had to be fed from a cow that was kept in the yard and gave milk to young ones in Belize City. He was the third child and the first boy in the family of 11 children. His father's name was William Cable Price and his mother was Irene Cecelia Escalante, married six years before he was born. Belize was then the capital of the country with a population of perhaps 10,000 and isolated from the rest of the country, except by sea and by river.

George Price likes to describe himself as a Central American man, "that is, made up of all the races that are in Belize - African, Mayan, Spanish, Welsh, Scottish, a bit of Hindu - in sum all the races."

George remembers Belize City as a small town. He was baptised at the Holy Redeemer Cathedral, his family being Catholic. He says he was baptised by the then Bishop, Bishop Hopkins, who was drowned on his way to Corozal town in 1923. George says his childhood was a happy one. There were no worries. Belize City was a small place and the whole world was then Belize City in the country of British Honduras, as it was then.

He went to a Parish School - the Holy Redeemer. In Belize the Church/ State school system was that the Churches had schools which were financed by the Government.

There were no rich people in Belize in those days, Premier Price recalls. Perhaps, he said, you could call his family middle-class. His father was an auctioneer and also an agent for a big landowner and he had some land in his own right. So in the family there was never any dire need, no extreme poverty, although "all of us lived, I think, very simply."

"All the neighbours seemed to live in the same way. The diet at home must have been tea and bread and butter and perhaps some fried beans or fried eggs for breakfast with a little fruit. That would be breakfast. The fruit could be mangoes, if mangoes were in season, or oranges or pineapples. Then off we went to school, where classes started at 9 o'clock in those days, and you had a break for lunch at 12 o'clock. We went home for lunch (which was called dinner really in those days). It was mostly rice, beef or fish and plantain. Some days my mother would come back from the Orange Walk district with fruits and other things and we would have as well yucatek and mestiza, a Spanish dish like tamales, escabeche, tortillas and relleno - chicken stuffed with bread and pepper; pork and eggs with a highly condimented sauce and eaten with corn tortillas for a meal.

"Well, we went back to schol from one to three o'clock and in the evening we had tea around five - bread and butter, a bit of cheese now and then, potted meat, tea. That was the diet of most families in Belize and that was the last meal of the day as a child."

George Price was not very much involved in games although he did play football in primary school and used to like to swim. The school was taught by the Sisters of Mercy and of course, the Priests at the Church were the members of the Society of Jesus. He remembers well that the books he used were the Granville Readers or Royal Readers. The subjects taught were Geography, English Grammar, English Composition, Arithmetic and Hygiene. The hygiene textbook was written by a Dr. Binns and it was very pertinent to our times, because it discussed things like malaria, dysentery, how to treat people and how to avoid getting ill.

Premier Price recalls that in the primary grade he thinks he must have been rated among the ones who got low marks. He wasn't too interested in reading or listening to world affairs. The little world he lived in was the home, the school, playing games with his school mates, interest in trees and in swimming.

The family had a vacation cottage on one of the Cays, St. Georg'es Cay, nine miles in the Caribbean Sea away from Belize City. They always looked forward to going there for two months in the summer as children, to live a carefree life, barefooted, running around, swinging in the trees, catching fish and being away from Belize for the months of May and June. The whole family went, though his father would stay at work in Belize City and come out to the Cay on Saturdays and Sundays. They used to have what is called a boop-boop, a little tramp boat with a one cylinder engine, 25 foot in length, that one could make the trip on. This they hired from Mr. Joe Collins or some other owner. The nine-mile trip took about an hour and a half. Of course, in these modern days, outboard motors and fast boats take 15 or 20 minutes.

Premier Price, recalling his school days, said "I think I just managed to graduate from primary school." In those days, the examining was done by the Director of Education, Mr. Dillon.

"If I recall rightly we didn't take personal written examinations. The class was brought before the Examiner and he would ask some questions; not all pupils were asked questions and on the answers of those who were asked questions, we were passed into another class. But we did learn to read and to write and perhaps to develop an interest in the world. Geography got me interested in a way, although my primary interest was in the community, Belize City, in which I lived.

"I graduated from primary school in 1931. I remember it very well, because that was the year of the big hurricane, which devastated Belize City and part of Stann Creek Town. It was a very violent, very strong hurricane, but not wide; it had a narrow path. I had just gone to St. John's College on scholarship. It is called a College, but it is a high school, was and still is one of the leading colleges in Belize, staffed by the Jesuits of the Missouri Province. At the time I went to school, it was a boarding school. The enrolment must have been two hundred, one hundred of them were boarders from the neighbouring countries, mostly from the Republic of Honduras and Guatemala, some from Mexico, some from El Salvador. The remaining one hundred were day scholars, Belizeans living in Belize City.

"We started classes in July and by September the 10th, the college was destroyed and about 22 or 25 teachers and students were killed in the hurricane. I think my escape was somewhat miraculous.

"It was a three-storeyed building on stilts and the breeze was blowing for a long time and I saw that the building was leaning over and getting off its posts. Many of us instinctively ran out of the building and the building came tumbling down and caught some who hadn't got away in time.

"That was the first half of the hurricane. The centre passed right over Belize. Then in the lull, I thought everything was over and began going home. St. John's College was about a mile and a half from where I lived. I used to live nearer the centre of Belize City and St. John's College was on the south side. My instinct told me to go home to see what was happening. I started off but did not get home. The tidal wave came, the second half, and I was caught in the centre of the city in Albert Street. I took refuge with some relatives next to the Methodist Church, the old Wesleyan Church in Albert Street. That was the second half of the hurricane and we were there taking shelter because the houses were falling down and the water was rising. I heard a noise like thunder and again instinctively I ran; the noise was the Wesleyan Church made of brick, just falling down on top of the people. Again, people were killed but I got away.

"When I got in the street, Albert Street must have had about five feet of water. There was zinc, flying roofs in the water, wire, electric wire and I was going along with the current floating. They said I was one of the good swimmers in those days. They took me in at some place, I think, the Palace Theatre. I was then 12 years old. That was the beginning of my high school days.

"After the hurricane, the high school opened in new quarters, temporary quarters near the Cathedral in the centre of the city."

He completed the high school course in four years. The teachers put him up for Preliminary Cambridge and he passed, but they said he couldn't make the Junior Cambridge or the Senior Cambridge so he was not put up for these examinations. He graduated in 1935.

"I remember that year again very well because it was the year King George V celebrated his Silver Jubilee. I know it was 1935. It was a very quiet graduation. The passing grade was 70 out of 100; we had to get 70 for pass. I passed with 70.1, just made it, just barely made it."

In High School, the Premier said, they had been taught the usual subjects, Mathematics, History - mostly English history - Geography, Literature - usually Shakespeare - and they did some Charles Lamb and some of the poets like Wordsworth.

"It was there I think I began to love reading, I loved reading although I wasn't too proficient in it. After we graduated in 1935 I had to make a choice of what I would do in life. I was 16 years old. I thought I wanted to help my fellowmen and I wanted to go into the Church. I went to the Bishop. At the time it was Bishop Murphy and I said I would like to be a priest to work in Belize. He gave me the opportunity and he sent me to the United States from 1936 to 1940.

"The course we did was mostly a college course, a lot of literature that they called American literature - today I say United States literature - some English Literature, a little bit of Science and Physics. For the first time I was taught how an engine works, a gasolene engine of a car, all the theory. My grades weren't the very highest and not the lowest, sort of mediocre. This was a seminary at Mississippi, known as St. Augustine."

Premier Price explained that the priesthood course was divided into minor studies and major studies. Major studies would be the philosophy and theology. He did not do that at St. Augustine; he did the minor studies, mostly college studies, Greek, Latin, French, German, the languages, literature, mathematics, a bit of science and biology. Then he graduated from the seminary, and he was to go to Rome in 1940, but the war had broken out, so he could not go to Rome. Then the Bishop of Belize called him back to Belize where he worked for a time. The Bishop said plainly it would give trouble to get him into a major seminary - the time was 1940 and a war was on.

"Incidentally," says Premier Price, "the boat we came back on from New Orleans to Belize was sunk a few months afterwards in Port Limon. It was the San Pablo; it was blown up by a German submarine right off Costa Rica."

From the seminary, in the San Pablo, Premier Price said, the trip was very educative. The ship left New Orleans and went to Santiago de Cuba; that was his first visit to Cuba way back in 1940, and from Cuba the ship went to Kingston.

"I stepped ashore in Kingston for the first time in 1940. I recall the wharf, it must have been the old United Fruit Company wharf; and I took a little old taxi to Holy Trinity Cathedral where the Jesuits are. The only high building in Kingston in those days was the Holy Trinity Cathedral with its dome. There I stayed a day, then came on to Belize.

"For me it was the beginning, the first visit to the Caribbean, the vision of what it was like there. Then when I got back home, I worked. The Bishop told me: You might as well get out and work. I worked in the library - the Jubilee Library had just started which is today the National Library Service. The work was to receive people, receive books, give out books and recommend books to readers. Before I went to the library to that job, I went to Corozal district to work for a month or two at the sugar mill that had just started there. They called it Pembroke Hall in those days and we corrupted it to Pembrokal. Now, it's called the Libertad. I worked as a warehouse keeper, then I went to the Library in Belize.

"By that time the Bishop said to me, 'I can get you into a seminary in Guatemala City, taught by the Jesuits, and you can study a little philosophy there, and, if necessary, go on to San Salvador. So I went in 1941 for about 9 months to the major seminary in Guatemala City taught by Spanish Jesuits. Most of it was Latin, Philosophy, and Ethics - Logic and Ethics. That was nine months, and curiously I could not stay in Guatemala City for the next year, because the same subjects I studied the first year would have been repeated the next year and the Philosophy there had at least six branches. Then I was to go to San Salvador. Arrangements were started but the teacher who was going to teach a certain branch of Philosophy died and so the course had to be changed again, and I came back to Belize. It was then that I decided not to go on to the priesthood. I saw where my help was needed and I decided to work and help my family."

In Belize young George Price looked around for a job. He says it was hard to get a job in those days. People didn't want to employ somebody who was studying for the priesthood. They would much prefer to hire someone who had done a commercial course or done some technical course.

"But there was this merchant, Mr. Robert Sidney Turton, who represented some firms in the United States - the Wrigley Company of Chicago (chewing gum) and Ichabod T. Williams & Sons of New York City, timber merchants, mostly mahogany and cedar. Mr. Turton's field of supply was not only Belize, but Mexico also and sometimes Guatemala, the Peten region. And a lot of his work was done in Spanish. He needed a Spanish translator, the job was offered to me and I took the job. That was in 1942 when I started to work as a translator."

The 13 years that he worked with Mr. Turton from 1942 until 1955 when Turton died, was like going to a university, says Premier Price. He visited New York three times a year, Chicago four times a year, Mexico City quite often, and other places. He had to see to worker problems, political problems, business problems and economic activities dealing with government departments in Mexico to get permits to do the trading. All this developed to the point where quite accidentally George Price got into politics.

Says he" Mr. Turton was one of the first elected members of the Brittish Hondural Legislative Council way back in the 1940's and he stood for the Corozal district and the Orange Walk district. Today it is the Northern district, the two of them. He represented the north and frequently I had to write his Minutes. In those days things were circulated among members of the Legislative Council, different papers and different Bills. Mr. Turton was a self-educated man. He had wonderful ideas, very constructive ideas but he needed someone to express these ideas for him. That became part of my work, to make some research into a subject and write a paper and then he could say whether it suited his ideas or not. It was then I got to meet some of the other Legislators of the time - Sir Harrison Courtney who was then a young lawyer; Gilbert Hulse, Archdeacon Hulse; Mr. Simeon Hassock; Mr. Otto Balderamos; and also the City Councillors in those days, the days of the Progressive Party.

"Mr. Turton at times did not see eye to eye with the Belize City Council and he had to oppose them, and I used to write some of his papers, some of his arguments. I remember in 1942 there was a hurricane which did great damage to North Corozal and the Orange Walk district, and there was a big argument going on between Mr. Turton, the representative in the legislature, and the acting Governor. The acting Governor was reported at that time as having said that government had not caused the hurricane; it was God who caused it therefore government should not be responsible for the work. Mr. Turton rightly opposed that false idea and there was a lot of correspondence going backwards and forwards and I was caught up in this.

"That was my education in politics, writing these papers, taking notes, preparing even a Budget Speech - though not a real Budget Speech, for in those days there was a Governor. There was no Ministerial system, it was a colonial government. The Governor was the government and he had his own executive which was appointed by him and were the only advisers to him. It was the beginning of the people's participation to have an elected Legislative Council.

"In those days in 1944 it seemed that the City Council was being taken over by non-Belizeans. One was a Guyanese, one was a St. Lucian, one was a Jamaican. The Belizean people felt: why should people from other countries come and manage our city? Mr. Fred Wesby (it used to be Westby but he took out the "t") who only died this year 1976, falling short of 100 years of life by three months - he was the Town Clerk of the Belize City Council in those days. And Mr. Wesby was a very staunch adversary of this sort of government by people who were not Belizians. And even though he was a Town Clerk he used to move around and try and prepare some other people to stand for election. He was a good friend of Mr. Turton, my employer, on the basis of Bob and Fred as they talked to each other. Mr. Wesby walked right into Mr. Turton's office one day and the next thing I knew was that Mr. Turton called me: 'George, come here.' I went in and he said: 'George, now you run for the Belize City Council.' That was a week before the election in 1944."

"I obeyed him and I went up for election. There was no real political party; there was a group of Belizeans, some young, some middle-aged, who called themselves the Independents, who grouped themselves into this political movement. I ran and they told me I lost by a few votes. There were about seven seats and I was number eight so I was not elected. But I got good experience. I saw what was needed in a campaign. Three years after there was another chance and I ran this time and happened to get the biggest number of votes. I did not become the Mayor because I was still working at Mr. Turton's. Someone else was Mayor. Curiously I think it was Mr. Karl Wade, who is in Jamaica at this time, he was the Mayor. That was in 1947."

During this service on the City Council, Premier Price says he began to see that the structures at that time could not change the country for the better. He came to realise that the whole system had to be changed for a better system, a system in which the people would have the real political power. Subconsciously, he may have been just getting ready for the opportunity when the people would be awakened. The occasion was 1949, December 31, when the Belize dollar was devalued. It was unlinked from the United States dollar and tied to the pound sterling at the rate of one dollar forty Belize for one dollar United States.

"I think what got us annoyed was not so much the fact that it was devalued, but the hypocrisy, the dishonesty of the system, the colonial system of the time which first assured the people that there would be no devaluation although the pound had been devalued a few months before. Now, looking back after twenty seven years, had I the experience and the information I now have, I would have known that it had to be devalued, despite what they were saying that the Belize dollar would not have to be devalued. There was no other consequence since it was tied to the pound. Although looking back I think we could have stayed with the United States dollar, but that's another question. The people were angry saying it was dishonesty to say it would not happen and it happened, also, the way it happened. It was done by the Governor's veto power in the Lesiglative Assembly against the vote of the elected members."

Premier Price says that on the 1st of January, 1950, they had a demonstration to "give us back our dollar"; an anti-devaluation demonstration. A group of about 20, including Price, formed a People's Committee.

"From this certain leaders emerged, for instance, Leigh Richardson, Phillip Goldson, Herman Jacques, Nicholas Pollard, Edward Austin, Joe Revere. There were several demonstrations, the biggest demonstrations ever witnessed in Belize City or in the whole country but it was all in vain; the dollar was not restored.

"We went to the United Nations, we wrote to the Central American nations, Mexico, the United States, Canada, protesting the high-handedness of the government. I visited the United Nations around that time and it was pointed out to me that the only effective way to win a political objective is to be organised. So we came back home and we founded the People's United Party in 1950, September 29th. We have just recently celebrated the 25th anniversary, 25 years of struggle and achievement."

In succeeding years George Price recalls that they were organising the people, not only in Belize City but out in the districts, everywhere. Mr. Price became secretary of the party, Phillip Goldson was the assistant secretary but, says Mr. Price: "The key man was Leigh Richardson. And really at the time I was prepared and willing and dedicated to support Mr. Richardson as the leader of the movement because I saw we needed a leader. I was with Mr. Turton and I could not give full time. So we organised the party and the first test, the electoral test, was when we had to face the first City Council elections. Of nine seats, we won five. We won a majority and we became the city's government."

Premier Price recalls some strange episodes in the ensuing years. They were critical of the war measures which, long after the war, were still being kept in force, causing hardship, and it was thought that one way to point it out was to refuse to hang up the King's picture in the City Council until these things, these evils, were righted.

"Then it was misrepresented that I was anti-British and radical. The Colonial government, I think, over-acted at the time and dissolved the City Council and appointed a new City Council. So we had to work from the outside and there were sedition trials. Goldson and Richardson and some other writers of the Belize Billboard were accused of sedition. It was at that time Mr. Goldson went to Jamaica and Mr. N.N. Nethersole came to defend them. They were convicted and they went to jail for eight months. While they were there we kept the Party going and they came out and we won adult suffrage. Our work was to register as many voters as possible, for the first elections under adult suffrage in 1954. There were nine seats in 1954 and we won eight, all except southern Toledo. That was in 1954. Later on we were being prepared for Ministerial system and the membership system was introduced whereby a member would be responsible for certain subjects. There was a member for Natural Resources, a member for Social Services and so on. But the real power was still with the Governor. But it was a way to accustom us as a people to manage our own affairs."

How this brave party of young politicians could break down after all that success is something that Premier Price tried to explain to me. He said that in 1956 there were defections from the party over Federation of the West Indies. He, Mr. Price, and others of the party opposed a federation with the West Indies.

"Why? The nature of the Constitution itself, the representation. We thought that Belize with its small population would have a very small representation in the Regional Congress or Parliament, whereas it would have the second largest area of land. Secondly there was the name. Geographically we are not West Indies, although the West Indies are our neighbours and they are our friends. And at the time it would not have been, as we foresaw it, a federation of independent countries, but a federation of colonial countries; and we did not see any political advancement in that.

"There was also the idea that we would have been swamped by the notion of immigration. Years of experience have taught me now that all that can be controlled by certain mechanisms in a constitution. But we opposed it. It was the time of the Caribbean Commission. And Mr. Richardson used to attend some Caribbean or West Indian regional meetings. Here we were opposed as a party with its manifesto to federation of the West Indies and there was our Minister attending these meetings without telling us what he went there to discuss. By accident he left his briefcase at some place. He left it either in one of the outer offices or some office of the party, and Mr. Nick Pollard got to know what the contents were. He accused Mr. Richardson and Mr. Goldson of deviation from the party's policy and there was a big row. They were expelled from the party and the party leadership; thus it emerged that I happened to become the Party Leader."

Such is the broad canvas of the beginnings of George Price as a servant of the people and as a politician. He has the modesty and stoicism of his upbringing in the discipline of the Church. Indeed, still a bachelor, he said: "At one time in my early life I contemplated marriage. But then I was so immersed in politics that there was actually no time for this. I tell my friends that I am married to politics and politics is my wife. I can therefore give full time to this great endeavour to advance the peaceful, constructive revolution of bringing a better life for all Belizeans."

Totally without ostentation, George Price lives a simple life. He attends Roman Catholic Mass every day. He has no fancy motor-car. He drives around in a Land-Rover suitable to the terrain of his country. When we last had lunch with some of his colleagues, it was a very tasty lunch, but it was Belizean. It was venison. The conversation was keen but not boastful from any of his colleagues, and George Price in a way sums it up.

Looking back at the progress of his country in roads, communications, infrastructure, land reform, he said: "Today, the people own the land. The revolution that we have conducted has changed the face of Belize when we compare it with twenty-five years ago. But it was a peaceful revolution. I look back and I see no blood on my hands. Yes, there have been demonstrations; there have been acts of unrest, signs of unrest, but it has always been a process within the law constitutionally - elections, demonstrations, meetings, public meetings, articles in the press, debates in the National Assembly. It is not bloody, it is constructive; we have built.   .

"Perhaps if Belize had a bigger population, perhaps we could go ahead faster with more people, more money, more aid per capita. What we are doing is purely Belizean - our own idiosyncracies, our own way of thinking. We take certain universal principles but apply them to the Belizean scene.

"I have been accused of being a Communist, of being a Guatemalan traitor; but I think in all truth the philosophy that we live by is one you could call a philosophy of social justice, where we create wealth but the wealth must be shared equally. Sometimes land reform is necessary. How can we allow a big landowner to own land where a community lives, with him in control of all those houses all the way back? How can we allow one foreigner to sell to another foreigner land where people have to live, the only means of earning a livelihood, where they would have to raise crops for the domestic market and for the foreign market?

I look to the day when I trust the revolution of Belize will go on. Recently there was a graduation in Belmopan, the new capital which we have built inland to save the capital from the worst ravages of hurricane and tidal wave. Belmopan is named for "Belize" and "Mopan", the river which flows by the new capital. The comprehensive school at Belmopan graduated 40 students recently. I spoke at the graduation on the revolution as having been peacefully constructed - the Belizean revoluton. I think there is a need to keep this revolution alive before the people . If not, the young people who come back will want to start their own revolution and there will be a continual process of turmoil and chaos.

"In my outlook on life, I think it would be the view of the world that there is a creator, a Supreme Being, that there is a plan in the whole universe, that creation was not finished at the dawn of this earth, but creation continues and we have a lot to do to make the world a better place. I think in this Caribbean region we should follow events in every country; we should know at least two or three languages. In Belize several languages are spoken. There is, of course, English, Spanish, Creole, Garifuna, and four Mayan languages - Mayapon, Mayamotec, Mayayucatece, Mayaketchi - and the Mennonite Community speak German.

"I think our economic plan is based on the family. We must provide good housing, all the amenities, the basic things a human being needs. Especially in the developing world, we have to make sure we do not only develop the metropolis or big cities; we must develop the countryside; put all the things there - schools, medical services, water. I agree with two decisions emerging out of HABITAT, and that is what we are doing - providing every community with pure water where possible, and land reform - people must be allowed to own at least their house lot where they live or the farm that they have. I believe, that and we are working towards that; that we must do everything possible to produce food for our tables and after that produce something for the export market so we can buy the things that we need.

"I believe that a country's first duty is to set its own house in order; and having set its own house in order, it can contribute better to the community of the world. Instead of being a weak link, it should be a strong link."

THE RIGHT HONOURABLE
DR. ERIC EUSTACE WILLIAMS,
D. PHIL, HON. D.C.L. (OXON)
HON. LL.D. (UNIVERSITY OF BRUNSWICK)
BORN PORT OF SPAIN, TRINIDAD, 25 SEPTEMBER, 1911
DIED: 30 MARCH 1981

CHIEF MINISTER OF TRINIDAD & TOBAGO (1956-1959)
PREMIER OF TRINIDAD & TOBAGO (1959-1962)
PRIME MINISTER OF TRINIDAD AND TOBAGO (1962-1981)

11

DR. ERIC EUSTACE WILLIAMS

SOMETIMES A SPHINX, often the articulate academician, always the politician, he was, a puzzle to friends but moreso to foes. A wizard, especially in crisis, he was as wizards are, naturally held in awe, rarely held in affection, but held totally in respect. The Rt. Hon. Dr. Eric Williams was completely different from any other Commonwealth Caribbean leader.

His government came close to an overthrow in 1970, yet he remained totally in command.

Eric Williams emerged from an administrative backroom of the Anglo-American Caribbean Commission to start the first effective political party in Trinidad. He remained unchallenged head of the Government from 1956 until his death in 1981, having his imprimatur re-endorsed continuously as Prime Minister of Trinidad and Tobago.

His emergence as a political party leader in 1956 ushered in a new and probably unique era in Commonwealth Caribbean political history. Besides being extolled as a renowned scholar (the masses called him 'di Doctor'), a Doctor of Philosophy, Oxford University, where he went as Trinidad's Island scholar and as a world-famed historian, (author of Capitalism and Slavery), Dr. Williams was also acclaimed for his wide-ranging grasp of international affairs as head of his country. He talked to his people as if they were an academic class, but he spiced his lectures and professorial talks with biting wit and sharp tongue.

He it was, in his popular phrase-making, who compressed the sociological condemnation of the past into the phrase "Massa day done", a reference to the

191

end of the colonial plantation system. And encompassing the multitudinous ethnic elements which constitute the Trinidad population, he also created the right aura in his statement: "All a we, a one" as he trumpeted Trinidad and Tobago's ascendancy to independence based on universal adult suffrage with equality of opportunity to all citizens regardless of race, colour, class or religion.

Opposition was not on ethnic racial lines, but opposition there was. Very good thing too. But perhaps the greatest of Eric Williams' achievements, was to avoid the separation of the ethnic elements into clear-cut political rivalry. Indeed, in the middle fifties there was thought that perhaps the East Indian communities of Trinidad and Guyana would polarise and create a new type of ethnic orientation of power in the region. Happily, this did not happen in either territory.

In Trinidad, polarisation was avoided because of Dr. Williams' leadership which depended on his genius for bridging the wide gap that existed between the politics of the East Indian and the politics of the African. He was able to create a cohesive society that was an example not only to the Commonwealth Caribbean, but to the world.

Eric Williams dedicated the "University of Woodford Square" to national political education. Generally, his audience held him in awe, but there was ribald laughter as his use of the creaole displayed a biting wit. In his straight passages, Eric Williams talked ex cathedra, papal. He did not suffer fools gladly, nor even less intelligent friends or supporters. Indeed, his own colleagues in his party very often came under fierce public slaughter. In a way, his total sense of superiority had a sad side to it in that he rarely acknowledged equals or people in their own right without some derision.

I remember being at Woodfford Square in 1959. Dr. Williams was impatient for the Federation of the West Indies to assume its full independence and give up the colonial constitution with which it was started on an experimental basis. His demand was that the West Indies Federation should declare its total sovereignty and independence and should set a date for it and not shilly-shally. In the context of this grand and admirable demand, listen to Eric Williams:

"We must fix a date for the Federation to be independent and the 22nd of April is as good a date as any, so let us fix the 22nd of April and since the Prime Minister of the West Indies cannot get up early in the morning, we can have it at eleven o'clock."

Even in a declamation of total national importance, he found the necessity to derogate old Grantley Adams, to subject him to contempt. That evening, I was in conversation with C.L.R. James who was at one time Dr. Williams' mentor in England. At that particular moment, he was riding high as one of Dr. Williams' principal adjutants, responsible for running the party newspaper and expecting to be put in charge of a much bigger journalist effort, a daily paper run for and by the

Trinidad people. I felt that that piece of contemptous public utterance by Dr. Williams about the Prime Minister of his own West Indies, was an indication of a character that needed watching, if one were just to accept him as colleague and leader. So I said to C.L.R. James that evening over a glass of wine: "You know, C.L.R., you had better watch yourself with Eric." C.L.R. considered it nonsense that there could ever be a rift and thought I was over-reading the mannerisms of Trinidad politics. I said: "No. No. A man who can publicly hold to contempt his own Prime Minister will do anything to strangers such as you and me."

Shortly after that, C.L.R. James was shaken out of his dreams. Instead of starting a national daily paper with C.L.R. James in charge, Dr. Williams persuaded the English newspaper magnate, Lord Thomson, to start a paper in Trinidad, and Thomson had instead bought the leading Trinidad publishing house, The Guardian. James had nothing to do with it and he got no share in all this. Indeed, not long after, when C.L.R. James sought to go back to Trinidad to report on international cricket, he was practically put under 'house arrest'.

This, perhaps a small matter, is I think, indicative of Dr. Williams' totalness in his public life. No wonder people held him in awe, even his blood relatives. It would seem sinister anywhere else that even a sister would be afraid to talk about a brother, about their childhood, without the brother's permission, for fear of his displeasure. Even a professional who was Eric's school-mate in the early days told me: "I could not talk about him without his permission."

Looking, however, at the other side, with a man such as Eric Williams as leader, the West Indian Federation could have been a power to reckon with. However, Eric Williams created a palsied Federation by his contempt for its leadership and by his own success and lonesome dominance of the Trinidad and Tobago atmosphere.

But, let it be said, Eric Williams had stronger and more practical ideas for the success of Federation than his contemporaries had. He had declared in his 'Economics of Nationhood':

"Only powerful and centrally directed economic co-ordination and interdependence can create the true foundation of a nation. Barbados will not unify with British Guiana, or Jamaica with Antigua. They will be knit together only through their common allegiance to a Central Government. Anything else will discredit the conception of a Federation and in the end leave the islands more divided than before."

Dr. Williams had made it plain over and over that he wanted a dynamic advance to Dominion Status. Prime Minister Grantley Adams was in agreement, but Jamaica's Norman Manley strongly disagreed, doubtless looking over his shoulder politically at the menace of Bustamante's anti-federal strategies. Instead, Manley called for the powers of the Federal Government to be restricted, the conflict coming to a head with the impasse with Adams over the establishment in Jamaica of the Esso Oil Refinery. In this, Adams and Williams for a rare event stood strongly side by side. So, while in the final event, Williams' tactics of harassment of federal politicians and personnel, and the inhospitable climate he and his supporters created for the federal inhabitants of Port of Spain, were pervading corrosives which destroyed the will to make a success of Federation, he had in fact the best formula for its success. He saw that with the colonial nature of the Federation, ineptly led as it was with a banal Governor General and a Prime Minister who did not come out to work early in the mornings, the only cure was "sink or swim" - total sovereignty for the Federation at once. The other West Indian leaders were timorous about this, and a great chance was muffed.

It must be remembered that Williams' party had been defeated in the federal elections (as had happened to Manley's party in Jamaica); also that Prime Minister Adams had waffled over Chaguaramas even when Dr. Williams had got the better of the Americans in persuading them to agree to joint US-WI control of the naval base. So he had national diffidence about a federal structure in on Port-of-Spain.

In the Chaguaramas dispute with the Americans (and with the Federal Government), Dr. Williams had won the admiration of the British Secretary of State, Iain MacLeod who, according to Nigel Fisher, established an excellent relationship with the Trinidad leader. MacLeod found that Dr. Williams was a man of rare intellectual quality and great ability, though officials found him enigmatic and sometimes difficult to get on with.

It was not only officials, however, who found Dr. Williams hard to get on with. Robert Bradshaw, the federal Minister of Finance reflecting on his association with Dr. Williams said:

"I have never had a personal confrontation or conflict with Eric, not really. He did something once, sending a delegation, the head of which was John O'Halloran, then Minister of Trade and Tourism, to Washington to obtain finance for some project or other, without first getting the Federal Government's permission for the Exchange Control aspect of it, over which the Federal Government had authority. I heard of it the morning after the delegation had gone. It was a Monday morning - I heard it on the radio - and shortly after I arrived in my office a chap from the Trinidad government came to my office seeking federal authority for it. I said to him 'Tell me something, what are you fellows doing?' So I rang Bill Williams and asked if I could see him on my way home for lunch. I went. John Mordecai was at that time acting Governor General. He and Solomon Hochoy, the Trinidad Governor, had been in contact as to what could be done about this, and so on. Grantley was not even in Trinidad at the time so I was senior federal minister there. So I went to Bill and asked him what was this all about. I said 'You know you should have Federal Government authority and you haven't done it; you make us look very small. This is not the sort of thing to do.' Bill replied, 'What federal authority! what federal government!' He shouted it at me. I then clashed with him and told him what was in my mind. I cannot remember the words but I told him he was just being rude, arrogant and offensive, unnecessarily so. I told him that, in contrast with this, when the Jamaican Government had to have foreign exchange for the building of the Sheraton Hotel, Wills Isaacs who had to do with it, either sent Egerton Richardson or sent a communication in advance about it. It was just a formality, but Jamaica was concerned to observe the formalities. But not Dr. Williams."

Incidentally, Wills Isaacs had himself told me of feeling hurt at treatment by Dr. Williams in Port-of-Spain when he went there during Federation on business for the Government of Jamaica. Wills Isaacs and his officials had been received in conference by Dr. Williams and the meeting had ended just before lunchtime. They went downstairs and were waiting on transport when Dr. Williams came down and passed through them to go to his car without saying a word to them. "He made us feel that he thought we were lepers", Wills Isaacs told me.

Whatever his acid ways, Eric Williams undoubtedly had the best chance (if he had accepted the challenge) to make the Federation a success. Perhaps he had not set his sights so high as to think he could step over Adams and Manley and his other seniors. Perhaps he was not super-ambitious and preferred to rule his own beloved Trinidad than lead a polyglot peoples who knew not "di doctor".

Eventually he witnessed the collapse of the Federation, and he almost seemed delighted. He was so quick to say of the ten units from which Jamaica had defected by the 1961 referendum, "One from ten leaves nought". But even this, according to a federal luminary of the time, had been an acid aphorism long considered and not really spontaneous. "It was not even clever" says this federalist, "it was something that had been told me long before by Ellis Clarke, special legal adviser to Dr. Williams." Without a doubt, Dr. Williams was glad to entomb the Federation with a bitter epitaph.

Dr. Williams was by common Caribbean consent somewhat of an enigma. A Jamaican civil servant says:

"Speaking with him and seeing him in action at conferences, one would think that he had lost interest in everything except his books, his politics and his daughter Erica. But there are other sides to him. During a Heads of Governments' Conference in Trinidad some years ago, there was a Test Match in progress in the Southern Caribbean. I would leave the Conference at 'respectable' intervals to get the news for my delegation, who would pass it on. Dr. Williams, who was in the Chair, did not appear interested but after about three trips, he looked directly at our delegation and without batting an eyelid said in his usual flat voice - 'I too am a cricket fan, gentlemen. What is the score?'

"Sometime about 1965, Sir Alexander Bustamante headed a delegation

195

to one of these conferences of Heads of Government. One afternoon, Dr. Williams was taking Sir Alexander on a tour of Port-of-Spain and its environs and, as usual, I went along as ADC. At one point a small crowd had gathered, but Dr. Williams appeared not to see them. Sir Alexander called it to his attention and enquired whether he did not intend to stop. His reply was 'Don't bother with them nuh - they just going to talk a lot of foolishness.' And we drove on.

"In 1967, Mr. Sangster, as acting Prime Minister, went to Palisadoes Airport in Jamaica to meet Dr. Williams who was intransit from Canada, where he had held talks with the Canadian Prime Minister. Arthur Brown and I accompanied Mr. Sangster. Dr. Williams was accompanied by two Ministers - Mr. O'Halloran and Mr. Montano. Dr. Williams and Mr. Sangster talked privately while the other Ministers stood aside. During the discussions one could discern that all was not well, and they ended with Mr. Sangster giving his usual little negative shrug of the shoulders. What had happened was that Dr. Williams was applying pressure on Mr. Sangster to agree that Jamaica would go along with certain understandings which he had arrived at with the Canadian Prime Minister and Mr. Sangster was telling him that in Jamaica we had a Cabinet system which worked. The result was that for nearly one year Dr. Williams refused to communicate with Jamaica on any matter. And believe it or not, neither of the two Trinidad Ministers had any knowledge of the matters discussed either with the Canadian Prime Minister or with Mr. Sangster.

"Dr. Williams had a rather unique way of dealing with top officers in the civil service who had incurred his displeasure. He would bring them into his Office, provide them with a desk, but no work. At one time he did this to one of his chief advisers because the officer had put his signature to a report signed by other members of a Commission to enquire into and report on the civil service. Reason: Dr. Williams did not agree with some of the Commission's recommendations."

Eric Williams, all this shows, was totally commited to himself, past, present and future. He analysed everything except himself but all his analyses and his pictures came out clear "I am that I am." Yet, in his book, Inward Hunger, one senses a deep insufficiency, a deep sadness. As an academician who had been very close to Dr. Williams puts it:

"The autobiographical memoir Inward Hunger is of enormous psychiatrical importance in an understanding of the Williams persona. It reveals at once a profound anguish and a deep rebelliousness: anguish at the historically determined role of the colonial in English society and rebelliousness against that role. It is ambivalent, for it, on the one hand, is full of the natural and necessary anger of a first-class 'Black' mind against white mediocrity, on the other, it is full of an eagerness to show the white man that his colonial competitor can play the white man's game even better than the white himself.

"There is an aggressive tone which, to the unsympathetic critic, means a 'chip on the shoulder' complex; to the more sympathetic reader, however, it can be seen as the mature, nationalist consciousness of a colonial intellectual reacting against the deep psychic wound that all racial prejudice and discrimination leave behind it.

"It has something of Fanon about it. However, it does not go as far as Fanon in its rejection of European culture. For the book also reveals Dr. Williams as a loyal Oxonian; and few things are more revealing than the confession that his life's dream, while a colonial at Oxford, was to become a permanent member of Oxonian society as an All Souls Fellow."

Our mutual friend concludes from all this that the collapse of Eric Williams' dream of becoming an All Souls Fellow at Oxford helped to explain much of the Williams personality in its later political embodiment. Dr. Williams was for the strenous life, intellectually speaking. He did not spare himself nor his colleagues in the strenuous life by which he led Trinidad and Tobago since 1956, and which has propelled him to the undisputed pinnacle of Commonwealth Caribbean life.

Who was this Eric Williams? Dr. Williams was the son of T.H. Williams and his wife, Eliza. T.H. Williams was a Post Office employee at the mid-level in the days when only an Englishmen could be appointed Postmaster General. A friend of mine recalls T.H. Williams as a short man about Eric's height but not as stocky. Eric was one of twelve children. Married three times, Dr. Williams' third marriage was sensational. It became public when a Guyanese-born dentist practising in Trinidad called in the newspapers and told them she was Dr. Williams' wife and said when and where the marriage took place. The reporters went to the Registrar General's Office and found the Marriage Certificate confirming the marriage and that it had taken place on an off-shore holiday island, Caledonia, with a Presbyterian parson officiating (although Eric Williams was a Roman Catholic). The couple had never been seen in public together before - and indeed, I am told, were hardly seen together afterwards. Before marriage, they were once at the same cocktail party given by the Indian High Commissioner in 1960. They stayed in opposite corners of the room and never looked at each other that anyone could see.

The report on this strange wedding made good newspaper copy for a few days, particularly because of the mystery of the certificate. It was only after the third Mrs. Williams made her own announcement that the certificate became available. For her part, Mrs. Eric Williams still practised her profession as a dentist on Frederick Street, Port-of-Spain. A mysterious atmosphere had always been part of the Eric Williams aura. One cannot read his own life-story of his childhood without feeling a great sadness for the total commitment of a young boy to a career, determined to show that the family could produce a leader, an outstanding person. It was as if the magnetism in father, mother, and brothers and sisters were combined to create in young Eric's mind a total commitment to success. The success was not always spontaneous because Dr. Williams himself says that sometimes it was only on the second try that he succeeded; but the sense of dedication went beyond what one would expect of a child, a lad growing up. It was dedication to the point of transformation; Eric Williams had been a transformed and utterly committed person all his years, all his life.

Normally, Dr. Williams was the quiet man at international conferences and meetings. He spoke as little as possible to the press. At cocktail parties it was even worse. He would go into a corner and stay there the whole evening until it was time to go home. Various people moved in to pay court to him and there was occasional laughter.

The Federation Conference in London in 1961, when the whole sky came tumbling down, was one of those occasions where it was impossible to get a word out of the Trinidad and Tobago delegation. One knew from the statements of other delegates that things were not going too well. So it was generally regarded that Dr. Williams held the key and one wanted to hear him opening the door.

The occasion came during a reception hosted by the Jamaican Premier and Mrs. Manley on behalf of the Government of Jamaica at the Connaught Rooms on the 15th of June., There was an undercurrent of tension in the atmosphere which persisted despite the music of a string orchestra and the buzz of conversation. Says a colleague: "I was overjoyed when Dr. Williams signalled me over to his corner. Just as he started to say something - and anything he said at that time would have been important and significant - Lady Molly Huggins tripped over: 'Ah, Dr. Williams,' she said, in a torrent of words. There was an amused smile on Premier Williams' face. He said not a word as she went on for at least five minutes non-stop. When she stopped and went away, he too, had turned off." All Dr. Williams then said to my friend was, "Yakkety-yak, yakkety-yak, yakkety-yak." The moment passed and my friend missed whatever Dr. Williams had intended to say.

Home in Trinidad, a newspaper colleague tells me Dr. Williams used his weekly press conference (recorded in his office at Whitehall and later broadcast unedited on government time on the radio stations) to speak to the Federal Ministers in Port-of-Spain. One had to be invited to be able to attend. The Chronicle, with which Dr. Williams had fallen out, was never invited. The Guardian - at that time not yet owned by Lord Thomson - boycotted it for a while because he was brusque and offensive to their reporters. The Gleaner from Jamaica, which had a resident representative in Trinidad, attended because, in spite of whatever went on at Federal House, Dr. Williams' press conference was were one could discover what was Trinidad and Tobago's attitude to this or that item of federal policy. The Gleaner's representative, when the Conference was over, would be asked to stay behind, and Dr. Williams would then insist that, if he had said anything about Jamaica, or the Federation, he was not referring to the Gleaner's, representative but "to those boys over there," waving his hand vaguely in the direction of Federal

House. Dr. Williams was always anxious to find out what was going on at Federal House. Our reporter was always careful to say that he did not know, that he only knew what other people told him, and they were not talking.

Dr. Williams' press conferences were as a rule long monologues. One short question could produce a response from five to seven to ten minutes long, but there was almost always a story in it somewhere. Nevertheless, there was one occasion when the Gleaner angered him. A Gleaner correspondent, writing in Kingston, expressed the view that Williams was pathological about Chaguaramas. Dr. Williams was very rude at the next press conference, and the Gleaner stayed away deliberately for the next three conferences, although begged to attend; and when the Gleaner resumed attending these conferences, Premier Williams gave no indication that he had even noticed its absence.

The foregoing would suggest that Eric Williams had always been a sombre, somewhat bitter person and personality. This was not altogether true. As a boy in school he wasn't the liveliest. A serious student he was, but he was adept at 'windball', the term used for football played with a tennis ball, and his colleagues remember in his youthful days mirthful moments. I myself met Dr. Williams just after he had graduated from Oxford. He had come to Kingston, and he entertained me to tea at the Myrtle Bank Hotel quite ornately. Then in 1955, after he had been to Howard where he was a lecturer and had joined the Caribbean Commission at Kent House in Port-of-Spain, I had occasion to go to Port-of-Spain, taking my two daughters on a trip on "The West Indian", the ship that was first on the run linking the Commonwealth Caribbean islands which were expected to be a federated. Dr. Williams was my guest at a dinner party with my children and others and he was quite gay and responsive to conversation. Of course, at that time, he did have rancour at the US Government's petty persecution of him over his matrimonial problems in America with his first wife and their children; still he was light-hearted and pleasant.

Yet, years later when he came to Jamaica and we had him to lunch at the Gleaner with the Board of Directors, he practically said nothing at all - all through lunch - and one wasn't sure whether he hadn't turned off his hearing aid. This habit grew and grew as his commitment to his work multiplied, and one must form the conclusion that Dr. Williams had at some early stage sublimated himself to his commitment to Trinidad because, for one, he was unhappy in his relationship with the United States Government and regarded Trinidad not only as his native land to serve but a means of showing that someone could deal with the U. S. Government. One wonders sometimes why a great nation like the U.S.A. carries out petty persecutions just because it has the power to do so. Of course, it is the bureaucracy that does this and not the people. But there are many people who can mirror Eric Williams' experience of a feeling, a sense of being hounded down, as a minor person in the world as Eric then was, hounded by that great nation.

There were other times during which he was rather more light-hearted. In the early days of his Premiership in Trinidad he was an avid follower of carnival. Dressed in jacket and without a tie, he patrolled the route leading to or away from the stage on the Queen's Park Savannah. One Carnival "last lap", the Tuesday night jump up on the street before the end of the festival at midnight, he followed the Invaders Steel Band. He was on the sidewalk just near the pans and smoking one of his endless chain of cigarettes, which later he abandoned for the pipe. At the next press conference, the Gleaner representative ribbed him, saying: "I saw you jumping up Tuesday night. Dr. Williams was in good humour. Said he sardonically: "I wasn't jumping up but you were".

As a family man, Eric always wanted to have the two children by his first marriage come and stay with him in Trinidad rather than with their American born mother in the United States. But that was not to happen. However, Pamela and Alistair, the two children, were reconciled to him. Erica, Dr. Williams' daughter by his second marriage was the apple of his eye and the comfort of his later years.

In the Trinidad Parliament, Dr. Williams had it much his own way because, for most of the time, there was no opposition and if opposition, it was largely inarticulate. There was a time when the Opposition made an attempt to maintain strong debate and, on one such occasion, an Opposition Member, Mr. Seukeran, was making what seemed a polished and well-informed attack on the policy of the Government. Dr. Williams rose two or three times to ask what was the Member reading. Mr. Seukeran retorted on each occasion that he did not have to read anything because he was perfectly capable of making his own speech. Seukeran persisted and then Dr. Williams rose and said: "Mr. Speaker, the Member is reading word for word the speech of the Leader of the Opposition in the British Budget debate and published in yesterday's London Times." Mr. Seukeran shut up and sat down.

Dr. Williams had always treated his own members with austere discipline and, indeed, this almost came to a crisis before the 1976 elections when he required his party to reconsider the list of candidates they had proposed and forced them to abandon some of them. He also required that members who were put up had to sign an undated letter of resignation to the Speaker of the House of Representatives to be given to him as political leader. This was to put an end to the notion that people could stand as members of his party, the People's National Movement, and then at a whim or to use some special opportunity, resign from the party, yet remain Members of the House.

At first, the panel of candidates who were to stand for election and many others in the party resented this, but eventually Dr. Williams had his way. He also enforced stringent financial requirements upon his members of Parliament and had his way. And his resounding and continuous victories in elections made him the longest continuous head of Government in the Commonwealth Caribbean.

Dour, sometimes bitter, always eloquent, Dr. Williams is the genius of the Caribbean. Said the late Norman Manley about him at one time: "Eric Williams should not be thought of as only a split personality. He is more than that. He is many personalities in one. He is the most complicated little man I have ever met." And Manley was speaking with feeling because he had, so to speak, taken Dr. Williams under his wing in the earliest days when 'little Eric', as he was popularly known, was going through the various tribulations of conjugal affairs and the United States Government harassment and was uncertain where he would eventually end up.

Norman Manley was always patron and god-father to him during all those years though, towards the end, the relationship was embittered. Manley told me finally when he had heard from Dr. Williams after an unsuccessful conference on Federation in Antigua: "I have just got a letter from Eric Williams. Nobody, nobody, nobody in my life has been as rude to me as he has been in this letter." That killed the friendship but made both Jamaica and Trinidad independent nations.

Dr. Williams would have benefitted from the earlier years spent at Kent House, headquarters of the Caribbean Commission,where he must have gained a tremendous amount of experience in administration and office executive work. This stood him in good stead as a Prime Minister. However, things had not been too happy for Dr. Williams at the Commissione. A parliamentary friend of Dr. Williams comments:

"On August 10, in 1955, he (Dr. Williams) was still at Kent House and he was addressing a meeting of teachers of which I was Chairman. At that moment he got the news that his contract with Kent House would not be renewed. For me that was good news for Trinidad because the great majority of island scholars had gone in either for medicine or law. It was at that moment that Eric Williams finally turned himself to public affairs. He would often lecture at the library and then Wilfrid Alexander came to me and said they were forming a party and would I be interested. And we came out in the open in January, 1956 and we won the elections in September. We used to meet for hours at Dr. Williams' house at Cornelius Street where he lived in a cottage to the back, on the same premises with his mother-in-law, mother of his second wife. There we discussed all kinds of things, and Dr. Williams was a wonderful man in that when he heard an idea which he accepted - in those days he used to accept ideas - he had a wonderful facility of putting into words the idea that had been accepted. Very often he had written something the day before we arrived - for he had nothing else to do but that. Then we would say what we thought and when we agreed he would put it all together and get it right. He was great at writing.

"He had a tremendous memory for history. I think I would describe him as a subjective historian. He fixed history to his pattern. I don't think he allowed for the weight on the one side as against the weight on the other side. He wrote rather subjectively and discoloured his history, a point about which Elsa Goveia has criticised him. He assimilated the matter to suit his political views. His politics were coloured by how it concerned Eric Williams. This is not to be unfair to him. He liked to write and wrote his speeches; so he had an accumulation of speeches. It was not that he could not deliver his speech without writing; he wrote it and that served him in good stead. We know he was very pragmatic; we know that he could not be held down to an ideology. He said: 'These fellows are talking about socialism. I don't know what they mean.' He was not concerned with any isms at all; this gave him a free hand.

"I think he needed a free hand because I think he was that sort of character. I do not think he was a methodical man. He showed it in his twenty years of leadership. He could not tie himself down. He is not going to talk about democratic socialism because, again he is going to say I don't know what that means. He bought out the Cement Company and he bought out Shell but I don't think he will want to buy out Texaco, though he will certainly want a voice in Texaco, maybe a major voice. He will condemn multi-nationals in one voice and in the next two, three months he will see good in a multi-national which can do good for his country. Indeed, his present philosophy towards the multi-national was described by Mr. Primus, the Chairman of IDC and other things, who said, 'at all times the Trinidad Government must be courageous and incorruptible when dealing with multi-nationals. This is the idea. So long as you have a courageous and incorruptible government, we can still make use for some time of the expertise of the multi-nationals. You can't put them all in the same category. Dr. Williams has himself made that quite clear.

"In some ways, he [Williams] has a tremendous broadness of mind, but the liberated mind we all expect, we do not find. We could do with a liberated approach to some of our problems in the whole region and this liberated mind is absent. Just remember how Dr. Williams went out of his way to criticise the recommendations of the Wooding Constitution Committee, he himself having chosen the members. He bragged about them when he picked them but he then criticised not only the recommendations when they were made but he criticised the people themselves. One does not know whether to call it intellectual dishonesty or what. You lambast colonialism although we left that long ago, and you lambast your own indigenous people. Everyone has reservations but do not accuse us of wanting to destroy him or to destroy the party. If he had a liberated mind, he would not begin to think that sort of thing."

Referring to the troubles of 1970, this commentator, said:

"The 1970 troubles were black-oriented. The black young men from universities mostly, men who had some education in the age group 18 to 22, having strong African feelings - this black power thing - and it was a very close thing. If the soldiers had not been afraid to die, those soldiers who had mutinied, they might have got through. They might have had a successful revolution there. The Government was very nervous, very nervous. It was lucky for the Government that

202

these insurrectionist soldiers had to pass by the Coast Guard to come into Port-of-Spain. And there was an Englishman in charge of the Coast Guard at the time who said: 'None of this damn nonsense.' And in order to come through some of them would have had to die. The Coast Guard actually started to fire on them.

"Now, the Black people have diverted their attention to Southern Africa, the Holy Land. So that their minds are now in Africa."

However, my political friend considered that Dr. Williams was destructive of the party system because "he says everyone else is ugly and he is the only pretty one"; and the people who will suffer from this in Trinidad ultimately will be the black people, not the Indians or the Chinese. Yet my friend, who is black, says that Dr. Williams as a person, as a politician, certainly twenty years as political leader and Prime Minister, was without any reservations a most outstanding performer.

In summary, another academic contemporary of great intuition and penetrative thought, compares or contrasts the Williams of the young days, wrapped up in Oxford as a pinnacle of golden clouds, and the modern Eric Williams, powerful politician, successsful, determined. He says:

"The collapse of that dream of Oxford helps explain much of the Williams personality in its later political embodiment. His has been the strenuous life, intellectually speaking. He does not suffer fools gladly; he does not suffer his equal gladly. He lives his own inner intellectual life; his open contempt for the University of the West Indies is in part based upon the fact that he does not know how to converse with other intellectuals as an equal in the community of scholars. The murderous incestuous give and take of Oxford senior common room wit is not his cup of tea; all the more surprising that he should at one time have wanted to join it. When you talk with him, you are on his wavelength alone; talk becomes a monologue because, quite simply, he knows that he knows all. His hearing-aid is just an alibi for that habit. He talks at you, not with you.

"He is the world's worst conversationalist. He lacks completely the gift of small talk; too bad, for small talk humanises us all and without it a man rapidly becomes a bore. His manner is that of the old time colonial school master or the old style English university lecturer - obviously shaped by his educational background in colonial Trinidad. C.L.R. James - with whom ideologically he has little in common - has the same autocratic cast of manner; he lectures you in a ponderous condescending manner, bringing to his devotees, as it were, the secret of the universe hitherto unrevealed to them. We are told that C.L.R. was a teacher of the youthful Williams at Queen's Royal College; as the Americans say, it figures.

"This temper of arrogant egocentricity - shared also in part by Norman Manley but absent in gentlemen of the old school like Grantley Adams - helps to explain the fierce combativeness of the Williams personality. Although doctrinally he is never and has never been a Marxist, he does share much of the Marxist personality; especially his theological readiness to have a fight any moment with any adversary; and in which fight you seek not merely to refute the adversary but also to crush him. As Mazzini said about Marx, so you can say about Williams - 'in his heart there is no love, only hate.' That is why Williams is at best respected but never held in affection by those who come into close contact with him. So it is open to serious doubt as to whether he has even had a close friend. And certainly there is no doubt about the elitist cast of his mind.

"He does not possess - as did, say Quintin O'Connor in Trinidad or Roger Mais in Jamaica - a real love and affection for the common man. Rather, for him, the common man is the crowd that in the manner of the University of Woodford Square, cheers the leader and hisses at the villain. He has, indeed, a scarcely contained contempt for the ordinary mass of people; his remark on Trinidadians as "a bunch of transients" reveals much, not least of all the curious tendency of some West Indian electorates to give their support to those leaders who show the greatest amount of contempt for them.

"Shaw once wrote a pamphlet on the Webbs in which he spoke of their cultural philistinism. Williams revealed the same disinterest in the arts. He is a book-man, before all else. It is doubtful if he knows the difference between the first and the fourth of the Vivaldi Seasons. I have never heard him cite a line of poetry or indicate that he had ever read a novel.

"His pleasures are modest. He is a moderate drinker (although he was at one time a heavy chain cigarette smoker until Dr. David Wyke told him to give up the habit). One suspects that he wastes little time on women (if he does, it must be the best kept secret in the Trinidadian society where there are no secrets). He is the perfect Benthamite; poetry and pushpin are equal pleasures. He is the puritan in Babylon."

Of his ideology, my colleague says:

"Williams is the complete radical black nationalist. Anti-colonial nationalism is his main doctrine. Like Duvalier in Haiti - with whom he shares much in common - he is the nationalist-scholar concerned to use his scholarship in the service of a real national pride against all the detractors of the Caribbean nation and Caribbean national personalities. His ideal is - as with Marti - the dream of a regional Caribbean community. That is why his scholarship is *fully* Caribbean, setting him apart from most of the University of the West Indies intelligensia who, however radical they may be, still work within the narrow framework of the so-called *Commonwealth* Caribbean. His early publications on West Indian documents - started when he was resident in the Puerto Rico of the 1940's with the old Anglo-America Caribbean Commission - showed that wide and very generous Caribbean sense.

"So it would be wrong to see Eric Williams as a radical in the Marxist sense. Sometimes <u>Capitalism and Slavery</u> is seen as a Marxist interpretation. But that I think is erroneous, for the doctrinal basis of the argument of that book is a combination of a revived negritude and a somewhat dry application of the doctrine of economic determinism. In that sense, the book is somewhat like Beard's 1913 <u>Economic Interpretation of the Constitution of the United States</u>. It recognises the primacy of the economic factor, but it avoids going further to say, as a Marxist would, that the economic factor is in its turn the expression of class struggle, only to be resolved by the elimination of classes. Beard's book is really an essay in the tradition of radical Jacksonian populism. Williams' book is an essay in radical anti-colonial nationalism. Thus, as one reads the Williams opus of published works, it becomes clear that it has a number of blind spots in terms of its ideological interests. He has no interest in socialism, either as an ideology or as a movement.

"One is reminded of C.L.R. James' remark that he could not remember ever having a conversation with Dr. Williams about socialism that lasted more than three minutes. This goes back to the early formative period in pre-war England. As one reads <u>Inward Hunger</u> one is struck by the fact that the young colonial undergraduate, Eric Williams, showed no interest at all in left wing movements of the time. His main mentor was Brogan, not Laski, not Cole, not Tawney. Dr. Williams was too busy proving to himself that the colonial version of Matthew Arnold's Scholar Gypsy could make it at Oxford. Williams, again, had no interest in the field of sociology. As a result, he was not interested in the multi-faceted expression of human nature and human behaviour patterns. When you read his work, the picture of people that emerges is, as it were, one-dimensional. He sees slavery, but not the slave. He sees the plantocracy, but not the planter. He sees capitalism, but not the businessman. He sees poverty, but not the poor. That is to say, the main emphasis is on institutions, not on people, with all of their variety and eccentricities.

"All this explains why the PNM in Trinidad has been throughout, a radical nationalist rather than a radical social class movement. The Williams argument is not against capitalism as such, only against its abuses, especially when it violates Caribbean sovereignty. So the PNM governmental programme has been based on the 'industrialisation by invitation' principle, using the outside capital investor, while at the same time its political leader will, from time to time, launch a spirited attack upon the multi-national corporations. It is, essentially, a pragmatic nationalism. And, like all pragmatisms, it ends up by arriving at a compromise with the established pattern of 'facts.' The world, for Dr. Williams, is divided vertically between nations and regions, not horizontally between international social classes. There is at once strength and weakness in that perspective.

"But let this final word be said. For all of his limitations, both on the personal and ideological level, if one does not agree with his lack of ideology, Dr. Williams has served his Caribbean nation very, very well. In his own person he

205

has married the academic scholar to the national political leader. As a professional historian, he has shown us how we cannot understand the present save as we understand its roots in the past. As a researcher in the archives, he has taught us that every generalisation must be based upon the concrete evidence that can only be provided by the historical record. And his books will always be read because of their exhaustive documentation, their dedication to the Caribbean cause, and not least of all for their savage wit and their polished sense of ironic comment."

For my part I have, as author of this monograph on Dr. Williams, relied extensively on persons of high academic quality and political perspicacity and penetrative observation, because the history of Eric Williams seems to me to fit into the pattern of their analysis and description. I myself cannot forget the younger Williams in his early days, the cheerfulness of the person at that time, his ability to be pleasant to everyone - young people - and now to see from a distance the transition, the transmutation of that debonair person into the totally dedicated national leader. It is awe-inspiring, but I still have affection for the man I first knew.

ATLANTIC

OCEAN

WEST INDI

CARIBBEAN SEA

LESSER ANTILL

GRE... ANTILLES

NORTH CAROLINA

SOUTH CAROLINA

C. Lookout
New Bern
Raleigh
Charlotte
Fayetteville
Jacksonville
Onslow
Wilmington
Long B.
Florence
Orangeburg
Charleston
Port Royal
Savannah
Darien
Brunswick
Fernandina
Jacksonville
St. Augustine
Ocala
Daytona
Titusville
C. Canaveral
Orlando
Kissimmee
Tampa
Okeechobee
Palm Beach
G. Bahama I.
Abaco
Miami
Key Largo
C. Sable
Florida Bay
Key West
Thousand I.
Nassau
New Providence
Berry Is.
Eleuthera
Cat I.
San Salvador I.
Watling I.
Rum Cay
Long I.
Exuma
Great Exuma
Andros I.
Great Bahama Bank
Crooked I.
Acklins
Mayaguana I.
Caicos Is.
Turks Is.
Lt. Inagua I.
Gt. Inagua I.

Bermuda

New York to Kingston 2705
New York to S. Thomas 2680
New York to S. Juan 2595
New York to La Guaira
New Orleans to Liverpool
Nassau to New York 1795
Havana to New York 2225
Florida Strait

CUBA
Matanzas
Cardenas
Sagua
Santa Clara
Cayo Romano
Moron
Sancti Spiritus
Nuevitas
Camaguey
Holguin
Banes
Trinidad
Cienfuegos
Batabano
G. de Batabano
C. Cruz
Santiago de Cuba
Sierra Maestra
G. de Guacanayabo
Manzanillo
Jardines de la Reina

HAITI
HISPANIOLA
DOMINICAN REPUBLIC
Sto. Domingo
Santiago
P. Plata
Monte Cristo
Samana
Port au Prince
Jeremie
Gonaives
Windward Passage
Mona Passage
Mayaguez
Ponce

PUERTO RICO
San Juan
Charlotte Amalie
St. Thomas
Leeward Isl.

JAMAICA
Montego Bay
Falmouth
Port Antonio
Savanna la Mar
Spanish Town
Kingston

Georgetown
Gt. Cayman
Lt. Cayman (UK)

Colon to New York
Colon to Kingston
Colon to S. Thomas
C. to C.
C. to Sta. Marta

S. Andres
I. de Providencia (Col.)
I. de San Andres (Col.)

VENEZUELA
Maracaibo
Coro
Pta. Gallinas
Aruba I.
Curacao
Bonaire I.
Los Roques
Orchila
Tortuga
Caracas
La Guaira
Barquisimeto
Valencia
Paraguana Pen.
Gulf of Maracaibo
Merida
R. Apure
S. Fernando de...

COLOMBIA
Barranquilla
Cartagena
Calamar
Sta. Marta
Magdalena
Bucaramanga

PANAMA
Colon
Portobelo
Gulf of Darien
Bocas del Toro
Chiriqui Lag.
David
Santiago
Gulf of Panama
Panama C.
Perlas
Las Perlas

Limon
San Juan del Norte (Greytown)

SOUTH AMERICA

www.ingramcontent.com/pod-product-compliance
Lightning Source LLC
Chambersburg PA
CBHW030925090426
42737CB00007B/328